The Quiet Professional

AMERICAN WARRIORS

Throughout the nation's history, numerous men and women of all ranks and branches of the U.S. military have served their country with honor and distinction. During times of war and peace, there are individuals whose exemplary achievements embody the highest standards of the U.S. armed forces. The aim of the American Warriors series is to examine the unique historical contributions of these individuals, whose legacies serve as enduring examples for soldiers and citizens alike. The series will promote a deeper and more comprehensive understanding of the U.S. armed forces.

Series editor: Roger Cirillo

An AUSA Book

THE
QUIET
PROFESSIONAL

Major Richard J. Meadows
of the
U.S. Army Special Forces

Alan Hoe

Foreword by
General Peter J. Schoomaker, USA (Ret.)

The University Press of Kentucky

Editorial and Sales Offices: The University Press of Kentucky
663 South Limestone Street, Lexington, Kentucky 40508-4008
www.kentuckypress.com

15 14 13 12 11   5 4 3 2 1

Maps by Dick Gilbreath

Library of Congress Cataloging-in-Publication Data

Hoe, Alan.
  The quiet professional : Major Richard J. Meadows of the U.S. Army special
forces / Alan Hoe ; foreword by General Peter J. Schoomaker.
     p. cm. — (American warriors)
  Includes bibliographical references and index.
  ISBN 978-0-8131-3399-7 (hardcover : alk. paper)
  ISBN 978-0-8131-3400-0 (ebook)
1. Meadows, Richard J., 1931-1995. 2. United States. Army—Officers—
Biography. 3. United States. Army—Commando troops—Biography.
4. United States. Army—Commando troops—History. 5. Special forces
(Military science)—United States—History. I. Title.
  UA34.S64H64 2011
  355.0092—dc23
  [B]   2011019760

This book is printed on acid-free paper meeting
the requirements of the American National Standard
for Permanence in Paper for Printed Library Materials.

Manufactured in the United States of America.

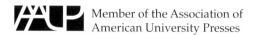 Member of the Association of
American University Presses

To the American soldier—wherever he serves.

If he'd been younger, I'd have wanted him for a son. If he'd been older, I'd have wanted him for a dad. But he wasn't either, so I had to settle for being his friend and confidant.

—Colonel Elliott P. Sydnor, USA (Ret.),
in his eulogy at Meadows's funeral,
August 1, 1995

God and the soldier we adore
in time of danger not before.
The danger passed and all things righted,
God is forgiven and the soldier slighted.

— Found on a scruffy piece of much-traveled paper
in Dick Meadows's military effects. He noted that
it was said to have been quoted by a veteran
of the Earl of Marlborough's army. It is probably
a misquote of the following epigram
by Francis Quarles (1592–1644).

Our God and soldiers we alike adore
Ev'n at the brink of danger, not before:
After deliverance, both alike requited,
Our God's forgotten, and our soldiers slighted.

Contents

Photographs follow page 128

Foreword

Most of us share some level of admiration and respect for the great achievers whom we read about in history or otherwise observe from a distance during our lifetimes. Some of us have been fortunate enough to meet and get to know some extraordinary people of whom legends are made. For whatever reason, I have had the honor and privilege of being surrounded by very special people for most of my adult professional life. Standing out . . . not really above (because he wouldn't want it that way) . . . but alone, in the unique way that he lived and worked, was Dick Meadows.

Dick and I shared a special friendship, nurtured by his desire to mentor and coach those willing to strive for excellence, and by my respect for him as a master craftsman of our business and my need to learn from the best.

Alan "Spike" Hoe knew Dick Meadows like very few others. Their professional association, growing to deep friendship, spanned over five decades beginning at Bradbury Lines in Hereford, the home of the famed British Special Air Service. The SAS was founded by Sir David Stirling during World War II in the deserts of North Africa. The rough counterpart of the U.S. Special Forces (Green Berets), the SAS gained much fame and respect on the road of hard knocks in the Dhofar Wars, Malaysia, Northern Ireland, the Falklands, and more recently Iraq and Afghanistan.

Dick Meadows was a natural fit. As a Special Forces noncommissioned officer, Dick spent an exchange tour in Hereford and was given command of an operational troop. Command of these premier units is normally reserved for "badged" commissioned officers—officers who have successfully completed the arduous SAS Assessment, Selection, and Training Program—not sergeants.

It was also during this period that Dick met Pam, his future wife, the daughter of the often feared regimental sergeant major. This is clear evidence that Dick was living the SAS motto, "Who Dares Wins!" . . . going boldly in every aspect of his life.

Spike was witness to all of this and more. He is uniquely qualified to report accurately on the extraordinary life of Dick Meadows, and does so brilliantly in the pages of this book. Spike captures the essence of this exceptional man, his friend, and the soldier/warrior role model from whom so many of us benefited.

Having known of the legendary Dick Meadows for several years, I met him for the first time in early 1978 when he was helping Colonel Charlie Beckwith form a special mission unit at Fort Bragg, North Carolina, of which I was a part. In true fashion, Dick's approaches were both subtle and often tangential. Before I knew it he had me under his wing, involving me in strange little assignments and activities designed to develop a young captain of nine years' service into a special operator and leader of very special men. He was a master teacher, patient yet demanding, and always probing, coaching, and coaxing a little more from his charges. He was never a cheerleader or backslapper. His rare compliments were like nuggets of 24-karat gold . . . and they didn't come easily. Among our ranks were a few veterans of World War II, Korea, and many from Vietnam. No one got any slack from Dick, and to be sure some didn't like it. But he had walked and survived a tough path and everyone knew it. He was the youngest master sergeant in the Korean War and the first direct battlefield commission that General Westmoreland awarded in Vietnam. He drove himself harder than anyone else, was always competitive at everything he tried, and most often he was the best at whatever he did, from handball to military free fall parachuting. His operational exploits from the Ho Chi Minh Trail to the Son Tay raid into North Vietnam to his daring work in Tehran during the 1979–1980 hostage crisis are incredible stories in their own right. His later accomplishments in Peru and elsewhere, where he continued to serve, are equally daunting and daring.

Mere days before Dick Meadows succumbed to cancer, General Wayne Downing, Paul Zeisman, Spike Hoe, and I spent several hours visiting with Pam and Dick in their Crestview, Florida, home. It was a Sunday afternoon and we reminisced about many wonderful times. Dick was going to try to hold on to life until the Son Tay Raiders' reunion the following Saturday. As it turned out, it was a reunion that he attended only in spirit. At the end of our visit he walked us out to our vehicle and we said our farewells. I asked him to send us his "angus report" when he got to the other side. This was standard operating procedure when a recon team was inserted into enemy territory, reporting that they were on the ground and continuing the mission. Dick's last words to me were: "Roger that, sir!" He was the bravest man that I have ever known.

A few years later, as the commanding general of the U.S. Army Special Operations Command, I had the privilege of hosting the ceremony to establish Meadows Field by our headquarters building at Fort Bragg, North Carolina. During the ceremony, Pam and the kids unveiled the larger-than-life statue of Dick Meadows. He is there at one end of the ceremonial field, entering the open space from the tree line, "on point" and leading his last patrol.

In the fall of 1997, I had the privilege of donning a fourth star for the first time as Commander-in-Chief, U.S. Special Operations Command, in the long shadow of Dick Meadows. He cast his shadow over many of us, and I for one will be forever grateful that he chose me as a friend.

> *De Oppresso Liber!* Who Dares Wins!
> General Peter J. Schoomaker, USA (Ret.)
> 35th Chief of Staff, Army (2003–2007)
> 5th Commander in Chief, USSOCOM (1997–2000)

Preface

This book is not an authoritative history of military actions. It is the story of a man who described himself as "just a soldier." However, Major Richard J. Meadows did not leave war behind when he retired from the U.S. Army—long afterward he continued to fight against the kidnap gangs and drug cartels of South America. He would have been the last man on earth to call himself a hero, but a hero he certainly was to the many North Americans whose lives he touched. He was also a hero to an even greater number of South Americans during his post-military activities in Peru and Colombia.

Meadows's reputation was international and his exploits have been recognized by the Special Forces of a number of countries. Indeed, it was while serving in the British Special Forces that I first met Dick, and I am fortunate to have had him as a friend and colleague for thirty-five years. In later life Dick met the founder of the British Special Air Service, Colonel Sir David Stirling, and it was the fact that I had written Stirling's biography that inspired Dick to ask me to set down his own story. In researching this book I met many others who felt themselves to be equally lucky in being able to call Dick a friend. I was honored when he asked me to write this book, and I was touched when a few days before his death he outlined the parameters for this agreement. He was never a bitter man, but he was sad that his nation did not always treat its soldiers with the honor that he felt they deserved. He was sad that some books and newspaper articles "threw rocks" at some fine soldiers who may have made a single mistake. He was sad that the Freedom of Information Act allowed former soldiers to divulge with impunity information that he thought was best kept secret.

Mentioned in this story are a number of noteworthy military missions, many of which have been recorded in depth in excellent books. There are few factual books written about the Special Operations aspects of the Vietnam War that do not include a mention of Dick Meadows. It has not been my intention to cover old ground.

Where these missions form part of his story, it is from the perspective of Dick Meadows that they are viewed. It was never difficult to get an opinion from Dick, but it could be extremely hard to get at the facts when the relation of those details seemed to him to put him in a heroic position. In putting the book together I have had many false starts, but I hope that with much help from his family and friends I have succeeded in getting into the mind of Dick Meadows and demonstrating his unique qualities. He also wished to send a message to the youngsters of the country that he loved so much. No matter what the misfortunes of youth and poverty may be, there is still space in America for a man to succeed with dignity. I have tried to mirror those wishes.

Further honors were heaped on Meadows just before his death. Some have said that this was too little, too late, but he murmured, "What's all the fuss about—I just did my job."

Dick and I spent many hours together recording his observations and opinions, often when he was extremely tired, as the leukemia took a rapidly progressive toll on his energy. To render my notes and recordings into accessible form, it was sometimes necessary to combine material from different parts of an interview. In other cases, I relied on my memory to reconstruct conversations that took place on an informal basis. I tried to minimize this practice and was careful not to alter the meaning of Dick's words. I am grateful to Dick's family for their support in this process.

In my last poignant interview with him, sitting on the porch of his fishing lodge overlooking the Alaqua River, he said that his one regret, now that he was about to go on his "last patrol," was that he had not achieved anything significant. He wished that he had had the chance to lead a hugely successful mission, to keep alive the honor with which he felt American soldiers should be regarded. Nothing significant? I leave the readers to judge that for themselves.

The Quiet Professional

Prologue

Changing the Course of the Vietnam War

The gleaming body of the soldier ant moved confidently along the length of the suppressed Swedish K submachine gun. The predator's head twitched incessantly from side to side, mandibles opening and closing, and with its antennae in constant searching motion for unseen threats. The ant showed no fear as it stepped from the cold woodwork of the weapon onto the warmer flesh of Master Sergeant Dick Meadows's hand. It hesitated as it encountered the fine human hairs, but sensing no threat it delicately picked its way through.

Meadows's cool blue eyes flicked back to the trail in front of him and he considered the situation yet again. Dammit, why couldn't he shake off the feeling of guilt? It was his selfish motive that had put RT Ohio into this tight spot. Two days ago he could have gotten them all killed. Sure, the briefing had been dressed up in fancy words, but the message was clear: "Prove that the North Vietnamese prime minister, Pham Van Dong, is a liar!" Four other teams had attended those briefings at Kontum in early June 1966, and although he couldn't be sure, it was likely that they had similar missions. Why was it that he had this burning need to be the one to succeed? Pride? Sheer cussedness? It made no difference who brought back the proof (if it existed), they were all in the same war. He sighed deeply. He still had to prove himself to himself even after all these years. Colonel Singlaub had been surprised when Meadows had asked for his team to be inserted into a recently bombed area, knowing that it was most likely to contain roving pockets of the enemy, who would be feeling secure—after all, lightning was unlikely to strike twice in the same place. They would assume that the area would be left alone for a while.

There had been no mistaking the urgency of the mission. Colonel Jack Singlaub, Chief of SOG (Studies and Observation Group) had taken his instructions directly from the Pentagon. It was June 1966 and for many months Pham Van Dong had been proclaiming to the world that no North Vietnamese regular soldiers were in South Vietnam. This was simply a peasants' revolt against a corrupt government and their aggressive American allies; it was none of his affair. General Westmoreland knew better, but he had no proof to put before the cynical congressmen in Washington, D.C.[1] Without hard evidence, he had consistently failed to get permission to relax the rules on conducting bombing raids and artillery strikes into the DMZ. In his view, this was critical to winning the war. More important, he sensed that the NVA was preparing a major offensive, and many frontline American positions were undermanned and ill-equipped to withstand determined assaults. He needed more troops—and fast.

A slight tickle at Meadows's wrist made him look down. At the cuff of his baggy shirtsleeve the ant had paused to contemplate the dark tunnel, made up its mind, and begun to enter. "That's enough, soldier boy," murmured Meadows as he reached over with his right hand to gently grasp the three-quarter-inch-long insect behind the head. The movement was unhurried as he deposited the invader on a length of fallen bamboo and watched it scurry on its way. The small movement caused his own body odors to reach his nostrils and he smiled.

There was no doubt that he stank in a very satisfactory manner. He smelled like his surroundings. There was no trace of soap, no toothpaste, no alien food smell, and no sign of the preservatives used in the pre-issue storage of his uniform. The whole of his group would be the same. They had stopped washing the day before they infiltrated. Looking to the left he could see Billy Antony, and over to the right Lieutenant Le Minh of the ARVN, and Nhouk, one of his most trusted Nungs; back to the rear would be Chuck Kerns, Jan Borek, Nguyen Canh Thach (his interpreter, known as "Ted"), and the other Nungs. They were in position around the rucksacks with the communications gear and securing the back door against unwelcome visitors. He shivered in the early morning chill. It had rained heavily the night before, and cold droplets of water still fell along the length of his body from the canopy of leaves above. He welcomed the icy drips. The heavy rainfall had given them partial security by obliterating most of their tracks. The guilt hit him again as he thought about the contact just after they had left the LZ. They had been moving across a fairly open area, which had once been some sort of cultivation, when they had come under small arms fire from the flank. With no hesitation he had turned into the fire and charged, making as much noise as he could and firing short bursts as he went. Billy and Minh had been close behind him. The six enemy soldiers who had ambushed them, surprised and frightened by the reaction, stood and then fled. Two fell to Meadows's gun and one to Billy's. The dead men were dressed in the classic black "pyjamas" of the Viet Cong. This was no proof for Westmoreland; it only supported Pham Van Dong's propaganda of a peasant war. Later the team had come under heavy fire from the rear, and after quickly breaking contact Meadows had brought down an artillery barrage so close to their position that debris had fallen on them. The nagging doubts persisted. Should he have inserted into a safer area? Should he have moved farther afield after the contact? Charlie could be quietly tracking them down as they lay here totally exposed from the rear.

Since the incident, it had taken them two patient days of slow movement to get to this position. They had heard shouting and signal shots in the background, but they had pressed on. They had spent many long minutes in total stillness. They had long ago mastered the technique of looking through the jungle vegetation rather than at it, an art that came more easily to the country-born soldier than the ex–city dweller. The nights had been spent snatching fitful spells of sleep as they remained with equipment belts on and rucksacks and rifles at hand. They had made it. Now they needed some luck. They had four days' food left and it would take them two days to reach their planned exfiltration LZ. They could stretch the food to last six days, but without the calories their pace would be even slower. "Well, let's just wait and see. What goes around comes around," he thought, using one of his English mother-in-law's sayings.

The Ho Chi Minh Trail lay in front of him. Fully five meters across at this point, it was more like a major road. In point of fact, this was Laotian Highway 110E, which was a tributary off the main arterial trail leading only into South Vietnam. Meadows looked up and marveled at the ingenuity and patience of the NVA soldiers. To keep the trail from being easily seen from the air they often shinned up the trees and tied together the branches overlapping the more open expanses of the route. Not an easy task but very effective. The place from which Meadows had chosen to observe was the end of a

U-shaped sector of the trail where it naturally followed the line of a narrow river. From this vantage point he and his team had a view of some 150 meters. He had selected this spot for visual concealment rather than physical protection—it was certainly no ambush site. He began to run over the exfiltration route in his mind again; if they had to move out under pursuit, then he wouldn't have the luxury of map-reading time. He was mentally halfway up the first spur leading to the main ridge when a faint noise snapped him back to full alert. He glanced along to Billy and then to Minh. Billy was stiff, his neck angled as though straining to hear. Minh seemed relaxed. That was it then. They were coming from Billy's direction. There it was again. Clearer now. There, again, it was the sound of laughter.

The point section of the enemy came giggling and chattering into view. Their AK-47s were slung over their shoulders and they paid no attention to the flanks of the trail. They were lightly laden with partly filled bandoleers of ammunition and small canvas packs. Meadows was both relieved and elated. Their attitude meant that they had received no radio warning of RT Ohio's presence in the area, but here was Westy's proof. The soldiers wore the uniforms of the NVA and their insignia clearly identified them as members of the 24th Regiment, a regiment that was positively marked on the Operations Center maps as being well inside North Vietnam. They hadn't a care in the world. One of them suddenly darted off the trail toward Billy, and Meadows eased his weapon into the aim position. He relaxed only slightly as the NVA soldier popped the buttons at his fly and began to urinate, looking over his shoulder to catch the ribald comments from the comrades who had paused to wait for him. He was within half a dozen meters of Billy, and Dick prayed that he wouldn't spot him. His own cover now seemed pathetically sparse. He had chosen to lie alongside a fallen tree and pull a few twigs over himself to break up his body outline. He knew that so long as the enemy stayed on the trail he was reasonably hard to see. He just hoped that no other bladders were straining right now. The NVA soldier moved back onto the trail with both hands busy at his buttons. Laying down his gun, Meadows carefully and slowly raised the Pen EE camera he had placed in readiness at his side. He sighted in on the group of men, hoping that their chatter would drown out the noise of the shutter release. Focus—click, focus—click; there was no reaction from the group as they passed directly in front of him and continued their cheerful banter. "Well, that's that," he thought, lowering the camera. "Four days and I go back with a photograph of half a dozen Charlies. Proof? Yeah, but that's not enough to produce a hard-on in the Pentagon." He considered taking out the soldiers or trying for a prisoner but decided to wait a little longer. They seemed safe enough for the time being.

He was about to give the signal to fall back to the rear for a short break when he sensed rather than saw Billy stiffen up again, and he turned to look down the track. To his delight he saw a line of black pyjama-clad figures with enormous loads begin to file around the corner. Eyes to the ground as they silently strained against the weight of their burdens, they trudged forward. There was no happy chattering from this sweating group. Focus—click; focus—click. Dick continued to shoot his film. The procession seemed endless. Interspersed among the black-clad Viet Cong were NVA regulars, weapons in hand and pushing and cajoling the porters to keep moving. Occasionally one of them would pause to look at the flanks, as if sensing a presence. More than once Meadows thought that he had direct eye contact with one of the soldiers, but they pressed on. They would know that the slow-moving group would be a heaven-sent ambush opportunity. He ignored the threat and carried on: focus—click, focus—click. Suddenly he was out of film. The 35mm Pen EE was a half-frame camera, so he had made a total of seventy-two exposures and still the men filed past. Their loads were a mixture of what could have been rice and other foodstuffs, tube-like containers that suggested artillery or mortar ammunition, and drums of communications wire. There was no doubt that this was a major supply column and that it was well into Laos on a trail that led only into South Vietnam, just a few kilometers distant.

Dick had a sudden thought. Chuck had with him an 8mm movie camera with which he had intended to get himself some souvenir footage of the Ho Chi Minh Trail. Could he get back to Chuck's position and return without being detected? Sure, most of the men were not alert as they sweated their way along, but the scattered regulars with them were certainly suspicious. His thoughts took no more than a second or two and then he acted. Leopard crawling, camera tucked into his shirt and gun across his arms, with remarkable quietness he eased out of his position and squirmed his way back up the hill to Chuck. It took him only a moment to warn the group what was going on, give Chuck the Pen EE, and relieve him of his precious movie camera, then he was on his way back.

This time he had to take a more exposed position, as it was impossible to frame a shot from any other angle. The porters had passed and now it was streams of regular NVA soldiers who were in the viewfinder. He knelt alongside the stump of the fallen tree in order get both the column and a clearly identifiable section of the trail into the shot. He could see Minh but not Billy and was pleased to note Minh's M16 in the aim position. Feeling very vulnerable, he set the camera running and, concentrating only on the focus, closed his mind to the dangers. The whirring of the camera motor seemed incredibly loud and alien against the muted background sounds of the jungle. If spotted, he would have no chance to reach for his gun before being shot down. Just as the film ran out he saw in the viewfinder the first of another full group of lightly laden NVA soldiers bringing up the rear of the column. Sinking back into the undergrowth, he held his breath as they passed. One of them, he noticed, was constantly looking over his shoulder and at one point their eyes seemed to meet. As the last one vanished from view Dick raised his hand, showed his five open fingers twice, and then put his hand on his head. If no other enemy appeared within ten minutes Billy and Minh would close with his position.

After the long vigil their joints were stiff and aching as they moved stealthily toward him. Moments later they were on their way to rejoin Jan and Chuck.

"Holy shit, Ricardo," breathed Billy, "That's gonna set 'em thinking back in the head shed. That musta been the stores for at least half a regiment." Dick did not answer. He was thinking. When he spoke it was in a low whisper. "Look guys, one of that last group kept looking back. Now, we know it wasn't because they were worried about enemy or the point section would've been a damned sight sharper. I guess that there's a few stragglers back there. What say we take some back with us?" His eyes were twinkling with mischief.

"But Dai Uý,"[2] objected Ted, "we know the main party won't be far away—they're moving very slowly. We know that there's enemy behind us. If there's any shooting we'll have a problem getting out of here."

"Well, I think it's a chance we've got to take. We'll try to do it without any shooting. We were told to look for positive signs of the NVA moving into the south, but nobody expected hundreds of them. We've got that on film—maybe. The goddam rain's been with us for three days now and we could've got wet film and no pictures at all. Do you think the spooks will take our word for it that the 24th Regiment's on the move? Like hell they will. Now, a prisoner, that's what I call evidence. Okay, here's what we do. We'll give it until last light. If no one turns up, fine, we'll move back a bit and hunker down for the night, then move to the exfiltration LZ starting at first light tomorrow. If someone does come along then we'll try to snatch a couple. We'll use the old drill. Up to three and I'll step out and cover them; Ted will cover me and invite them to drop their loads and come along with us. Don't shout Ted; talk real low, the rest might've decided to take a break just around the corner. Between three and ten we'll try to take most of them out with the silenced 'K,' leaving a couple to join us on the walk back. More than ten and we just spring the ambush and hope that we keep one alive to take back. Okay?"

Meadows was happy to see the grins of anticipation on the faces of the team. Leaving a frustrated Jan, Chuck, and half a dozen more Nungs with the heavy gear, he moved his team back to the point of the U-bend where he had earlier taken the film. They did not have long to wait. Two men staggered slowly down the track, and when a smiling Meadows stepped out in front of them they dropped their loads immediately and raised their hands. The packs contained rice and dried food, which the team took away from the trail, scattering it among the leaves, then brushing jungle debris over it. The weapons consisted of an AK-47 with five rounds and a .30 carbine with only a few corroded bullets. The weapons were tied together to be disposed of at a suitable point in the river they would cross later. The prisoners' hands were tied and RT Ohio began to pull out. Meadows considered calling for an air strike on the area where he reckoned that the enemy column would now be. No, it was not worth it. The evidence he had was too valuable to risk losing. Apart from Ted's whispered injunction to the prisoners, everything had been done in comparative silence.

There were four hours of daylight left when the rain began again and Meadows sighed with satisfaction. Any tracks they had inadvertently left by the Ho Chi Minh Trail would fade quickly. There was no telling how long it would be before the regular NVA soldiers began to search for the missing men, but by then RT Ohio would be well on their way to the exfiltration LZ with two prisoners and hopefully some good film. When they got close to the LZ they would be safe enough to report an accurate target location for air and artillery bombardment.

Master Sergeant Dick Meadows was quietly satisfied with the results of his patrol, though in truth he would have preferred more real action. He could not even begin to anticipate what far-reaching effects his irrefutable evidence of a large NVA presence in South Vietnam would have on the U.S. war effort and his own career. Neither did he know at the time that this mission would earn him his first Silver Star.[3]

In the annals of the U.S. Special Forces there are many heroes, but the name of Dick Meadows still stands out as the ultimate "quiet professional." The "great American dream" is a hackneyed phrase nowadays, but this man of humble origin lived that dream to become a name synonymous with Special Operations. What molded him? What inspired him? How did he get there?

1

The Early Years

1932–1947

In the early 1930s America was still in the grip of the economic depression which was to last almost until the decision to enter World War II in December 1941. Nowhere was this worse than in the valleys, forests, and mountains of West Virginia. The state lagged well behind the national average in respect to personal income and overall development. One of the reasons for this is a freak of nature. West Virginia is well-named the "Mountain State," for almost the whole of it is part of the great Appalachian mountain range.

The earthquakes that formed the Appalachians gave West Virginia two important features. First, the small valleys and, lower down in the foothills, large flood plains are all richly fertile. Second, those tectonic plate collisions exposed some of the heaviest soft coal deposits in America. The majority of the state's labor force was thus divided between farming and mining. The mountains also locked the folk into small communities in the narrow valleys, where family farms sprang up in the "hollows" along the creeks and rivers.

However, nature mainly benefited the wealthy and powerful who were able to purchase huge tracts of land and exploit the ready supply of cheap labor. They were able to control local commerce through company-owned stores and the application of credit lines to coal workers and small farmers alike. Coal was expensive to transport; therefore, many light industrial factories were established close to the source of power. The result was a sprawling mess of coal camps and factories spewing out the smoke and grime which choked the atmosphere and lent an air of gloomy despair to the once beautiful valleys.

In some ways the character of the West Virginians worsened the situation. Mountain dwellers throughout the world tend to be fiercely independent and inward looking. In West Virginia much of this spirit can be ascribed to the Celtic characteristics of the many Scots and Irish who settled the more inaccessible areas in the 1700s.

This history is still detectable today in the speech patterns, musical instruments, ballads, and handicrafts of the area. These people were staunch unionists who refused to accept the Secession Convention in 1861, and in 1863 the new state of West Virginia was accepted into the Union. Tightly knit communities meant that few people looked outside the state to compare their way of life with that of others more affluent. A condition of hopeless acceptance was reached. Some youngsters left the state in search of work, but in the main, the West Virginians of the 1930s divided into three categories. Some eked a living from family farms, some opted for the rigors of the coal camps, and a small percentage lived on the proceeds of bootlegging.

The farmers had chosen a hard life. The rugged terrain made workable land plots small and their priority was to feed their families. Meat was plentiful for the hunters, and many became expert backwoodsmen. White-tailed deer, rabbits, squirrels, and groundhogs were in good supply, along with some of the finest trout fishing in the South. The vegetables and fruit left over after the family had been fed would be sold on the sidewalks in the small towns or bartered for commodities in the few independent stores. Money was scarce. There were slim pickings from these sales. Life was a matter of subsistence, with little money left over for luxuries.

The men who elected to work in the coal industry had an even harder life. This was coal mining at its most basic, and little attention was paid to safety. The coal camps were no more than shantytowns. A gritty black dust penetrated every crack and crevice of the company-owned shacks. The owners of the mines kept a tight grip on their labor force through cleverly imposed debts. What finer way to keep a man bound to the coal faces than by holding his "mark" against groceries and clothing bought at the company store on onerous credit terms: "Saint Peter don't you call me 'cause I can't go / I owe my soul to the company store."

Life was hard and often short. Those who did not die in accidents at the coal face stood a fair chance of succumbing to "black lung" disease (pneumoconiosis), caused by the constant inhalation of the fine, pervasive dust. Conditions were so bad that six times in its history the coal mining areas of West Virginia had been subjected to intervention by the National Guard, which was used to quell riots. In the early 1930s the miners won the right to organize labor unions, but it took years for conditions to improve significantly.

Declare something illegal and it becomes more attractive. The

National Prohibition Act of 1919 increased the value of bootleg corn liquor. There were those who risked life and freedom to make a living from moonshine whiskey. Many of the farmers indulged in it as a sideline to supplement their meager incomes. Even after prohibition ended it remained illegal to distill without a license, but the mountain men of West Virginia perfected the art of evading the ever-vigilant revenuers.

This was the West Virginia into which Bernard J. Meadows Jr. moved in 1938. Before this transfer the Meadows's lifestyle had been very basic but on a par with their neighbors in the Allegheny country, where Junior had been born six years earlier. Bernie Meadows Sr. scraped a living as best he could working in the coal camps and supplementing his income by selling moonshine. Junior's memories of that part of his childhood were vivid and mixed. There were hard times with an always belligerent and often violent father who was prone to taking a little too much of his own illegal brew. His mother, Hattie, suffered as much if not more than Junior at those times.

It is a strange thing that humans sometimes remember more easily the good times than the bad ones. Junior readily appreciated the love and affection that he found within the home of his grandparents, John W. and Fanny Booth. During Bernie Senior's many absences at the coal camps Junior spent much of his time with John and Fanny. A memory that stayed with him typifies the warm relationship. One of his childhood pleasures was lying in bed in the biting, pre-dawn cold and hearing Grandpa Booth get up to light the fire. The smell of the wood smoke from the potbellied stove would slowly permeate the house as he huddled into the comforting warmth of his rough blanket. Reluctant to face the dawn chill, he strained his ears for a familiar sound. One of his grandfather's early morning habits was to heat the water for his first hot toddy of the day. The tinkle of spoon against glass was the signal for Junior to rise. Still wrapped in his blanket, he would climb onto his grandfather's knee, where he would enjoy the treat of being handed the glass and spoon to scoop out the warming residue. In Meadows's own words: "It was a purely private time. Grandpa would put his arm around me and begin to tell stories as I enjoyed the taste of sugar and the remains of the warm whiskey. He was a gentle man and still had a British accent—forever telling jokes against the Irish in that very precise way of speaking that he had. Those were some of the happiest times of my childhood."

Junior was a shy boy, which was natural enough considering his environment. The community was very small and strangers were unusual in the hollows (sometimes they would be revenuers looking for moonshine stills), and so the family was his main experience of the adult world.

He remembered the happy days spent with Grandpa Booth. Though his clothes were poor, usually hand-me-downs, his food was wholesome. There was a wild aspect to the life that appealed to him—the days were spent hunting squirrels, deer, and turkeys. He would catch crawdads to bait his raccoon traps—raccoons being considered good food. In the evenings, before the advent of the radio, the family would gather on the veranda to tell tales and sing.

Meadows did not build a close relationship with his older sister, Verna Lee. She moved everywhere with her mother, and so they met only on those occasions when Meadows spent time at whatever place his mother was. In later years, Verna Lee would be of great assistance to her brother.

Meadows did not have a good relationship with his mother, and his happiest months were spent with the Booths. There was no way to get a good living from the farms, but at that age Junior had no need of money. Most of the Meadows and Booths (the maternal side of the family) were moonshiners, and the competition to produce the best corn liquor was fierce. Both families had a reputation for making a fine drink. They made their own special brew with peaches and apricots. Straight corn liquor could fetch around $8 a gallon then, but the peach and apricot "brandy" was good for about $15. All the family drank on those evenings sitting on the veranda, "porching" as they called it. The liquor would make the songs and stories more prolific, and in the flickering glow of the kerosene lamp the screeches of the bobcats and cries of the whippoorwills created an eerie atmosphere. The arrival of the radio, known locally as the "squeaky box," rather changed that way of life.

When not with his grandparents, Junior lived in a company-owned shack in one of the coal camps. It was a far cry from Grandpa Booth's home at Johnson's Creek. The atmosphere was violent. The frustration of the miners in never being able to get financially ahead of the owners due to the enforced credit system and meager wages led to drunkenness and fighting. Bernie Meadows, tough and violent himself, was never far from the action. In Junior's words:

Nothing was ever so true as the lines from the song, "I loaded sixteen tons and what did I get? Another day older and deeper in debt." Life was pretty tough until the day Dad said: "To hell with this. No more coal towns." In truth he'd just had his still busted up by the law for about the thirtieth time and he'd been told by the deputy sheriff to get out of West Virginia or die. That deputy meant it too. Dad often told me that the deputies would take all the moonshine back to the jailhouse to destroy it, but the quality was so good that usually they drank it or sold it themselves. Anyway, soon after that he moved on and got himself a job in the coal mining company at Besoco. That was all he could get in spite of saying "no more coal towns." Somehow he eventually raised enough money to lease about one hundred acres of farmland—he was always a country boy at heart and never a true miner. He sent for Mom and me, and a lot of the Booths and Meadows clan followed us.

He bought some stock. A cow, some chickens, ducks, and a horse and life was pretty good for a while. We were into the foothills of the mountains and the moonshine stills were set up again, but this time Dad wasn't a part of it—he never brewed another drop as far as I know. I didn't mind that one little bit—I'd spent too many hours at one end of a crosscut saw turning out cordwood for the stills. This was the biggest give-away to the revenuers. A moonshine still burns up a whole heap of wood in a short time and they'd look for piles of cordwood or places where the moonshiners had been felling and know they were in the right area. Sometimes we hauled timber for what seemed miles to cut down the odds of discovery. When Dad's moonshining days came to an end it was because his sentry fell asleep and got himself whacked over the head. Good military lesson there. He might have stopped brewing but he sure as heck didn't stop drinking the stuff.

Junior was turning six years old when he started his formal education, though life was far from settled. His mother and father were going through a bad patch; separations were frequent and often violent, and Junior saw Hattie only occasionally. The farm didn't work out and Bernie Senior was forced to keep returning to the Besoco coal camps he hated. Junior spent much of his time with his grandparents. Often his father would return from Besoco to try to take him back, but Junior would usually manage to hide out in the woods until he left. Aware of his own tendency to violence when he was drinking, Bernie Meadows went through long periods of abstinence, but these were not peaceful times as he then became prone to bouts of religious mania that were as disturbing as his drunkenness. Junior felt sorry for his father, but he just couldn't face the move to the coal camps again or the atmosphere at home. During the school vacations and on weekends he was hired out as a farmhand (he received none of the pay himself). He did not like farming: "It always seemed to me that more work went into maintaining the horse than the horse put into the farm." His family had thought that he should become either a farmer or a builder, but to Junior life was much sweeter hunting groundhog than "pulling corn" or "laying planks."

Those halcyon days in the mountains were responsible for the real birth of the "point man." The writer who captured Junior's imagination was Zane Grey. One of his heroes in particular was the legendary Louis Wetzel, intrepid hunter of the Huron, Shawnee, and Delaware Indians, who inhabited the forests bordering the Ohio River. The woodlands of the Virginias provided a living theater within which Junior could reenact the stories of the frontiersmen. The young warrior, now (in his own mind at least) the very reincarnation of Louis Wetzel, was to carry out many a daring mission as he stealthily took himself foot by careful foot through the undergrowth. Not a leaf would he disturb, not a branch would he shake as he closed with his deadly foe. All the odds were against him in these Indian-infested forests, but, dammit, he was going to win through. Zane Grey's characters were not the only examples to him in the art of fieldcraft. Grandpa Booth and Uncles Oscar and Henderson, all hard-muscled men of whipcord strength, were also accomplished hunters eager to pass on their skills to such a willing youth. He learned well lessons that would never desert him.

A boy given these surroundings and home life either uses his imagination or develops into a dull and uninteresting individual. Junior let his thoughts run rife as he invented secret and dangerous missions for himself. A squirrel would become the dreaded Silvertip, chief of the Shawnee nation and arch enemy of Wetzel. After a long stalk it would be dropped with a single shot to the head. Sometimes he would be Wetzel, sometimes Colonel Zane or maybe even

Major Sam McColoch bent on doing good for his country. Whatever the self-imposed mission, it is apparent that the frontiersmen of legend and book really lived in the mind of the young backwoodsman. His Uncle Oscar gave him his introduction into tracking and he took it seriously. He would lie down to look along a fading spoor, knowing that the light patterns change from that perspective, where he might pick up the trail from a leaf or bent twig that reflected the sun differently from its neighbors. He knew that if he carefully removed the leaves from around a slight indentation there was a good chance that underneath there would be a near-perfect print in the soft earth. All these and many of the tricks of the woodsman were learned from books and relatives and all helped him in his frequent games of make-believe.

Patriotism arrived early to become a part of Junior's makeup. In the main this was due to the stories told by his kinfolk and the school system, which at that time still required the daily Pledge of Allegiance. One of Junior's early decisions during his schooldays was to rid himself of the name "Bernard," which he hated. Instead he assumed the mantle of "Richard" (after a favorite cousin) and used the name from then on.

The young Richard was receiving other lessons in life, though at the time he did not recognize them for what they were. Sometimes he would accompany Grandpa Booth to town to sell eggs—a veritable fortune was to be made at ten cents a dozen. Grandpa Booth also had a little sideline that he kept to himself. He sold perfume. He would carry with him a small case containing tiny sample bottles, take orders, deliver the next week, and hope to collect the money at the same time. Most of the women who placed orders were trying in a pathetic way to escape the harsh realities and drudgery of life and for a few brief moments imagine themselves in a place far removed from the coal camps. The luxury of a perfume (even an inexpensive one) was hard for them to ignore, though few of them could really afford the purchase. After selling his eggs, Richard would meet up with his grandfather along the road and go with him to the various shacks and houses.

Sometimes there would be a little shuffling and blushing as the lady of the house said that she had no money, and Grandpa would say that in that case he couldn't leave the perfume. Sometimes he would be invited inside to discuss the matter and he would turn to me and tell me to wait down the road a piece. He'd then appear a little later looking sort of red-faced and a bit breathless. He wouldn't say anything and he'd avoid meeting my eyes directly and we'd go off down the road again. This could happen two or three times, and it was a long while before I realized just how those ladies were paying for their perfume and why he was getting so darned tired!

The see-saw of life took young Richard to stay once more with his father, who was now back in the Johnson's Creek area and mixing his work between carpentry (at which he was untrained but expert) and laboring on another rented farm. His violence was as unpredictable as ever, though Richard knew the warning signs and avoided him as much as possible if he was drinking or quoting loudly from the Bible. School activity was to bring the next clash. Richard had become very good at basketball and had made the school first team. As is the way with youth, he now saw in himself the ability to become a basketball star, and the school coach, Mr. McNish, gave him every encouragement. Not so Bernie Meadows. To him, if school was to deprive him of his son's availability as a source of cheap labor, then it was a place for learning to read and calculate—not for wasting time with ball games. Bernie steadfastly refused to let his boy stay late at school to take part in ball practice. The coach, recognizing a real talent, fixed things so that training took place during the noontime break. All went well until an important match was scheduled to take place one evening. This match was for championship points and the team was pitted against their old rival, Beckley High School. Richard decided to ignore parental protest and stay late to play anyway:

> I did let Dad know that I would be a little late, but I didn't say it was for a ball game. It was a real important match and even though my tennis shoes, which someone had given me, were too small and painful to wear, I got very excited about it. The captain of the team, the best scorer, was prone to violent migraine and it hit him that night. Every now and then I'd see him hunching over and wincing as one of his headaches struck. My big chance came in the closing seconds of the game as he shot for basket. I could see he was

in trouble as he shot and the ball was falling short when I managed to get a hand to it and flip it home. It was great. Everyone was on their feet and clapping and shouting. Although we hadn't won, my shot held the game to a draw. Damn it felt good.

It was when I had to go home that the problems started. It was dark by then and starting to snow. I couldn't find my darned boots, so all I had was my too-tight tennis shoes and thin clothing and it was darned cold. I decided to try to hitch a ride back toward home, and every time a car came along I'd dash out into the road and stick up my thumb. When it had passed I'd duck back into the shelter of the wall again. Eventually a car did stop.

"Meadows. What are you doing here?" It was McNish, the basketball coach.

"Trying to get home, coach."

"What. No one to give you a ride?"

"No. I guess my Dad doesn't much approve of ball games." There was no point telling him that Dad didn't have a car anyway.

"Jump in then. I'll take you."

Meadows got into the car and they headed out of town. Soon the snow was getting worse and deepening on the road. At a point about three miles out of town was the turn off to home, and Meadows asked to be dropped off.

"No. I'll take you home."

"But it's no problem, coach. It's only about a mile and I usually run from here anyway."

"Okay. Well done on the running young Meadows, but you're not doing it in this snow and dressed like that. I'm taking you all the way. I'll come along and say 'hello' to your father."

This was Meadows's worst fear. He was embarrassed and did not want his coach to see the one-room house where he lived. But there was nothing he could do. The car slithered up the deeply pot-holed track and eventually the Meadows home came into view. There were no lights—no welcome home from Dad. He thanked his rescuer and mumbled something about it not being a good idea for Coach McNish to wake up his father. Relieved, he scurried inside.

In the house both parents seemed to be in their bed, which was separated from the main room by a suspended blanket.

> I was expecting an ass-kicking but got a real surprise. Dad was in bed but not asleep, and he turned over and asked me where I'd been. I told him that I'd played basketball for the first team and that I'd saved the match from being lost. He said that was good and invited me into his bed to get warmed up and he told me that he guessed it was okay if I played some ball now and again. I didn't tell him about the missing boots. They turned up the next day anyway. I went to sleep happy.

For a while life was relatively relaxed, but that state of affairs was not to last. Spring came and one morning Bernie sent Richard off to do his daily chores, which included spraying the bean crop. After finishing all the other tasks Richard found that the sprayer was not working, so he left the beans and took himself off to hunt groundhog. On his return there was an angry scene with his father, who accused him of being a lazy good-for-nothing and squared up to give him a beating. The scrawny Meadows Junior stood his ground and his father relented. Richard thought about the business overnight and decided he did not want another confrontation. Early the next morning he took his dog and headed "Wetzel-style" over the mountains to his mother's house (she having moved out once again after a brutal argument witnessed by Richard, who narrowly escaped injuries himself). She told him that it would be best if he went to his grandfather's house for the time being, and despite his father's efforts to reclaim him, Richard stayed there for some months.

So the boy's education continued. Throughout all the movement between his father's, mother's, and grandfather's homes, he managed to reach ninth grade. Apart from the eighth (and part of ninth) grade, most of his education took place at the same school, which lay at the center point of a triangle formed by his three abodes. Meadows had some fond memories of school and especially of his teacher, Jane Foster. She, at the age of about thirty-five years, was a firm but compassionate woman who tried to teach girls to be ladies but was tolerant enough to let the boys be boys. The system of schooling was not uncommon in country areas at that time, with several grades of students all being taught by the same teacher in the one large classroom. (When Meadows visited the school some forty years later, he was surprised at just how small the old building was.)

> I guess you'd call it a self-help school. The girls were taught home economics (but it was called something else then) and all the kids were asked to bring in different ingredients for the girls to provide a hot lunch for everyone. I usually took what I could forage from the fields or something I'd shot the night before. Boy, on a cold winter's day when the smell of that cooking came into the classroom it was hard to remember that you were there to learn as the hunger pangs started and your mouth began to water.
>
> Christmas was a big occasion at school and we had to act out various plays, like *Scrooge.* I was shy and could never remember my lines, so I usually got the part of some dumb ghost. I remember one Christmas when it was our duty to get the Christmas tree; I and two of my buddies decided to have a little fun. Remember I told you the whole area was full of moonshiners and we all had a little drink from time to time. Well, we took about a half of a bottle along with us when we went off for the tree and we got a little happy. By the time we got back with the biggest darned tree the school had ever seen we had spent most of the day drinking. It didn't take Jane Foster long to spot that we were drunk.
>
> She lined us up in front of the class so the kids could watch. "Breathe on me," she said. Well, the other two let out great breaths but I just blew a little air through my nose and I got away with it. Then when it came to punishment I felt kind of guilty, so I admitted to her that I'd been drinking too. "I know that," she said. I guess she'd just been waiting for me to own up, and I'm glad that I did. I can't remember what the punishment was, but I had a pretty rough headache on the walk home that night. You know, lots of folk laugh when someone says that he walked miles through waist-deep snow to get to the bus point for school—but, man, I did that regularly.

It was at school that Meadows experienced the first of Cupid's arrows:

> I can remember when Jane Foster's daughter, Mary Ellen, arrived at the school. She was a lovely blonde girl with her hair in pigtails. She had bright brown eyes and a smile that lit up her whole face. I was smitten, but I was also very, very shy. Boy, was she a flirt, and it was lost on me because I was tongue-tied with her. One day we were all sat down and told to read *Topsy Turvey* or some such book and warned that at the end of the session we would have to give a recitation. I was sat next to Mary Ellen and for some reason my shyness suddenly left me and we talked and talked. Jane Foster was constantly telling us to shut up. Well, it came to my turn to read aloud and much to Jane Foster's surprise I did a darned near perfect job of it. This was the guy who couldn't remember a single line and had to play dumb ghosts in the Christmas plays. All the time Mary Ellen was looking up adoringly at me. Man, I was in love.
>
> We became pen pals, with Jane acting as the courier. I'm pretty sure she opened all our letters, but all through those years I was too shy to ask for a date or to let her know how I lived. She would write to me on beautiful paper with little flowers or butterflies and such at the top. My paper was pretty cheap and to make it look better I'd place it over the patterns on the oilcloth table covering and spend ages with a stubby bit of pencil tracing the outlines onto it. Later, after I joined the army, I looked her up and asked her out, but by that time she was married and had kids. I was pretty crushed but we stayed friends for a long time.

Throughout the latter part of Meadows's education, World War II was raging and the sight of the volunteers parading in the towns further stirred his patriotic instincts. They were full of the bravado of such recruits as they shouted victory slogans. The early volunteers from the coal camps were typical of the mountain men, with their macho mockery of the unknown dangers to come. His own cousin Richard Keith, whom he greatly admired, at the age of twenty-one had been such a man. He just had to get into the war. (It was this cousin's name that Meadows had taken when he decided

to shed the title of Bernard.) Sadly, Richard Keith was killed in action. The mountain men sang patriotic songs on the porches with
great feeling as they cheered their kinfolk going off on the Great
Adventure. The "squeaky boxes" were full of the war news and the
newspapers heralded the exploits of Audie Murphy and a thousand
other heroes. This entire atmosphere served to inflame the patriotic
fervor of the young Meadows.

The veterans who did return were feted, some reluctantly and
some with great enjoyment. Some told glorified versions of their
exploits, but many were quiet and introspective as they reviewed
their own private images of the horrors of war.

There is no surprise, given the lack of a proper home life and his
exposure to the wild men of fiction, that Meadows begin to think of
the army as a career. So it was that in the summer of 1947 Meadows
and two friends, Jimmy Trail and "Dink" Smith, decided to enlist.
For Meadows, however, there was the small matter of his age—he
was only fifteen years old. To sort out that little problem he visited his mother. Together they went to see the recruiting sergeant.
"I guess Ma really wanted rid of me anyway and the recruiting sergeant must have been down on his quota for the month, because
between them they changed the date on my birth certificate to 1930.
This was great news for me and I didn't even feel a day older. Pretty
soon Jimmy, Dink, and I were on our way to Camp Lee, Virginia,
with a whole $10 in our pockets. I'd never been so rich."

2

The Young Soldier and Korea

1947–1952

On arrival at Fort Lee the three youngsters were put through a series of basic tests, but Jimmy and Dink didn't make it. Meadows felt exposed and lonely at their departure. The isolation experienced during his childhood did not allow him to make friends easily, but nonetheless it was not too long before he found a kindred spirit and linked up with Floyd Payne, another West Virginian, and an easygoing man with a sharp sense of humor. They became constant companions. Meadows wanted to be an infantryman in the best traditions of the Zane Grey characters, and when Payne stated that he intended to join the 82nd Airborne, Meadows was quick to go along with that. He had no idea whatsoever what the 82nd was all about. In truth, neither of them knew much about it. In August 1947 they arrived at Fort Jackson to begin basic infantry training.

Most soldiers remember their basic training days with some horror and misery. This was not the case with Meadows. The training was tough, sometimes very tough, but with his background he took to it easily enough. What some recruits saw as deprivation he accepted as a life better than any he had known so far. He reveled in the physical aspects, soaked up military knowledge, and marveled at the fact that he was getting three square meals a day with as much milk as he could drink. On top of this he was being paid a regular wage for the first time in his life. During this period Meadows picked up one of his first military role models in the form of SFC Stanley. Stanley also was from West Virginia, a hard but basically kind soldier with constant encouragement for deserving cases. Meadows was not having an easy time. The smallest and youngest in the class, he was having difficulty performing the intricacies of foot drill while wearing big boots for the first time and manipulating a heavy rifle.

All he wanted to do in the evenings was fall into his bed and sleep; it was Payne who made him get his act together and clean his boots and equipment for the next day. The constant tiredness made Meadows think that he was ill, but he dared not see a doctor for fear of being sent off the course. He was aware that some of the instructors were not happy about his age, and he knew that any excuse would serve to have him dismissed. The tiredness was just a result of exercising and growing while his body was demanding recovery time.

Basic training eventually came to an end, and in pursuit of their Airborne dreams Payne and Meadows should have shipped out to Fort Benning together. Payne went alone as Meadows, shocked to the core, was told that he had failed the necessary physical examination. Why? He weighed only 125 pounds against the 130 that was then reckoned to be the optimum weight to ensure that a static line parachute deployed properly. So Payne was on his way and Meadows was consigned to KP duties in order to pack on some body weight. Forty-eight years later, Floyd Payne,[1] who was to serve with Meadows many times in later years, could still remember the shock of the moment: "Hell, I didn't know what had happened to him. I didn't know why he failed the entrance. He just stammered out that he'd failed. I can recall the look on his face and it was tragic. That young guy [Payne was only a year older than Meadows himself] just soaked up every bit of information the army threw at him. He was like a damn sponge. He never forgot a single thing."

Meadows's slight stature let him down once again when he failed a second physical for the same reason as before—too light-weight. Another spell on KP duty at last got him up to the required weight, but it was a struggle to maintain it against all the physical exercise that was taking place. He ate vast quantities of food but lost all the value on the rigorous training schedule. He actually enjoyed this period and could feel himself getting stronger day by day; soon he was qualified to start Airborne training proper. He was only a few weeks behind his good buddy, Floyd Payne.

At Benning he came under the critical eye of Sergeant Charlie Craig. Craig was a tough guy of the old school. He was a strict disciplinarian and a fitness fanatic. He would perform one-handed push-ups with ease, and he had the ability of many of the old drill sergeants to cuss a man out with great finesse. Sergeant Craig got plenty of practice on young Meadows.

In those days the first phase of Airborne training was in gliders, and Meadows did not have fond memories of that experience. Flying in a military glider is a gut-wrenching business. The thing bumps into the air behind the towing aircraft, and those unfortunates in the passenger hold are subjected to a feeling of abject helplessness as the violent dips and yaws throw the contents of stomachs from side to side. The roar of the towing aircraft fills the hold, and then there is a momentary silence seconds after the towline is slipped. The soft whistle of the slipstream takes over and there is a sense of nothingness. Then there is the thrill of fear as the nose points earthward at a seemingly impossible angle. The passengers are blind to the outside world and imagination runs riot. The motion can be turbulent with a great sensation of uncontrolled speed as the flimsy craft plummets downward, apparently out of control. Suddenly terra firma is reached with a sickening thud and the creaking airframe bounces along the ground doing, it seems, whatever it wants to do before coming to a juddering stop and lazily flopping over to one side.

And so the training went on. If Craig was a hard man, then First Sergeant Bradshaw was even harder (at least he was more vindictive), and it was under his watchful eye that Meadows began his Jump School. The seasoned World War II veteran of the 82nd Airborne appeared to dislike Meadows intensely. He didn't want skinny young brats in the Airborne—he wanted *men*. He constantly harassed the youngster who had dared to attempt to get into his great unit and did his best to make him quit. Life for Meadows was punctuated by commands of: "Gimme 10," "Gimme 20," and "Gimme 50." Meadows probably became the push-up expert of all time. But despite Bradshaw's harassment he continued through the school, making some friends along the way.

Two he recalled well were Julio Neguera and Bud Malone. Another man he was extremely grateful to was a huge Hopi Indian whose name he could not bring to mind. He was the first true American Indian that Meadows had met; but it is not for that that he was remembered. That big, amiable soldier managed to keep Bradshaw off Meadows's back on many occasions when he thought that the first sergeant was giving the youth too hard a time. If he saw Bradshaw heading toward the lad, he would commit some obvious "sin," such as dropping his rifle, and divert the punishment onto his own shoulders. This informal protection lasted through the hardest part of Jump School, the thirty-four-foot tower. This soulless piece of equipment was enough to strain the nerves of any novice.

Designed for the practice of aircraft exit, in-flight techniques, and landing positions, it is a device from which many men shrink. From a high tower a steel cable runs at an angle of about 30 degrees down to earth. The hapless soldier is suspended from a rolling pulley in a parachute harness; he leaps from the platform of the tower and hurtles to earth, trying to remember to hit the sandpit with his feet and knees together and go into a natural roll. It is probably worse than the first parachute jump.

At last they were through. At the graduation parade, during which it is customary for members of the recipient's family to pin the wings on the successful soldier's chest, Richard Meadows and Julio Neguera, having no kinfolk present, solemnly performed the courtesy on each other. The parade then opened ranks so that congratulations could be made, and at that point Meadows saw First Sergeant Bradshaw heading toward him in a very determined fashion. His immediate thought was that he had committed some sin and was about to be chewed out again. He was delighted and surprised when Bradshaw thrust out his hand and said, "Son, you're going to be one hell of a paratrooper." At that moment Meadows loved him.

"Those were hard but happy days, and I'll never forget how effective and moving the beating of retreat and the lowering of the flag were. They brought back all the feelings and memories of the Civil War, World War II, and everything a soldier stands for. At those moments I'm sure that we were all prepared to give up our lives willingly."

The newly trained men shipped to Fort Bragg, a post with which Meadows was destined to become very familiar in later years. They were billeted in old wooden barracks and put into a holding pattern. All of Meadows's money was being spent on Hershey bars to bolster the food which was nowhere near as good as that served up at Jump School. He was growing fast, always desperately hungry, and usually broke. At last there was some movement and much to his disappointment Meadows, the would-be infantryman, was sent off to the artillery.

He was despondent to be going to the artillery, but his feelings were eased somewhat when he arrived on station. Master Sergeant Eddie Powers, a leg (nonjumper), met the incoming soldiers. They were shown into barracks where the beds were already made up and they were given an initial brief. At dinner that night the mess hall was spick and span and the new intakes were treated like broth-ers and with respect. They ate from plates, not trays, and the food was excellent. Meadows remembered thinking for the first time that the army was now his home and family.

What followed was good living after the rigors of basic and jump training. By the time he had reached his sixteenth birthday Meadows had completed eight more jumps with the artillery. Work for the most part consisted of stripping, packing, and loading the howitzers until it was second nature. There was a lot of demon-stration work, and though it eventually became boring there were many good experienced senior NCOs and commanders from whom Meadows was able to soak up information. He was as eager to learn as ever and believed that no military knowledge, even if it were not pertinent to the job at hand, would ever be wasted. He began to move up the promotion ladder despite his youth. The feeling of having found his true home persisted and grew.

No matter how pleasant and fun-loving his nature may be, ev-ery soldier worth his salt has to have his first fistfight. Meadows was no exception, and it was to happen after he had been given the act-ing rank of "buck" sergeant. He was sitting with a group of friends in the Rainbow Room in Phenix City, Alabama. They had purchased their whiskey in a store and taken it to the Rainbow Room, where they bought their mixers. Meadows's thoughts were far away as he spotted a pretty young waitress who looked remarkably like his childhood sweetheart, Mary Ellen Foster. He became aware of a fig-ure standing by him and looked up to see Roberts, a tough ex–coal miner in his thirties. Roberts was well known to be a troublemaker in barracks (though highly rated as a soldier in the field). He knew that Meadows was to be the Corporal of the Guard the next night and he demanded that he be given the favored twelve-hour post.

Meadows had already given the post to someone else, but, sens-ing trouble, he just shrugged and appeared to agree. Roberts then took the bottle of whiskey off their table and returned to his own. A couple of the friends protested, but Meadows calmed them down and went out for another bottle. In truth he was scared of the mus-cular, mean-talking Roberts.

True to form, Roberts came back to the table and said that he wanted to make sure that Meadows understood his demand for the best post the next night. He then reached out for the new bottle of whiskey. This time Meadows reacted. He grabbed the bottle and told Roberts that there was no way he would be getting the twelve-hour post. This was too much for Roberts, and he invited Meadows outside to "get his ass whipped." As they took off their jackets and squared up Meadows knew fear. He later said that he had had some sort of "blackout"; he hit Roberts with a good hard punch and then just kept swinging and flailing until Roberts collapsed on the ground. Meadows was not about to let him get up, and it was only the whistles of the MPs in the background that made him beat a retreat. When Roberts came out of the hospital, the first thing he did was find Meadows, who thought that the whole thing would have to start again, but Roberts shook his hand and declared that he was now firmly on the side of Meadows.

The fight with Roberts created something of the "gunslinger" syndrome of the old Wild West. Many fighters wanted to test themselves against Meadows. There was quite a bit of disgruntlement about his youth and rank. A lot of World War II veterans had earned their rank based on their size, toughness, and combat experience. Some of them were not too bright, and a fight was always a welcome diversion. Meadows took his share of knocks and had his nose broken a couple of times—but he learned from each encounter, and they became less frequent as time wore on.

He was now a gun team commander and his team was known to be among the best, but he was having problems with Lieutenant Kirk, who always seemed to be on his back. By now the Korean War had broken out and Meadows wanted nothing more than to prove himself in combat. His chance came when the call went out from the 187th Regimental Combat Team (RCT) for volunteers for six-month tours of duty in Korea. He did not hesitate, but after two weeks he had received no news, and when he checked he was told that his papers had been lost and that he should resubmit them. Lieutenant Kirk was not making things easy. His second application was not approved, and Meadows went home on a thirty-day furlough a very unhappy man.

He had a very unsatisfactory furlough. His father was bitter and uncommunicative, feeling that he had somehow been let down and deprived of help on what he for the first time called the "family farm." Hattie was living in Charleston and there was no space in her life for the young soldier. After a couple of desultory weeks with old school friends Meadows returned to barracks early.

That was a good move because he found out very quickly that

his first application for duty in Korea had in fact been approved, so, despite the second one being turned down, he was all set to go into combat and learn that his romantic illusions of war bore little resemblance to reality. When he shipped out to the Far East he knew only a little about the "police action" taking place there. On June 26, 1950, the UN Security Council had approved a resolution that called the North Korean communist-inspired invasion of South Korea a "breach of the peace and an action of aggression." It called upon all UN members to assist in the restoration of peace. Seoul, the South Korean capital, fell to the communists on June 28. June 30 saw President Harry Truman sanctioning the commitment of the first U.S. ground forces from their bases in Japan into Korea, from where they reached the battlefield on July 4. Shortly after this the UN approved the creation of a unified command in Korea and General Douglas MacArthur was appointed commander. Although there was a commitment of troops from sixteen nations, the United States was to supply the bulk of the air units, naval forces, military supplies, and hard cash.

The North Koreans, trained and supplied by the Soviet Union and China, forced a rapid retreat by the UN forces right back to a defensive perimeter along the Naktong River line. MacArthur made a brilliant counterattack on the flanks of the North Korean army into Inchon, where he successfully trapped the majority of the enemy forces. The main force either surrendered or fled, allowing MacArthur's soldiers to march back north to the 38th parallel. By October 26, the UN forces had reached the Manchurian border at the Yalu River via the North Korean capital of P'yongyang. The situation was short-lived.

In November 1950, the Chinese, who had moved troops along the Yalu after the Inchon landing, entered Korea. The UN troops were forced to retreat in disorder. Seoul was reevacuated in January 1951, but the Chinese advance was halted at P'yongt'aek in February. By March 31, the UN forces had again reached the 38th parallel. MacArthur's advocacy of taking the war into China, against the political desires of President Truman, resulted in his dismissal. General Matthew B. Ridgeway took command and continued to fight the holding action along the 38th parallel. That was the state of the war when Meadows arrived in Japan to join the 187th Regimental Combat Team.[2]

The 187th RCT was a combined infantry and artillery team.

Meadows, already a sergeant first class, got his own gun immediately and was sent for combat training to Teague, in Japan. He was good at his work and was well received by the unit. Enjoying the training, which was enhanced in his mind by the closeness of the battlefield, Meadows was both fascinated by and apprehensive about the horror stories told in the NCO's club each evening by the veterans on R&R. Despite the blood-curdling tales, the situation still seemed unreal. Not for long. The reinforcements were moved in to join the 7th Division south of Seoul, which was in the process of recovering an airfield, and the guns were soon into action. Meadows remembered seeing shell holes with bodies in them but had no time to think about it; that came later, when the troops had to move the corpses. His earlier feelings of excitement soon dissipated. Attacking unseen targets and laying and firing the guns became one long mindless flog, and at the end of each barrage the guns were cleaned, ammunition was made ready, and the gunners slept where they could, grabbing a bite to eat whenever they were able. He was conscious of the fact that he and his comrades stank: often water was scarce and there were more uses to put it to than washing and shaving.

Soon the team was moved to join the 3rd Division, which had orders to retake the Inji Valley, which had been lost by the 2nd Division. That was arduous infantry work, with the guns supporting long, hard attacks in which a lot of men died. There were also short, sharp retreats where dead men's foxholes were used. Now Meadows had men dying alongside him—some friends and some unknown; some survived with terrible injuries. The full horrors of war became clear to the young man, though he learned quickly to accept it as soldiers do. Eventually the position was surrounded by the Chinese, and Meadows marveled at the attacks as the long, extended lines of approaching soldiers seemed to absorb all the artillery and small arms fire without ever faltering or getting thinner.

For the frontline soldiers the nights were the worst. Every shadow was the enemy; every creak and rustle was a Chinese soldier. Sleep was measured in snatched minutes and the pervasive tiredness was draining. When forced awake after a short nap it was difficult to focus intelligently unless the position was under attack, at which point the adrenalin would work its magic only to leave a person even more desperately tired afterward. Rumors were rife and every night the word was that twenty thousand Chinese were going to break through the next day.

The days were not much better, but at least they were keeping the guns in action. Sometimes it was almost direct fire, the elevation was so low. In the trenches beside the artillery pieces there were medium machine guns, M1 Garand rifles, and grenades. Many of these weapons had been taken from the dead. The Chinese assaults seemed interminable despite great numbers falling to the heavy defensive fire. Death was not the only fear on the Korean front line. Stories abounded about how the Chinese tortured their prisoners, and for many death was preferable to capture.

The U.S. armor eventually broke through, but not before the division had lost about two-thirds of its strength. Meadows witnessed a direct hit on one of the guns and was appalled by the carnage, but still found this easier to deal with than the constant sniping. In that landscape it was almost impossible to do more than guess at the direction the sniper fire was coming from. There were no giveaway puffs of dust. The snipers dampened the ground around them before they opened fire. Men would be chatting away about the sort of pointless things soldiers talk about when suddenly one of them would drop with a bullet hole in him. The Chinese snipers were good, and the demoralizing effect was tremendous. Meadows was interested in the fact that men with World War II experience had the ability to laugh, joke, and make comments about life having been worse on the Normandy beaches, but he eventually realized that they were as scared as anyone else. However, they had learned to hide their fear. It was a valuable lesson for him.

A respite followed the relief of 3rd Division shortly afterward and Meadows was sent back to Kyushu, Japan, with the other survivors for rest and recuperation. He recalled:

It was a great place. There were hot springs there. We were in a place called Imoluchi as far as I can remember. We were training as the first 6-gun battery in history and we had the 105 howitzer. That was a honey of a gun. It was about that time that Lieutenant Krepps (a fine guy) called me in and said, "Well, Master Sergeant Meadows. How are you doing?" "Sir, I'm no master sergeant," I said. "Oh yes you are," he replied. And that was that. Master sergeant at twenty years old![3] I was pretty darned proud, but I was a bit nervous as well. It meant that guys like "Bull" McGuire and "Mac" McIntosh had been passed over, and they were pretty tough old World War II veterans. In fact, I guess it was a shock to the whole battery and I made two more enemies without even trying. Over the years they both made sergeant major, but they gave me some hard times back there in Japan.

The next ten months or so saw Meadows deployed with the restructured battery undergoing intensive training, which included packing the guns for parachuting and also preparing and devising diversionary tactics for what they were led to believe would be a combat jump into Korea. During this time Meadows witnessed parachuting fatalities for the first time—not just one but three, all on the same jump:

> Of course we all knew about parachuting fatalities, but we'd never actually seen them. All parachutists put such thoughts to the backs of their minds because they know it can't happen to them. Well, when you see three buy it at the same time it sort of rocks your confidence a little and the next jump tends to be something of nervous affair. You know, when I think back on it, I think those guys fell in total silence. Maybe my memory's playing tricks. I think if it had been me I might have given a pretty loud howl.

It was a period of quiet maturing for the young master sergeant. Constantly seeking to perfect his knowledge, he did a lot of homework on the gun mechanisms and not always with the desired results. He would take the guns apart and try to devise ways of getting them working again if they were damaged in action. On a number of occasions he had to call in the mechanics to fix things, but he did get to know the pieces well. The mechanics complained that once Meadows had gotten them to a gun he would not release them until they had gone through every technical detail he wanted to know.

Meadows was emerging as a knowledgeable and confident young leader, but in his own mind he was still hampered by his self-perceived inability to write as well as he thought he should as a master sergeant. There were no military facilities available for him to take instruction. Even if there had been, it is doubtful whether his pride would have allowed him to participate in them at that time. This explains to a large degree why he was so determined to excel in as many technical matters as he could. Asking a technical question was one thing, but asking how to spell or construct grammar was quite another. Meadows's pride led him to conceal his lack of formal education from everyone. On a number of occasions he was asked to consider going forward to Officer Candidate School (OCS), and he always countered these suggestions by saying that he was perfectly happy as a senior NCO. Secretly he feared exposure if he went along with the idea. He began developing his spoken briefings to the point that he rarely used notes at all; on those occasions when he did, they were simply one-word or one-line cues to assist in fluidity. In this respect his memory was quite remarkable.

Mid-1953 saw Meadows with the 674th Field Artillery Battalion back in the combat zone of Korea. This time the unit was in support of infantry along the DMZ, but negotiations for the armistice were well under way and life was relatively quiet. When the time for rotation back to the States came around, they were well and truly bored. Transport back was by troopship, and Meadows, with a massive hangover from the night before, made one of his few tactical errors: he pulled rank when a couple of senior NCOs tried to choose their own bunks. He took a top bunk, which is about the worst position to be in if there is a heavy sea, and he got a long and uncomfortable bout of seasickness that lasted for much of the journey home. Once back in the United States, but as yet unknown to him, his life was on course for another change.

3

Special Forces

1952–1960

Meadows's first assignment back in the United States took him to Fort Pitman, California. SFC Julio Neguera and First Sergeant Joe Candy, whom he had also met at Jump School, were with him at this time, three buddies with friendship born of mutual experience in basic training and the shared hardships of combat. It was back to the old routine of clean the guns, disassemble the guns, pack the guns, parachute with the guns, assemble the guns, fire the guns, and clean the guns again. Though Meadows was still taking a pride in his work, peacetime soldiering's lack of pressure made it a matter of no great persuasion for him to be tempted into the downtown attractions of the local dance halls.

Life was full of surprises for a still young set of soldiers, and there was an occasion remembered by Meadows when all three of the modern-day musketeers were vying for the attention of a single girl in one of the downtown dance halls. Such places catered mostly to the soldiers from Fort Pitman, and the girls were eager to separate the men from their money in the time-honored fashion. On the whole, Korean veterans were treated in a friendly manner and life was rosy. All the girls were out for drinks and no doubt had a racket organized with the owners, but one girl caught the eye of all three warriors and a little competition sprang up between them for her favors. Maybe the whiskey made her even prettier, but Meadows was determined to be first in line.

As they joked and flirted with the girl, Meadows noticed a big, unpleasant-looking master sergeant approaching their table. He wore the Master Jumper insignia and had an impressive collection of World War II medal ribbons. He reached the table and curtly told the girl to go away. Julio Neguera jumped up and protested that he was about to kiss the lady. With a grin the master sergeant responded: "Well, sonny, you go right ahead, but I'm here to tell you that the son of a bitch has a set of balls in his panties!" All feelings of passion soon dispersed and the young soldiers got an object lesson in life. Later, in a different bar, Meadows got another shock when a waitress appeared topless. He was with some friends older than himself who lacked his shyness. Each time he stared at the waitress she would look him in the eye and smile, causing him to look down in embarrassment. She then came over and asked him what he was staring at, and all he could think of was to blurt out that he wanted to buy her a drink but that he was a year short of the age when it was legal to buy alcohol in California. His friends started laughing at this, but it was short-lived. The lady told him that the drink would be on her as it had been such a long time since a guy had stared so longingly at her equipment.

Shortly after that Meadows, Candy, and Neguera were split up and sent on different assignments. Meadows was sent to the East Coast to Fort Bragg to experience a different taste of post-Korea life. In the Fayetteville bars, many of which had antiblack and antisoldier posters on the walls, there was a good chance of an aggressive approach from a civilian demanding to know why a soldier had been fighting someone else's war. Though the situation would get worse in the years of the Vietnam War, those were the days of the "McCarthy madness" and the "reds under the beds" era.

At Fort Bragg he was due to take over as first sergeant of an artillery battery with the 82nd Airborne. But the army grapevine is good and he had heard rumors of the formation of a new outfit. His curiosity was aroused. He was now a combat veteran with the badges and medals to prove it. He was a soldier fully on top of his trade. He was confident in his ability to move into the new responsibilities of a first sergeant, but he wondered if there was something else out there. He was eager for a change from the eternal gun drills. With furlough to come before he signed in for duty, he took time out to look for an old friend. He knew that Ed Denton was somewhere in Fort Bragg and would probably know something about the rumors. He made his way across the post to seek his old friend's advice.

Denton was a tough soldier for whom Meadows had a great deal of respect. When he eventually found him, in a barrack room on Smoke Bomb Hill, Denton was flat out on his bed, having just returned from a field exercise. Meadows woke him up, expecting to be congratulated on his promotion to master sergeant and to have some acknowledgment made about his combat badges. That did not happen. Denton seemed exhausted but glad to see his old buddy. He explained that he had joined the new outfit but that he could not talk much about it. What he did say, however, was to change Meadows's life as a soldier: "We need guys like you, Dick, you oughta join, but it's not easy." It didn't take Meadows long to find out a bit more about the Special Forces, and it caught his imagination immediately.

In common with all the allied countries that had made victory possible in World War II, the United States had discontinued special operations shortly after the cessation of hostilities. Under the control of General "Wild Bill" Donovan of the Office of Strategic Services (OSS), individuals, groups, and units had worked behind enemy lines in Europe, the Balkans, Africa, and Burma. The West had not expected the rapid spread of communism and the enthusiastic maintenance of that political ideal. After Eastern Europe fell to the Soviet Union, some third-world countries became ripe targets. The Soviet Union and the People's Republic of China inexorably extended their grip.

A conventional army has severe limitations when sent into action in an insurgent scenario. The collection, collation, and precise exploitation of intelligence, the ability to operate aggressively in small numbers, mobility, and the means through which to conduct "hearts and minds" operations became the key factors in some of the many "wars of liberation" that were beginning to emerge. Britain had recognized the need during the Malayan Emergency and acted by re-forming the Special Air Service Regiment, which in 1952 was beginning to prove the effectiveness of small patrol operations deep behind enemy lines in counterinsurgency operations.

In mid-1952, under command of the U.S. Army Chief of Psychological Warfare, the 10th Special Forces Group (SFG) began calling for volunteers for a new and exciting challenge.[1] Ed Denton was one of many outstanding officers and noncommissioned officers who responded to the call, and the concept also caught the imagination of Meadows.

As he had not yet "signed-in" for his assignment with 82nd Airborne, Meadows had no difficulty in getting a transfer to the 10th SFG. He was initially looked at a little askance, but this was because of his youth. He was into a selective process within which there were World War II veterans of Special Forces, former members of resistance groups, and a few ex-OSS men, all of them experienced and parachute qualified.

The concrete indications of professionalism attracted him instantly. Despite the disparity in ages, education, and experience, the young Meadows fit in well with his fellow contenders for admission into the new force, but not without his own ever-present doubts. He had no problems with the long marches and navigation tests; what worried him most at the time were the seemingly formidable academic requirements. The tests designed to show how the students would cope with learning intelligence operations, medical work, communications, and demolitions appeared to be complex. Every man was expected to specialize in one main skill but also had to master a secondary skill to bolster the team's efficiency. There just seemed to be such a lot to learn and understand. In the early stages Meadows, true to form, learned things parrot fashion, but full understanding was quick to follow.

Dick's natural curiosity and pride gave him the edge he needed to become a star pupil. He had fought his own lonely battle against his lack of formal education, but once he realized that his natural learning ability and acute memory put him on an equal footing with his peers, there was no barrier to his acceptance into the organization. To him Special Forces represented a whole different way of soldiering, one that gave scope for initiative beyond anything he had ever dreamed could be available in the military.

The teams of the 10th SFG were designed for long-range penetration operations into potentially hostile areas behind enemy lines, where they could be expected to work for long periods with little or no formal support. Making contact with indigenous resistance or guerrilla groups, training them, and, if necessary, leading them into action were all part of a day's work. There were escape and evasion tactics to learn, resistance to interrogation methods to remember, sabotage techniques and operational planning skills to master. Above all, though, were the leadership qualities required to become a dependable, respected member of a team without losing the ability to command in the field.

The selection, training, formal organization, and validation operations for the 10th SFG took a whole year before they were to be committed to active duty in Europe. When the proud members of the new Special Forces' "flagship" moved out to their new base in Europe, they left behind a number of disappointed men who were to be tasked with the business of selecting, training, and forming a new group of specialists, the 77th SFG.

The 10th SFG was destined to set up shop in Flint Kaserne at Bad Tölz, Bavaria. This beautiful country made a perfect setting for the missions they were to undertake. It bordered Czechoslovakia and was within striking distance of the southern boundaries of East Germany that suited very well the primary role of the unit. Here the group trained to support resistance movements and operate with guerrilla forces in the Soviet-dominated Eastern European satellites to the U.S.S.R. If necessary, they could be deployed with relative ease to the Middle East or even Africa. The training had a real military and political purpose in those days of Soviet postwar ambitions.

The countryside itself was perfect for training in the many skills required to fulfill the SFG role. There were high mountains, dense forests, clear summer skies for parachuting, self-contained airfields, and lakes aplenty. On top of this was the close proximity of the border with a Soviet-controlled country. Bavaria, in the years just after World War II, had still not shaken off the fact that it had been a hotbed of Nazi intrigue. Bad Tölz, nearby Lenggries, and Munich had been at the center of Hitler's early public appearances, and there was still a quite firm resistance to the presence of U.S. troops, albeit hidden under a thin veneer of acceptance. What to the troops was little more than generosity, to the locals was largesse; the Bavarians took all that was offered but despised the troops for their constant show of hospitality, which they felt was demeaning.

The local farmers had their own way of showing their displeasure at this army of "occupation." They had a very good intelligence network among the civilian workers in Flint Kaserne. When it became known that the troops were about to take part in a parachute operation they would quickly load up their "honey wagons" with human fertilizer from the cesspits and spread the loads over the drop zones. Clip joints began to appear in the town of Bad Tölz, with girls flooding in from nearby Munich. There would be anonymous tip-offs made about troops fraternizing in out-of-bounds areas. Gradually these things diminished, but for a while life was not as pleasant as it could have been. For Meadows, though, these were treasured days. The freedom he had as a small detachment master sergeant to devise tactics and unconventional methods to resolve problems gave him extreme satisfaction. Insofar as any soldier ever can be, he seemed to be in charge of his own destiny.

Aware that he could learn not only from the books, manuals, and courses, but also from some of the highly effective soldiers who surrounded him, he made up his own dictum. The Meadows recipe for military success was "Seek out the top 10 percent of the officers and soldiers around you. They are the ones to study and rub shoulders with, to learn from and to go into competition against."

The inferiority complex that Meadows had wrongly borne for some years began to fade, although he remained hampered by the difficulty he found in quickly writing fluent military reports. To get over this he continued to expand his verbal abilities and to turn himself into as complete a soldier as he could. The shy boy from West Virginia was gone and a confident, seasoned leader was emerging. His exhaustive reading and natural curiosity produced another facet to his character of which he was hardly aware. His vocabulary had expanded enormously from that provided by his meager education. He was able to express himself with a rare clarity that left no listener in any doubt as to his requirements. His calm delivery of orders and his total composure inspired immediate and full confidence. In short, he was already a formidable leader. Known as a man of action, Meadows began to pick up another reputation—that of a thinking man. If all of this makes him seem to be a man who did not enjoy himself, then it has to be said that that was not so. Meadows would party hard with the best of his comrades and had an eye for a pretty fraülein to match that of any Casanova. And certainly pretty girls were in abundance in Bad Tölz and nearby Munich.

The tour of duty in Bavaria came to an end in July 1956, and Meadows was routed back to the States to join the 77th SFG at the now familiar Smoke Bomb Hill complex in Fort Bragg. Life did not stand still at Fort Bragg; Special Forces was expanding and in 1957 the 1st SFG was formed in Okinawa to conduct support operations for unconventional warfare in the Far East. Meadows was in demand as a well-respected trainer and leader. There were many temporary missions to far-flung places, during which he built up a reputation as the man who always made things work despite the odds. In his book, *Code Name: Copperhead*, Sergeant Major Joe Garner says: "MSG Dick Meadows was our NCOIC for training and in charge of jungle navigation. Meadows was the elite of the elite when it came to training and conditioning and was a walking example of the best that SF put into the field."

When then-Captain Elliott "Bud" Sydnor was taking his indoctrination tour on joining the 77th SFG, he noticed the tall, confident soldier and asked his escort who he was. The reply was: "Oh. That's

Master Sergeant Dick Meadows; he gets all the best missions because he always succeeds."[2]

The successful activation of the U.S. Special Forces attracted the attention of the Special Forces in the United Kingdom, and Colonel Dare Wilson, then the Commanding Officer of the British 22nd Special Air Service Regiment, began to explore cross-training possibilities with General William P. Yarborough, then commanding the Special Warfare Center at Fort Bragg. One outcome to this liaison came as something of a surprise to Meadows. In late May 1960, he was summoned by his commanding officer and told to prepare himself for a one-year tour of duty in the UK as an exchange NCO with the SAS. His officer counterpart in this was to be Captain Sydnor.

4

A Lighthearted Interlude with the Brits

1960–1961

Meadows, though delighted at the prospect of serving with another Special Forces unit, was conscious that he knew little about the British SAS. Indeed, there was not much available information on the organization at that time. (Right up until the relief of the Iranian embassy siege in London in May 1980, the SAS managed to keep a very low profile despite deep involvement in many successful actions around the world.) Meadows researched the subject and found out that the SAS's origins had been in the Western Desert of North Africa during World War II, and that they had subsequently fought through the Aegean, Italy, France, and Germany before being disbanded at the end of the war. He discovered that they had been raised again in 1950 (as the Malayan Scouts) to carry out unconventional operations against the Chinese communists on the Malayan Peninsula; they had fought there for ten years and were covertly acknowledged both in military and political circles as a major ingredient of the success. He knew that they had the reputation at that time of being the finest postwar jungle fighting force in existence.

He had read that they had showed a remarkable talent for switching from one terrain to another at very short notice; in one case they had routed a strong rebel force in the high mountains of the Sultanate of Oman having come directly from the jungles of Malaya.[1] He had been warned that theirs was one of the toughest physical selection courses in the world, with only a 5 percent pass rate. Outside of this his knowledge was scant.

Meadows by this time knew and respected Sydnor, and he was delighted that the two of them would be forming this first and critical exchange partnership. Sydnor was a tough, straight-talking officer from Kentucky who had already impressed the 77th SFG with his leadership abilities and his calm, unflappable approach to any problem. He was an impressive man, physically fit and in those days rarely seen without a cigar clamped between his teeth. Sydnor was married and would be taking his wife, Jean, to the UK with him. Meadows almost didn't make it.

On a training run one evening he suffered a sudden pain in his chest that intensified alarmingly quickly. He found himself struggling for breath and could not understand why. He slowed down and began the walk back to his barrack block with the pain worsening all the time. He staggered to his bed and collapsed on it, wondering what was happening to him. As the pain began to ease he put it down to some sort of mild infection. He was not used to illness. After a few hours he got up to take a shower and the pain hit him again; fortunately one of his friends was there and had Meadows taken immediately to the dispensary. Within minutes a collapsed lung was diagnosed. The cure: surgery, followed by complete rest. After the surgery Meadows pushed himself physically, against all medical advice. He was determined not to miss the assignment to Britain. At the medical examination before he went, the doctors expressed amazement at the speed of his recovery and pronounced him fit for active duty.

Hereford, which lies in the west of England in an area known as the "Marches" and bordering with Wales, was then the SAS base. Very much an agricultural area, the countryside is soft, rolling hills divided by beautiful, forested river valleys holding charming old villages. The barracks at Bradbury Lines was a surprise to Meadows; he had expected something more modern to house a special regiment that had been established for ten years. In fact the regiment had just moved to the town and the camp was one of the typical World War II leftovers which many of the country's soldiers occupied at that time. The wooden clinker-built barrack blocks conformed to the dated "spider" system, with three legs spreading out of each side of a central block that housed the communal latrines and ablution facilities.

The barrack rooms, each holding about a dozen men and heated by a sparse network of inefficient radiators, were reminiscent of a Rudyard Kipling ballad. Hot in the summer, these billets were extremely cold in the winter. The Warrant Officers' and Sergeants' Mess which was to be Meadows's home for the next fifteen months was built to a similar principle, but he had the benefit of a small single room and access to a bar that seemed never to close. As a married man, Sydnor fared a little better, having a brick built house for his family adjacent to the Officers' Mess.

The central parade square is a feature that dominates every military barracks in Britain; in the case of Hereford it seemed to be more in demand as a car park than as an area for demonstrating the intricacies of foot drill. Meadows observed that the morning "muster" parade seemed to be little more than a formality to check that everyone was present. The troops fell into line and the only movement thereafter was that of soldiers coming to attention as they answered their names. When the order to dismiss was given they all seemed to vanish to the four corners of the camp with no sense of urgency. Although there was a "guard room" at the entrance to the camp, it seemed to serve little purpose since there were as many ways into the compound as there were facets to a man's imagination. These were the days before terrorism hit mainland Britain. The soldiers who strolled around the camp were clean but hardly well polished; only the officers seemed to wear rank insignia, and there was an incredible number of long, handlebar mustaches adorning the faces of some of the obvious veterans. Their overall manner was one of familiarity, and officers and men alike seemed to know each other well.

The first hurdle for Meadows was the selection course for which he had volunteered. The system then in operation was an initial two-week period spent in assessing the course volunteers. This took the form of some basic navigational instruction and then a series of ever-increasing marches with ever-greater loads to carry, the whole of these marches being conducted in the mountains of Central Wales. Those mountains are not high, but they are steep, and the pressure was on to complete the marches against the clock. The culminating point of this part of the course was the endurance march, approximately forty miles across hard, broken terrain carrying a load of about fifty pounds, a heavy belt kit, and a rifle with no sling. Probably the most difficult aspect of the course was that the aspirants mainly operated alone; they were dropped off in different places and often had to make the rendezvous points in a different order. The result was that the loneliness and the lack of a buddy with whom to cross-check navigational decisions would begin to erode the confidence of some soldiers. If the movement was during the night or one of the heavy fogs for which the area is famous, then the effects of disorientation compounded the erosion. Add to this the extremes of weather and it will be understood how demanding the course could be. If a man's navigation was not good he wasted time and had to walk farther. The factor that surprised Meadows was the lack of urging on by the instructors:

> I found that course very hard, but the instructors never tried to persuade a volunteer to go faster; there was no shouting at them and no advice of any kind given. They were simply checked through the various rendezvous [RV] points and had their rucksacks weighed and water bottles checked, usually in silence. Their attitude indicated that they didn't really care whether you passed or not. Occasionally if the instructors wanted to put someone to the test they may try to persuade a guy that he'd had enough and wouldn't it be a good idea if he packed it in. Sometimes this worked.
>
> You never ever knew which of the RVs would be the final one. I remember finishing the endurance march confident that I had arrived at the final RV because the trucks were there and an urn of tea, only to be told that the tea was for the instructors and that I had more miles to cover. I hoped that my disappointment didn't show as I shouldered my rucksack and moved off again. They let me go about two hundred meters before they laughingly called me back. If you were not at the final RV on time then you had to make your own way back to the base and this could be quite a distance. I once was on a vehicle which pulled away from the RV even though one soldier was only a couple of hundred meters away. We were based in the city of Hereford. Each morning began with a cold, two-hour truck drive to the mountains of Wales. The average time to depart was about 5 o'clock in the morning. There were no early calls for the soldiers on selection. If they didn't wake up in time to have breakfast or start the day's exercise—tough—they went hungry or they failed. It was sobering to know that certainly one, and I think it might have been two guys, had died on the winter course before ours.

By the time the first part of the course was ended the volunteers were usually down to a dozen or so soldiers from about one hundred starters. The second part of the course, which Meadows was not required to complete due to his existing experience, was a form of continuation training with navigation, weapon handling, basic medical, patrolling, and other skills being taught. The arduous field exercises continued. Those who made it through this were then reckoned to be ready to join a SAS troop, where they would continue to be assessed for at least another year.

Meadows passed the course and was assigned to a saber (active duty) squadron. Bud Sydnor's recollection of initial assignments is interesting:

> Speaking primarily of Dick's and my reception into the SAS, I was asked by the second-in-command if I wanted to work or watch. I don't know what he may have said to Dick but they assigned him and gave him a leadership position as they had me.
>
> I think that nearly everyone that he [Dick] had any kind of contact with was impressed by all those things he had learned in Special Forces. And this is the time to say this: when I describe Dick to friends of mine I say, "Well, here's this guy who has everything to be immodest about and yet he's the most modest person that I know." So Dick wasn't claiming any expertise, he was just demonstrating it all the time. And because they [SAS] were jungle fighters and only that at that time, because of the ten years of the Malayan war. That's where he stepped in and I believe he was probably the role model for a number of the NCOs who wished that they knew or had been exposed to all those learning experiences that Dick had. He looked the part and he acted the part.

The two men became the first foreigners to be awarded the coveted SAS wings, badge, and beret since its postwar re-formation. Sydnor was assigned as a troop commander and Meadows as a troop sergeant. The rank structures of the British and U.S. armies do not equate simply. Sydnor and Meadows were appointed to commands exactly equal to those that their British counterparts would take. Though this sounds perfectly fair and reasonable, it has to be borne in mind that these commands were taking place in a "foreign" army and within a regiment which had its own pride, prejudices, and other quirks.

Once Meadows had proven himself on the selection course he had no problems in getting on with the Brits. His charm, friendliness, and obvious professionalism ensured his total acceptance. He kept many of his thoughts to himself and showed great tact in passing on his experiences. He realized that although the SAS at that time lagged well behind the U.S. Special Forces in terms of foreign weapons, explosives handling, and language training, they also had things to teach him. The ten-year war in Malaya had made them masters in the art of silent patrolling. They were very good field communicators with radios, which were tailor-made for their job, and they would experiment a lot with techniques and tactics. Meadows liked the doctrine that it was the man that made the difference, not the equipment he was carrying. Many of their training methods would have given a U.S. Army range safety officer headaches, but they were effective and he was to use many of them in Laos and Vietnam in the years to follow. One thing in particular he liked was the way that they used little models of the ground made in mud or wet sand to show routes to the indigenous aborigines they worked with in Malaya. Those natives could not read maps, but they could recognize the ground formations very easily.

At that time the SAS had their own ideas on personal equipment. They reckoned that a man had to be able to survive for four or five days with what he carried on his belt. If they had to scoot out of a situation or were surprised when resting, then there was a good chance that the rucksack would be lost. Most of them carried a pouch with a few emergency rations, ammunition, water, a parang or a good knife, and a small survival kit for fishing or repairing clothes. Much of this equipment was homemade from whatever they could scrounge. At night the belt was looped over a handy tree branch from which it could be slung quickly over the shoulder if they had to bug out. No litter was ever left at a campsite. Everything was policed up and carried back to base.

Meadows recalled that a lot of the focus and training of U.S. Special Forces at the time was on dealing with indigenous people and training them to fight. The SAS had vast experience with the aborigines of Malaya. They did not train them to fight, but they did convert them from helping the Chinese communists and they set up excellent intelligence networks. He enjoyed talking to some of those veterans who had even learned the aboriginal language. Frank Williams, Frankie Hague, Lawrence Smith, Bob Turnbull, John Cann, and Len Bullock all knew an awful lot about what is now termed "hearts and minds," but it was all in a day's work for them. They didn't think it was any special kind of skill.

Meadows also adopted their method of hand-signaling while patrolling. The signs were clear and simple enough for anyone to remember in any language. On patrol in fours, they used a buddy system where one man cooked and the other kept sentry. One man would handle the communications call and the other would prepare his meal. Their trailcraft was very good; they had some good trackers and their jungle lore was worth listening to. There were some pretty tough characters among them, but it was still a great family atmosphere. At a briefing for a mission every man had his voice, though the leader made the final decisions. They called it a "Chinese parliament." This Chinese parliament was not an uncontrolled element. One of the SAS's great strengths was that its volunteers came from all walks of military life, from all of the logistics corps as well as infantry regiments, so there was a big span of knowledge—particularly in technical matters. By letting every man have his say the commander knew that he would not miss out on any good ideas. But at the end of the session there was never any quibbling about the decisions made—everyone knew that he had had his chance to contribute.

Self-discipline was a characteristic looked for during the selection course, and this became evident to Meadows after he took command of his troop. There was no compulsory fitness training, and when he decided to organize a run he was taken aside by a corporal and told, "Hey, Dick, we get fit and stay fit in our own time, not the army's time." If a man became unfit then he went. There was no argument. If he couldn't do his job at any time then he was of no use to the SAS. Meadows appreciated that one of the biggest differences between the USSF and SAS was that the SAS ground commanders were allowed much more flexibility in achieving their missions. They had a saying that "the man on the ground is right," and he liked that approach.

The SAS was in an early stage of its post-Malaya development when Meadows and Sydnor arrived on the scene, and their input was of immense value to the regiment. It was Sydnor and Meadows who started off the first new look at demolition techniques, and it was Meadows himself who ran the field survival section of the first of the combat survival courses which became a British Army-wide responsibility for the SAS in the years that followed. He had some interesting memories of that course:

> One of the pieces I remember best was the one bit that the Brits wouldn't let us take part in. That was the resistance to interrogation phase. Mostly an ex-RAF odd guy called Squadron Leader Parker ran it, and I'm not too sure that the guy was alright in the head. When soldiers were captured they went through some of the most realistic interrogation that I've ever seen. They were kept in boxes where they couldn't stand up. They were hosed down with cold water. They got continual abuse from guards who seemed to be talking Russian and they were generally given hell. Some of them, after a couple of days, began to hallucinate and think it was for real. Those men who happened to be in the regiment were sent back to their own units if they gave more than date of birth, number, rank, and name. I remember being told that Parker used to bring his wife along and she'd be paraded in front of naked soldiers and briefed to giggle at what she'd call their "tiny dicks." I think the course really tested the determination of some of the young soldiers who attended it. It was certainly realism at its best.

Other people remember Meadows's backwoods expertise with some humor. In the northeast of England lies the Army Training Area of Otterburn. It is a wild area, heavily forested in parts and with large stretches of open, wind-blasted moorland. Shaping its contours are many rivers and streams containing small but tasty river trout. On a squadron field exercise in 1960, Meadows was quick to show his prowess at trout "tickling." This is the art of laying on the riverbank, putting one's arm and hand into the water, and gently searching along the bank for a resting trout. The fisherman gently strokes along the length of the fish until his hand is in the right position. At the right time he quickly flicks the fish out of the water and onto the bank. On hearing that the "A" Squadron sergeants had enjoyed a delicious fish supper provided by the skilled hands of Dick Meadows, Major Peter Walter, Squadron Commander and a country boy himself, summoned Meadows. With a stern face he pointed out to the embarrassed soldier that all the rivers in Great Britain are either privately owned or are the possessions of government. To fish with neither the owner's permission nor a government license was a crime punishable by heavy fines. Walter suggested that the only thing that could dissuade him from reporting this heinous crime would be if a dozen or so trout were to be produced for the officers' supper. That night Meadows had very cold hands! Another famous SAS officer recalled that when he was being instructed in the finer arts of fishing by Meadows he accidentally grabbed a water rat by mistake. The water rat is an aggressive and tenacious little beast with long, very sharp fangs, and that officer bears the scars of his misadventure to this day.

A consensus of opinion among those SAS soldiers who knew him at the time can be encapsulated by a quotation from a notable SAS soldier, Corporal Maurice Tudor (later lieutenant colonel), who said, "Meadows was the most complete soldier I ever met." Sydnor was right—many British SAS soldiers soaked up everything Meadows could pass on, and more than a few modeled themselves on him.

Meadows's off-duty home with the SAS was that uniquely British military institution known as the Warrant Officers' and Sergeants' Mess. In those days the Mess, as it is familiarly called, had two bars. One was a long bar in a room with bar stools, tables, and chairs along with the usual dartboard and "one-armed bandit." The other bar was the "Inner Sanctum," a small, intimate room holding only about eight to ten people in any degree of comfort. The Inner Sanctum was for the proven "warriors," who each purchased his own pewter tankard that hung on the wall. Entrance was by invitation and not by right of being a senior NCO. Almost a Masonic institution, within the walls of the Inner Sanctum discussions of a very private nature took place—maybe a rehash of a recent exercise, maybe the agenda for the next promotion conference, or maybe a verdict on a new young officer's or soldier's suitability for the SAS. An invitation to join the Inner Sanctum in those days signaled full acceptance into the brotherhood of the Mess. It was probably unique in the British Army.

It was fairly early on in his days there that it was noticed that the tall, blue-eyed, handsome "Yank" had as much of an eye for the Hereford ladies as they had for him. The Warrant Officers' and Sergeants' Mess of 22nd SAS Regiment was a local legend. The bar closed when the last man ordained it so, and the girls were always keen to get an invitation to the place—and not always just for the drinks. The weekends could be riotous occasions. Meadows remembered one weekend in particular that took place shortly after he had taken command of his troop:

> Arthur Watchus came up to me and said that there was a particularly attractive girl in town who had been asking about me and that he had taken the liberty of inviting her to the Mess on that Saturday night to meet me. He hoped I didn't mind but would I turn up, just for a couple of hours, so that he didn't get saddled with her, as his wife was also attending the Mess that night. Well, I sure wasn't going to object and I joined Arthur and his wife at their table and met the lady. She, Phyllis, was very, very pretty and she seemed to take to me. She pulled her chair up closer when I sat down and we had a drink or two.
>
> Someone started up the jukebox and she asked me to dance. Well, I'm no great dancer but it sounded good to me. We had a dance or two and without her actually saying anything, I thought she was making it pretty plain that she was interested in making a night of it. We went to the bar and I got some more drinks, the lights were low and we moved back to the table. Arthur and his wife had gone and I supposed they were dancing. We sat as close as we could and we were talking about this and that and I was feeling pretty pleased with myself. As I bent across to say something or other I saw the shadow come over the table and I turned round to see this big, drunk, and very angry guy behind me with a chair raised over his head as though to bring it down on me. I didn't know what to do. I guess I was still a visitor in the Mess and I sure didn't want a fight. My feelings must have showed in my face because suddenly there was a great burst of laughter and a round of applause. The guy with the chair put it down and started grinning, stuck out his hand, and said something like: "Good to meet you, Yank." Of course the lady in question was his wife and I'd been set up. That was my introduction to "Gypsy" Smith, one of the SAS legends. That same night Gypsy invited me into the Inner Sanctum.

Although not operationally busy at that time, the SAS was still in a position to conduct regular overseas exercises, which both Syd-

nor and Meadows were able to participate in. Norway and Den-
mark were both very interesting, but it was the Sultanate of Oman
that Meadows enjoyed the most. It was not easy to get permission
for him to enter the Sultanate. The country was still under the des-
potic control of Sultan Said bin Taimur, to whom the Western way
of life was anathema. He tolerated the British having an occasional
presence and the SAS in particular, because of their action in quell-
ing the rebellion in his country against all odds in 1958–1959. He
was highly suspicious of anything American, as he saw them only
as oil-seekers who would bring ruin to his country; an American
soldier, therefore, could only be an oil company spy. He didn't mention the fact that British oil companies were already in his country
with his blessing. It took the solemn word of the commanding officer to promise that Meadows would never be out of sight of British eyes while he was in Oman to secure his entry. In fact, the SAS
did have a rather furtive mission on that occasion, in that it was
suspected that a further rebellion was brewing and that the oil companies did not have totally clean hands and might be giving money
to the rebellious faction. One part of the mission was to check out
the rumors of gunrunning.

The country was still wild and the occasional band of dissidents
would take potshots at military patrols, and there were still many
land mines on the various tracks that criss-crossed the deserts. There
was no air support and no mechanical support, so the vehicle-borne
patrols had to rely on their own initiative to get themselves out of
trouble. Meadows enjoyed his time in Oman; the wild, inhospitable
deserts and mountains and the lack of creature comforts appealed
to him:

> It was a great experience. It was the first time I'd had the
> chance to tackle astral-navigation, which took a bit of time
> to master. Too much math involved for my liking, but it was
> certainly precise. The desert's a great leveler where a man
> can feel truly insignificant, just a great bunch of nothing, but
> it's still alive with all sorts of creeping, crawling things and
> you wonder what they're there for. It was a bit sad for me
> when I had to be taken off the patrol. The British embassy
> got cold feet in case the SAS got caught up in a firefight with
> dissidents and I got injured. I hadn't realized that though the
> Brits had got permission from the Sultan for me to go along,

they hadn't bothered to get permission from the American embassy in London.

In fact, Meadows did not leave Oman. Instead, he was put into the company of one Colonel Johnny Cooper,[2] who was commanding an outpost of the Sultan's Armed Forces at Saiq. Saiq lay at the top of the eight-thousand-foot-high Jebel Akhdar (Green Mountain), which was the very stronghold from which the 22nd SAS had ousted the rebels just over two years earlier. As Meadows remarked:

> For me it was a bit of history come true. I was able to climb the same mountain by the same route as some of the patrols and appreciate the conditions faced by the regiment not that long ago and I met an amazing soldier of whom I'd only read. Saiq was a complete contrast to the dry desert. There were tiers of bright green foliage, date palms, and running water. If there is a heaven, then I guess it would look a bit like that. It was bright but cool during the day and very cold at night. Johnny Cooper and I ate with his Arab guys at night and we fed from a communal pot of meat and rice. After they'd eaten, some of the Arabs would wander off hand in hand into the darkness and I asked Johnny what it was all about. "Oh. It's just their way," Johnny replied. "They'll go off and sit in the cool of the night and share a cigarette and talk. The Arabs are great talkers. Don't get offended if one comes up to you and takes you by the hand and pulls you into the dark. Just go along with him." Johnny said all this with a straight face, but I didn't notice him going off with anyone and sure as hell this country boy wasn't going to.[3]

On his return to the United Kingdom, Meadows was once again to meet someone who would change his life. Pamela Thompson was one of the three strikingly attractive daughters of Sergeant Major "Spud" Thompson and his wife, Sadie. Thompson was a tough, powerfully built World War II veteran. Originally a Grenadier Guardsman, he was also an early Parachute Regiment soldier and an SAS veteran of Malaya. Hard and uncompromising as a soldier, Thompson also kept an eye on his daughters like a suspicious old eagle. His attitude toward "Yanks" could be compared to the wartime slogan of "Over-paid, over-sexed, and over here." Meadows's dates with Pamela became almost like planning a covert operation. Thompson's efforts to keep the pair apart came to naught. Pamela is a strong-minded lady, just as tough as her father. Many members of the Sergeants' Mess became willing conspirators in the following months. Dave Haley made constant requests for seventeen-year-old Pam's services as a babysitter, whether he and his wife wanted to go out or not. It is a measure of the sympathy with which their friends viewed the romance that when, late one Saturday evening, a distraught Spud Thompson burst into the Mess and shouted, "Where's the bloody Yank?" he was greeted by the calm reply that Meadows was on a weekend exercise. The exercise, of course, was in looking after Haley's children in the peace and privacy of their army quarters not very far from where Spud stood.

In those days of the very early 1960s, some members of the SAS were informally getting themselves interested in free fall parachuting. The ringleaders of the group were Cliff Eastwood and Pete Sherman, both of whom became good friends of Meadows. At one of the regular Saturday night sessions in the Sergeants' Mess they mentioned to Meadows that they were going off the next day to Thruxton, a nearby airfield, to do a couple of jumps. They asked if he would care to go along and do one. "Well, with a few pints of bitter under my belt I was game for anything and I secretly knew that they weren't serious. I knew that they couldn't risk a Yank casualty from a jump when he'd had no ground training for free fall. In the morning they'd change their minds. Of course they didn't change their minds. They woke me up and, nursing king-sized hangovers, we drove down to Thruxton. It was a beautiful day, warm sun and clear blue skies. I thought that I'd just lie in the sun and watch them perform."

Meadows was surprised when they arrived at Thruxton and were greeted by what seemed to be a pretty old pilot wearing a scuffed leather jacket, leather boots, and a little leather flying helmet with goggles pushed up on his forehead. A huge handlebar mustache which appeared to be plugged into both ears completed the archaic picture. "Biggles" said that he was ready to go and Sherman handed Meadows a parachute. Still thinking it was all a big joke and that he would be told to haul off and sit down any minute, he put it on. Eastwood pointed out the ripcord handle and told him to pull it after he had counted to five slowly. The pilot got into the tiny two-seater aircraft and beckoned him over.

"Any minute now and they'll call me back" was the thought in

Meadows's mind as he swaggered over to the flimsy little machine. He was talked through the procedure for getting in and out of the single forward passenger seat in front of the pilot and shown the only strut that he was allowed to stand on and suddenly they were away and bouncing over the grass. A few minutes later they were airborne.

Knowing that it was a joke, Meadows was surprised as they continued to gain height. It seemed to be a waste of expensive fuel. He turned to look at "Biggles" in the back seat. His goggles were down and his great mustache was pressed back in the wind till it seemed that the ends were wrapping around the back of his head. Meadows returned the pilot's thumbs-up, then turned to face the front again. There was a thump on his shoulder and he turned to see "Biggles" half-standing and pointing to the wing. Well, the wing looked okay to Meadows, so he faced front once more, only to feel another thump as "Biggles" gestured to the wing again and pointed down.

Determined not to show his concern, Meadows decided to play the joke for all it was worth. He struggled out of the cockpit and onto the strut, hanging on for grim life but trying to look unconcerned. "Biggles" gave him another thumbs-up, and thinking the jest was over Meadows began to clamber back into his seat, only to get another, harder thump from a puzzled-looking pilot as he pointed downward again. With trepidation Meadows suddenly realized that he was serious. Taking a deep breath, he let go his grip and fell off into the nothingness. Somehow he got himself turned round to face the ground and realized that he had forgotten to count. How far had he fallen? The ground looked damned close. He let it go for maybe another second and pulled the ripcord. The chute had hardly opened it seemed when he was landing.

Sherman and Eastwood were looking distinctly white-faced when they came up to him, and Meadows realized that he had opened far too low. "I guess that's what we call a combat jump in the States," he said. He was glad that the pair walked back to the truck in front of him because they would have undoubtedly noticed that his legs were still trembling. But the joke paid off for Meadows. He was hooked on free fall from that point on and did as much as he could during his remaining time there.

It was not only in free fall parachuting that Meadows distinguished himself. He was the first American to represent a British regiment in the semifinals of the Army Rugby Union Football competition. With his high-stepping sprint and his ability to turn on a sixpence, Meadows was a very difficult man to catch and tackle. He made his place on the SAS rugby team after only one practice session. He had no need to master the intricacies of the game. His speed and accurate passing made him a great natural asset. The regiment won the semifinals and were drawn against the Welsh Regiment, one of the British Army's great rugby teams. After watching the SAS play in the semifinals, and noting the speed of Meadows, their coach lodged a complaint that it was not proper for an American to play in a British competition. Their objection was sustained and they won the match by a short margin.

All too quickly for both participating partners in the exchange, the time came in July 1961 for Sydnor and Meadows to return to the United States. For Meadows it meant an assignment to the newly activated 7th SFG at Fort Bragg. He was to be there for only a few short months before finding himself in the jungles of Laos.

With the exception of 1960, the SAS had been on continual active service since their re-formation in 1951. The British definition of active service differs from the American. In the UK the term signifies combat conditions. It was a light-hearted year with much humor even though professionalism prevailed in terms of learning and preparing for the future. The characters of both Meadows and Sydnor lent themselves to wholeheartedly joining in the balanced mixture of fun and serious preparation for future wars.

Did Meadows and Sydnor leave a legacy to the SAS? I was there at the time and can say that they had a marked effect on the outlook of many SAS senior NCOs, who were put into a competitive frame of mind by their expertise and energy. A much greater understanding of the U.S. Special Forces was gained and built on. The program was an unqualified success and paved the way for repeat exchanges of officers and senior NCOs over the years. A program was set up to allow SAS medics to train at Fort Bragg, where the U.S. Special Forces already benefited from probably the finest combat medical training in the world. Through this, many SAS casualties were saved. The SAS hearts and minds missions that followed were much enhanced. In later years there has been a mutual cooperation that would have been unheard of forty years earlier, and the understanding that initiated this mutual support sprang from the early SAS/USSF cross-fertilization of ideas. Yes, Meadows and Sydnor left a legacy of professionalism. It was also a case of the first exchange soldiers being the best.

5

Laos and the Learning Curve

1962

In July 1959 the first U.S. Special Forces personnel were committed to Laos as USSF Mobile Training Teams. The United States had been providing the major part of the Laotian defense budget since about 1955, but overt military intervention or assistance was precluded by the 1954 Geneva Accord. Washington's only viable method of giving physical help was to provide an "aid" program. This was done under the aegis of the Programs Evaluation Office that was initiated in the capital city of Vientiane. The role was a classic Special Forces mission. They were to train the disorganized remnants of the Forces Armée Laotienne (FAL). A complication was the fact that France had been allowed by the Geneva Accord to maintain a military presence in its former colony. This unwieldy arrangement left the French in charge of "tactical" training and the USSF with the heavy weapons and logistical responsibilities.[1] FAL was the renamed version of the Armée Nationale Laotienne (ALN), as raised by the Royal Laotian Government that had been reconstituted in 1949.

The ALN had a fairly peaceful existence until mid-1953, when the People's Army of Vietnam attacked across the northeastern borders of Laos. The subsequent rapid expansion of the ALN in order to contain the Viet Minh activities led to a weakened, ill-trained, and largely inefficient army. Not only were the Viet Minh controlling the North Vietnamese resistance groups, they were also directing and supplying the communist Laotian resistance movement, the Pathet Lao. Despite the signing of an accord for a coalition government between the Royal Laotian Government and the Pathet Lao in 1957, the uneasy truce fell apart quickly. The coalition disintegrated and thousands of trained Pathet Lao troops openly switched their allegiance to North Vietnam. In 1959 Laos looked ripe to be taken over by North Vietnam. The intention of the U.S. government was to build a force in Laos that would make it impossible for the Viet

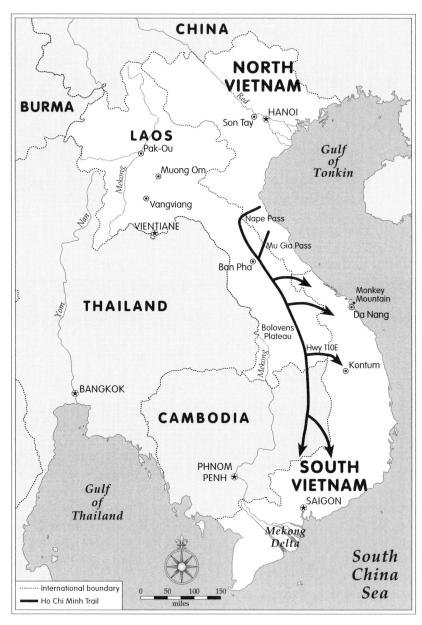

The Ho Chi Minh Trail and its many branches.

Minh and Pathet Lao to conquer the country, and the concept of the Mobile Training Teams evolved.

In principle, the Hotfoot teams, as they were known initially, were provided from the 77th SFG, then under the command of the highly regarded Colonel Donald Blackburn. Later the responsibility for the provision of the teams was to fall on the 1st SFG. The total SFG commitment was to be twelve modified A Teams, designated as Field Training Teams (FTTs). The eight-strong teams represented all major SF military occupational specialities. After four months of training at Fort Bragg the teams deployed to Laos, ostensibly as civilians. Rotation of troops was to be strictly controlled. With the exception of one chosen member per team, the other personnel would rotate back to the United States after six months. The team member who stayed behind for up to a further three months was there to provide the necessary continuity on a mission where knowledge of individuals, and an understanding of their culture and methods, was an essential ingredient to success.

Immediately upon his return to Fort Bragg from England, Meadows volunteered for a tour of duty in Laos. His application was accepted. After the training session he left for Southeast Asia in September 1961 (interestingly, he was only a month ahead of his now good friend Bud Sydnor, who was to be located at Plaine de Bolevens). Meadows was deployed to the training base at Muong Om Camp with FTT-59. Like the rest of the training bases, Muong Om was necessarily in a remote area.

He recalled that seven soldiers arrived together at the training base. Captain Charles Judge was the detachment commander, Meadows was the team sergeant, and three SFCs, Chuck Cooke, Jimmy Cooper, and Al Taylor, along with "Sparky" Walker and Ted Berlett,[2] made up the party. The XO, Jan Rush, got there a few days later. Meadows was not absolutely certain about the names. He thought that they were probably the fifth or sixth rotation. They were under the overall command of Bull Simons,[3] who had his own Mobile Control Team that operated out of Vientiane. By this time the operation had been renamed White Star. Since about April of that year the government had gone overt and a Military Assistance and Advisory Group (MAAG) was formed. The early soldiers had worn civilian clothes, but the replacements now wore their uniforms.

One of the White Star roles was to act as stay behind teams to carry on the operational direction of the men they were training. In that event, in theory at least, they would be free to fight alongside the trainees. The program was well under way when Meadows arrived, and his men did not experience the teething problems of earlier teams. The emphasis had switched from formal training of the Laotian Army to training local Kao and Meo (also know as Hmong) tribesmen on the village basis upon which their traditions and loyalties were formed. This was much closer to the classic SF role, and there is little doubt that the teams were more at home in this context than they had been with the formal Laotian Army. Training for combat was the first priority, but intelligence gathering was also a necessity, and much of the early impetus of the missions was geared toward gaining more information on the Ho Chi Minh Trail.

"Ho Chi Minh Trail" is something of a misnomer, as it implies a single route. In reality, it consisted of many tracks, small trails, and wide passageways along which heavy vehicles could pass. A supply route for personnel, arms, food, and other war equipment, it stretched for over a thousand kilometers from the Nape Pass on the Laos–North Vietnam border southward into Cambodia. Along the way there were many trails of varying dimensions branching off into South Vietnam south of the Demilitarized Zone. The jungle canopy provided good cover from the air, and even the use of defoliants did little to alleviate the problem. Many dummy routes were created and there were also a great number of loops and bypasses the insurgents could use to evade contact, pursuit, and air strikes. All of the SF soldiers then in Laos would come to know the Ho Chi Minh Trail in the years that followed. Some offshoots of the Trail which led into Vietnam were used for the purposes of building up stocks of food and ammunition that later became a secondary target for reconnaissance team (RT) missions. Some of the wider areas of the Trail were used to stockpile heavy transports and even artillery pieces.

The great frustration for all of the White Star teams was the fact that they could train the Hmong teams and plan an operation for them but were not allowed to participate. Meadows with a small group was moved further toward Vangviang to train Colonel Vang Pao's[4] command staff, which had been put together hastily by Major Johnson and Captain George Stewart.

The training went well enough, and after about two months the troops were ready for action. The only problem was that at that time there was no operational plan to put them to work, and so the SF team was moved to Pak-Ou with instructions to train a full battalion as a Ranger-type unit. This battalion was to be trained to attack rather than just reconnoiter the Ho Chi Minh Trail. The cease-fire agreement reached in May that year had been totally ignored by the Pathet Lao. Nam Tha had been overwhelmed by the communists again and the Laotian Army, or what was left of it, had taken heavy casualties.

Vang Pao's army consisted mainly of Hmong tribesmen. With U.S. assistance they had been trained as "Auto Defense d'Choc" companies to operate using guerrilla tactics against the Pathet Lao. The Hmongs were hill tribesmen—stocky, tough, and courageous. They were loyal to the king and their deep hatred of the Viet Minh made them tenacious fighters.

The SF teams did not have a peaceful existence by any means. Most of the training bases were known to the enemy and many were within artillery and mortar range. The bases had to be close to the action, as many missions by the Hmong companies were launched on foot directly from the base. The operational performance of the irregulars was questionable only because they lacked the solid and experienced leadership that the SF men could have so willingly provided.

Meadows and his team found it to be a soul-destroying business. They trained their soldiers for weeks on end, reassuring them that the tactics and planning systems would work. Then, when the time came to launch a mission, they had to tell the men that they were not allowed to accompany them. Neither party could understand it. Meadows enjoyed training the tribesmen. He found them willing and capable and would have liked nothing better than to lead them into action. He recalled:

We sometimes got switched around for a while, but basically the team stayed together for most of the time. We all had our special areas to instruct and camp chores we took in turn. When it was Chuck's turn to cook, it was great trying to get the Hmongs to say, "Chuck Cooke the cook cooked cookies today." The weapons and demolitions guys had some real challenges with outdated and broken weapons and mines, but I don't remember them ever being beaten by a problem. Technically, of course, we were teaching the Hmongs to become instructors themselves, though what difference this made politically I never did work out.

Meadows was full of praise for the SF medics and thought it probable that their duties impacted more on the Hmong than any other. They had to understand and not offend the "witch doctors" and they had to contend with diseases they had never encountered before. There were language problems that didn't make diagnosis easy, and the Hmong's disregard for camp sanitation was a continuing problem. The medics even had opium addiction to treat. Within the Hmong communities opium was accepted, especially among the older people. The young ones would tend to laugh a bit when the elders went off to the opium dens. Vang Pao had several camps with such facilities, and it was rumored that he made considerable money from the opium trade. The Hmong also brewed some potent liquor as Meadows remembered. Colonel Little was handing over, and Major Johnson, Meadows, and some others went along to the party in the local village. Although everyone turned down the invitation to visit the opium den, they drank so freely of the "moonshine" that they all had trouble walking back to the base and the hangovers were memorable. For Meadows it was the first and last time that he drank the local brew.

Meadows recalled a very frustrating occasion when Captain Harvey Moon and Sergeant Orville Ballinger[5] were captured when the base at Ban Pha (northwest of Vang Vieng) was overrun on July 27, 1961. The team received information that Ballinger was being held captive along with a news reporter in an American-owned house. The house was identified by a helicopter recon, and it just happened that there was a small airstrip close by. A CIA asset reported that a French priest had talked to Ballinger, and he was able to pinpoint the man's location in the house. From the owner of the house the CIA procured a detailed description of the interior, and Meadows was itching to do something about the situation. Bull Simons instructed the team to go ahead and make a plan. The ploy that was decided upon required Meadows and one other to insert by free fall parachute, observe the place, and possibly take out any guards prior to an all-U.S. helicopter assault. Simons approved the plan, but he was obliged to put it to the U.S. ambassador, who refused point-blank. It is an understatement to say that the team was very unhappy. Not only was the plan sound, but it would have been the first time that HALO techniques had been used in action. Probably Bull Simons was equally aggrieved by Sullivan's refusal. He was a remarkable man and often acted against higher authority. Meadows remembered an occasion when they picked up on the radio the fact that one of the Hmong units was under attack and having a hard time. Simons ignored his orders and told the CIA helicopters go to the rescue.

During the three-year life of Hotfoot and White Star, many members of the SF experienced their first combat conditions in a jungle environment. Not only that, they were carrying out their primary role of training indigenous personnel in an active theater of operations. They experienced many of the problems that go hand in glove with such work: faulty equipment, slow supply lines, language and cultural difficulties, and the acute frustrations of training men to peak performance status and then being barred from accompanying them on missions. It is a huge credit to the SF that their aims were met. When soldiers are committed to training others, the situation makes them look to their own preparations for combat, and a lot of new tactics were devised in Laos.

They were gaining a real feel for Southeast Asia. They absorbed a great deal of knowledge about the Ho Chi Minh Trail and how it was being used. Many useful lessons were learned from the Hmong, who were closely related to the Montagnards with whom they would work so closely in Vietnam. Modifications were made to personal and team equipment that had been designed by non-soldiers. Navigation skills were honed to a high degree. An immense amount was learned about the use of helicopters in a jungle environment, and a healthy mutual respect grew between SF soldiers and the pilots. In particular Meadows perfected his own patrolling skills and methods of briefing and training indigenous soldiers:

> I got used to making sand models to follow map contours as an aid to teaching some basic navigation, and these were very useful later on when we started to work with the Yards. We used jungle lane shooting ranges to improve observation and reactions and developed a lot of simple hand signals that were suitable for working with indigenous soldiers. It also gave us experience of a different sort of jungle from Florida and South America. You know, I once read a book by a guy called Freddy Spencer Chapman.[6] It was called *The Jungle Is Neutral,* and I guess that's a pretty good statement, but I preferred to try to turn the jungle into a friend by getting to understand it and be at home in it.

Perhaps the greatest feeling of satisfaction for the SF soldiers was the knowledge that all the training and field exercises carried out in North Carolina had been to good purpose; on the ground the system worked and worked well. But there was more, much more, which was to stand them in good stead as the war escalated in Vietnam. First, for political and "face" reasons it was necessary for the RTs to be seemingly under the command of a Vietnamese officer; after all, the Americans were advisors weren't they? Particularly in Laos this required the SF advisor to take an apparent back seat while the national commander supposedly planned, organized, and led the mission. In reality the "advisor" often had to use some skill in subliminally implanting the right ideas and decisions into the mind of the "commander." The SF advisor was the man who wrote the after action reports always implying that the leadership and organizational abilities of the local commander had been the mainstay of the mission. Due deference had to be made to local customs and traditions. In the RT missions in Vietnam there was never any doubt as to who was in command, but nonetheless the protocols had to be followed. Second, in Laos, there was the unique opportunity to get to know the nature of the terrain, improve navigational skills in badly mapped areas, practice in the operational use of helicopters, artillery, and strike aircraft, devise small patrol tactics, and perfect communications skills without being under intense pressure.

In 1962 the United States forced the Pathet Lao and the Laotian Army to the conference table and a coalition was formed once again. Under the neutral prime ministership of Souvanna Phouma, a further Geneva Agreement was signed. This time the agreement contained clauses that all foreign military forces would be obliged to leave Laos. In October of that year the MAAG disbanded and all SF personnel returned home.

Meadows, in fact, had returned to the United States on May 25, 1962, and reported for duty with the 7th SFG at the now very familiar Fort Bragg. He was not to remain there long. Dick was on station for less than a month when he was personally requested by Bull Simons to form part of an advance party to move down to Fort Gulick in the Panama Canal Zone.

6

Panama and the Fun Years

1962–1965

The activities of Fidel Castro in Cuba created a new awareness in political and military circles that Central and South America were potential hotbeds of unrest which, particularly in the field of drug smuggling and possible military coups, could impact the United States. Simons had, therefore, been given the mission to move to Panama and set up a training base at which Delta Company, 7th SFG, would create the 8th SFG. He hand-picked his team from the contenders recommended by an examining board. Meadows was selected as one of only three from 150 candidates, and the advance party headed to Fort Gulick in July 1962. The 8th SFG, when trained and validated, would be the first into action if clandestine missions in Latin America became a reality. Fort Gulick, Panama, was not a new place to many Special Forces soldiers. For some years it had been the central point for SF jungle training, and it had also been the site for the School of the Americas,[1] where many SF soldiers had instructed in the past.

Meadows, to his pleasure, was placed in charge of jungle navigation and tactics. He had only two months to design and test the course prior to the arrival of the first SF company. The training had hardly gotten under way, however, before the whole of U.S. Special Forces was put on alert as the Cuban Missile Crisis worsened.[2] With Bull Simons in command there was bound to be action. Meadows's contingent was tasked with knocking out the Soviet SS-4 and SS-5 medium- and intermediate-range ballistic missile sites. The plan was to infiltrate by parachute, create as much damage as possible, and then get out by whatever means presented itself. As history tells us, that particular SF contingent did not invade Cuba, but it was a close run thing, as their aircraft did take off and adopt a holding pattern for some hours before standing down.

In between Mobile Training Teams (MTTs) and jungle training, life in Panama was fun. There were some vintage SF characters around at that time; many, like Meadows, had returned from tours of duty in Laos. There were still large numbers of soldiers with World War II and Korea combat experience, and they tended to enjoy life to the fullest when the opportunity arose. Jim Paxton provided a glimpse of life typical of the times:

> I guess it would have been in February or March of '63. I remember waking up early one Sunday morning just as dawn was breaking and I heard the sounds of .22 caliber rifle shooting. I looked outside through the barrack room window and spotted a lone rifleman. Throwing on the uniform of the day, which happened to be a pair of shorts and shower shoes, I approached the solitary figure and recognized Master Sergeant Meadows. He was seated on a horizontal telephone pole which had been placed there as a barrier alongside a steep, muddy embankment leading into a swamp after "Pappy" Barnett drove his brand new Cadillac convertible a bit too far into his chosen parking slot.
>
> I asked Dick what he was firing at, and he explained that he was shooting iguanas out of a very large tree in front of the barracks. I asked if he would mind company, and he asked me if I had a rifle. I told him that I had a .22 caliber rifle and several other personal weapons in the company arms room. He said that was fine and I quickly got a rifle and returned to join him sitting on the pole.
>
> It was one of those lazy, hot, muggy mornings and we were totally relaxed. As the barracks came to life others began to join us, and with each new arrival the variety and caliber of the weapons increased. Everything was fine until "Dirty Shirt" Johnson brought out his 59mm Madson mortar and let fly with three rounds of high explosive. Our line of fire included the Military Police post at the entrance to Fort Gulick and the rounds landed somewhere between them and us—close enough for them to think they were under attack. We all scattered before the first mortar round hit the ground and were calmly eating breakfast in the Mess Hall before the last round struck. Actually, I'm sure our exodus couldn't have been that fast—but it was damned close.

Life settled in to some form of routine while the group was being trained. Leisure pursuits were plentiful, with excellent fishing, swimming, and hunting. Meadows, a strong swimmer, took a perverse delight in taking long swims outside the protection offered by the anti-shark nets. In between training sessions with the early nucleus of the 8th SFG he was assigned to conduct counterinsurgency exercises and training for the Panamanian National Guard, and it was his mixing with the soldiers of Latin America that began to create his long-lasting interest in those nations. The success of those early training missions in Panama led to more commitments of a similar type. It was during this period, on November 22, 1963, that the Special Forces lost a firm friend when President John F. Kennedy was assassinated in Dallas. Apart from mourning the tragic loss of a great supporter, the 8th SFG also began to speculate on what might happen in Cuba—would the next president cope with Castro and the Russians in the same implacable style? The situation put a new note of seriousness on the regular missions that the 8th SFG was given to test the security precautions of the Canal Zone. All such missions led to the successful penetration of all the targets.

Just a month before the tragedy of Kennedy's death Meadows had received some good news. Everything necessary was now in place and he was free to follow up on something that had been blossoming since 1960. He was able to marry Pamela Thompson, and they didn't waste time. The wedding took place at the Canal Zone on November 30, 1963, and after a huge party a new life began. Meadows, in true SF style, almost didn't make it. He had been free-falling with his good friend and best man to be, Joe Garner, and a slight delay over the DZ caused them to arrive at the last second. Pamela remembered being "officially" interviewed by Bull Simons as to why she wanted to marry "one of his boys." Indeed, it almost fell to Bull Simons to give Pamela away at the ceremony. Her parents, fully in favor of the marriage by now, could not make the journey from England. Pamela, a little nervous of the big gruff soldier, was quite relieved when other arrangements were made. Later she was to get to know the "Bull" well and they became firm friends until the end of Simons's life.

The events preceding the wedding had not exactly followed a copybook plan. Making the arrangements in Panama was the easy part. From the moment that Meadows had left England, Pamela had been warned by all and sundry that that was the last she would see of the "Yank." Americans, she was told, had a habit of making promises and then leaving the country never to be heard of again. There were, after all, many instances of this in the months and years following the end of World War II. Meadows, however, was not cut from that cloth. He sent letters whenever he could, and all of them indicated that he saw Pamela as a permanent part of his life. Pamela was certainly convinced of his good intentions because on February 13, 1962, after completing all the necessary paperwork, she moved to the United States. She got a job as a legal secretary and all she then needed was a permanent U.S. address. To make the move possible, Meadows made arrangements for Pamela to stay with his sister, Verna Lee, and her husband, Eugene Smith, who at that time lived in Miami. Pamela recalls the period with much warmth.

> On the journey to Miami I realized that I didn't even know what Gene and Verna Lee looked like. It all turned out well though and we met up okay. I really admired those folks. They opened up their home to me with no hesitation at all and made me very welcome. At that time, in order for me to live with them, they had to virtually bare their souls to the authorities; all their personal details, including their financial accounts, had to be scrutinized and their lives were made an open book. They were extremely kind. After all, they had never even met me.

Thanks to Gene and Verna Lee, Pamela was given the necessary authorization and documents that enabled the marriage to go ahead.

A soldier's pay was not overly generous in those days, and the festive season of 1963 promised to be a bleak one as far as money was concerned. Pamela had wanted a formal wedding, and this along with the costs of the reception had left the couple with only $50 to their name. There were not going to be any Christmas presents. Pamela was quite capable of handling a situation like that. On Christmas morning she presented herself, naked except for a big red bow, to a surprised but appreciative Meadows. This became a family joke for many years when she or her husband were stuck for ideas for a Christmas present: "There's always the red bow," one of them would quip.

If Pamela had expected to see a lot of Meadows during a three-

and-a-half-year tour of duty in Panama, then she was to be disappointed. The MTTs around Latin America frequently required
periods of separation for up to two months. Home to the newly-
weds was an apartment in an old-style house in what was known
as the American Complex in downtown Colón. The large house was
set in formal gardens and surrounded by an iron fence. Their apartment was to the rear of the house with its own small walled garden.
Originally the houses had stood in well-spaced isolation, but now
the slums had encroached right up to the walls and between each
home. Colón, in keeping with many Latin American cities, shows
the huge difference between the "haves" and "have-nots." Wealth
rules and poverty restricts. Violence was common on the city streets
and an anti-American atmosphere had been bubbling quietly since
the riots of 1958.[3] The Panamanians considered the comparatively
prosperous Canal Zone to be theirs by right. In short, there was an
uneasiness that detracted from what would otherwise have been an
idyllic life.

One slightly off-the-wall mission that came Meadows's way
was to take part in a team that deployed to the Dominican Republic
to train a two-hundred-man company of specially selected personnel in the arts of riot control. This was not a skill within the SF reper-
toire. The authorities believed that the election of Juan Bosch as the
new president could lead to rioting. The mission was so successful
that the Army Chief of Staff of the Dominican Republic Army requested that the team be extended for a two-month period in order
to train the Mountain Battalion in counterinsurgency operations.
This training was conducted under very lifelike conditions in the
area of Castanza, deep in the interior, and culminated in the very
first operation where all military services of the republic worked together in a common cause. Such missions as these took place in Costa Rica, Nicaragua, Bolivia, Chile, Peru, and Colombia. One such
team, under command of Captain Ron Shakelford (?),[4] was responsible for training the Bolivian light infantry Manchego Battalion,
which was later to take out Che Guevara. The tasks were widely di-
versified. A team under command of SFC Herman Blume was sent
to Colombia to train elements of the army involved in civil action
projects. Their task was to teach the Colombian soldiers to handle
heavy plant equipment, such as graders, bulldozers, and cranes. Interesting though these missions were, once the 8th SFG was fully
validated there was more time on Meadows's hands, which he was

to utilize in a way which gave him great personal satisfaction. But before that was to happen there was the small matter of the 1964 uprising to contend with.

Approximately ten thousand Panamanians lived and worked within the Canal Zone and were paid in U.S. dollars that they were able to exchange at good rates. Satisfaction should have been the order of the day, but nationalistic pride took over. Clashes between Panamanian and American students had been occurring intermittently since 1958. Lives had been senselessly lost over the years, but an uneasy stalemate was reached when the U.S. government, between 1960 and 1964, allowed the Panamanian flag to be flown alongside that of the United States at a selected number of sites. Students at the American high school were angry and in protest flew only the flag of the United States at the school. It was the trigger that sparked off a massive riot in January 1964.

Twenty thousand Panamanians went on the rampage in Panama City, and shooting eventually broke out. Meadows got news of this at the same time as he was told that the rioting had spread to Colón. His first thoughts were for Pamela, who was two months pregnant with their first child. It would naturally be the slum areas where the riot picked up impetus, and U.S. homes could become prime targets for looting and worse. With his free fall parachuting colleague, Joe Garner, Meadows sought urgent permission to go to Pamela's rescue. They were refused both ammunition for their service weapons and military vehicles. Taking their private shotguns and a borrowed car, they sped the four miles or so to Colón. Using back streets and grimly noting the smoke from burning buildings and listening to increasing numbers of shots, they made it to the house. It was immediately obvious that it had been visited already. The fence was down and windows were broken. There was no sign of Pamela or the car. Meadows recalled:

> Now I was really worried. Had Pam made it away or had both she and the car been abducted? There was no way to tell. We rushed around the houses of friends in Colón but there was no sign of her. The only thing to do was get back to Gulick and listen out for news, but I was sure as heck going to get myself a proper weapon as soon as I got back to base. When we got back I found out that Pam had made it out by the skin of her teeth. The rioters had downed the

fence and were at the back door when she got away in that little old Triumph car of ours.

Tense security situations were not entirely new to a girl who had started life under the restrictive conditions of the Malayan Emergency.

Much to their chagrin, the 8th SFG soldiers were refused permission to take any offensive action. They were officially committed only as observers at various points to report on the rioters' activities. Unofficially, there are probably other stories to tell. The net result was that after three days of rioting followed by a couple of weeks of high alert, all U.S. troops were confined to barracks. The enjoyable hunting and fishing trips virtually came to an end, though Meadows and his friends made a number of illegal trips by night to collect lobsters. The enforced confinement made even more time for the sport parachuting that Meadows had come to love.

In Britain, Meadows had dabbled in free fall parachuting but in a very unscientific way. Those members of the 22nd SAS Regiment at that time who were hooked on the sport were coping with a shortage of money and very limited military support. They had only rudimentary ideas on the stable flight techniques and precise maneuverings that were being developed in the United States. Nonetheless, Meadows had enjoyed what he had done and when he was invited by Joe Garner to make a weekend jump with the sport parachute club, he took little persuading:

> We just jumped at every opportunity and at the maximum altitudes we could achieve. Pam tried her hand at it as well. I think she might have been the only woman to jump out there. Hey, Pam was more than a wife, you know. She was also my best buddy.
>
> The new military free fall techniques were getting a lot of attention in the Special Forces, but we were a bit limited by knowledge and equipment at that time. We did all of our own chute conversions. But things got better and it was a great time. Even a soldier's gotta have some fun.

Pam recalled those jumping days. "When I became pregnant, Dick wouldn't let me jump any more, so I spent my time on the DZ packing parachutes for the guys for $1 each."

The principal enthusiasts at that time, apart from Joe Garner, were Lieutenant Chuck Fry, Jim Perry, Captain Jesse Ramos, and later Captain Jim Pearson. The U.S. Army Sport Parachute Team was beginning to build up a formidable reputation and competition with the French was intense. Techniques were shared freely and the army as a whole was beginning to see the possibilities of free fall parachuting for covert insertion into hostile areas. Probably the major key to the acceptance of military free fall was the persistence of people like General Joe Stilwell and the enthusiasm of the early SF sport parachutists. When the techniques were brought together under the acronym of HALO (High Altitude Low Opening), the future was set. HALO schools were opened up in Fort Bragg and then in Okinawa with the 1st SFG. Chuck Fry was elected as the man to put the idea to Bull Simons that the 8th SFG should also have its own school. Extracts from a letter written by Chuck Fry cast an interesting light on the evolution of HALO at the 8th SFG and also demonstrate the intense but friendly rivalry extant between SF teams in the late 1950s and early 1960s.[5] The letter is addressed to a former comrade in arms of Fry:

Dear . . . [name omitted],

Pursuant to our conversation at the SFA Reunion, reference HALO, I will relate a bit of history that led to my assertion that Dick Meadows and I were the first "officially" trained and qualified HALO Jumpmaster Instructors in the US Army. I will add some background that you may find interesting, if not; forgive a "simple old soldier from Missouri" for his nostalgia. Here goes and I apply the standard disclaimers such as—"to the best of my memory."

My first awareness of HALO parachute infiltration techniques was in the mid-fifties when I heard talk that Jacques Estel had been contracted to train some guys at Fort Bragg in free fall parachute techniques. . . .

We had a fledgling sport parachute club at Bad Tölz which I thought about joining but never seemed to bite the bullet. . . .

I remember quite clearly when the bug finally bit me and I made the decision to become a free fall jumper. It was based more on my ego than for professional enrichment.

We had just finished a good field exercise (early spring 1960) and Jerry Babb, the best heavy weapons man that I knew, and I were sitting out back of the NCO Club imbibing "red-eye." We looked up and observed the "dream team" circle overhead in their state of the art orange and white modified B-12 HALO canopies and descend for a landing on the old Herbst Fest grounds. Jerry looked at me and quipped, "I will if you will." We joined the Parachute Club. . . .

I left Germany to attend OCS in September of 1960 and, following graduation as a 2nd Lt., was assigned as an instructor to the Airborne Department at Fort Benning for a couple of years. I continued with sport parachuting but not fanatically as I was making six or seven parachute jumps a week as part of my instructing job. I did accumulate several free falls by the time I was assigned to the Special Forces at Fort Gulick, Canal Zone, as the S-3 Air Officer in March, 1963. MSG Meadows, who I had worked for, when I was an NCO, came to my office soon after I arrived to recruit me to jump with him and Sgt. Joe Garner. As I look back, I believe that they were looking for an officer to run interference for them as they began to think of military free fall techniques. They convinced me to apply for the Parachute Club of America (PCA) Class B License that was required by Army Regulations, to make demonstration jumps. They wanted a third man for a demonstration jump planned for the Fort Gulick parade field and, according to them, the zone was restricted to Class B or higher parachutists. I later reviewed the Army Regulations and PCA drop zone restrictions for the different classes and believe me when I say that the regulation would have to be stretched for even a Class D parachutist to legally make the jump.

As you might assume, we made the demonstration jump on May 4, 1963 in spite of what the regulations said. I hadn't jumped in a year, had never made a 60-second delay and had never tried to enter a tiny DZ surrounded by three storey buildings, jungle and streets with electrical light posts around the ball fields. And the field was occupied by Youth Day activities of all kinds. At 12,500 feet, the pucker factor was in place and I asked Dick to share his experience with this particular drop zone. His answer was vintage Meadows but anything but allaying. He said that we would be the very first parachutists to attempt to land on the field! He also said not to worry, just follow Joe Garner, who had good instincts. I was last out and I saw that Dick was right on Joe's tail so I played follow the leader. We made it in but I had to raise my feet to pass over the roof of one of the buildings. The demonstration impressed our leaders, one of them being the Commander of USARSA. This paved the way for the USARSA Command Parachute Team, later to become known and respected throughout Latin America as the "Jumping Ambassadors." At the same time it was the beginning of the 8th SFG HALO Team.

Just a few days after the parade field jump, we started receiving requests from different Latin American governments, military commands, US Embassies and civic groups to make demonstration jumps. I convinced Colonel Arthur "Bull" Simons that we should practice to hone our skills in order to make positive public relations for the 8th SFG. I got his "grunt" which I interpreted as an "OK" to co-ordinate with the 605th Air Commandos for support aircraft and my parachute log book soon began to show what are now hundreds of entries for jumps from their assigned WWII aircraft; C-47, C-46, T-6, A1E, B-26 and the newer STOL U-10. We seldom jumped under 12,500 feet and most were from 16,000 and above. Soon the Bull began programming us to participate in his "Sell SF capabilities to Latin America" demonstrations and we were billed as "HALO" parachutists. The 8th SFG (Abn) had the 9th Psyops Detachment assigned as part of its Special Action Force and they published a great newsletter. Of course it was circulated to Fort Bragg reporting on the results of the multi-faceted counter insurgency, nation building MTTs that the 8th deployed throughout Latin America. One can be sure that the Fort Bragg operators were reading these stories with envy; a SF soldier's reason for existing is to deploy on a meaningful MTT. The editors began writing of our HALO accomplishments and soon we came under the jaundiced eye of the Special Forces Training Group who had the HALO School under their auspices.

In late 1963, we performed a number of demonstrations in Panama, Chile and Peru and got a lot of publicity. We set records on consecutive baton passes and altitude records for Latin America. Those in Bragg read about it. Soon the Bull received a phone call from Brigadier General Joe Stilwell Jr., the Special Warfare Center Commander, telling him that none of us were HALO qualified so he couldn't use us for demonstration purposes and bill us as "HALO"! The Bull made a deal with the General, he would send two of us to Fort Bragg to the HALO course with the proviso that we return qualified as Jumpmasters and Instructors. . . . In February, following the 1964 Panama riots, MSG Richard Meadows and 1st Lt Charles Fry arrived at Fort Bragg to attend basic HALO Course 64-4. If my memory serves, Dick had enough jumps for his C License (C-1695) and I applied for mine and received it (C-1790) soon after we arrived at Fort Bragg. Dick and I spent hours "on the job" training in the HALO rigger shed preparing ourselves for 8th SFG HALO training courses that we would launch when we returned to Panama.

We graduated from the basic course on March 27, 1964 after completing 29 jumps. When I inquired about the Jumpmaster/Instructor Course, I was told that there was no such course and that was a fact. There had never been a course and none was planned. I talked to the Committee Chairman, LTC Farrington, and told him of the agreement the Bull had made with the General and was told it was impossible to conduct such a course. I used his phone to call Panama and break the news to the Bull. We didn't need the receiver to hear his response. He told me in no uncertain terms to "Stand the f$@% by." He called the general and a few minutes later LTC Eb Smith, Commander of the Training Group entered and told Farrington to "qualify Fry and Meadows as Jumpmaster/Instructors." I was told later that the Bull told the General to live up to his agreement or "eat" the cost of our training and TDY. There were some unhappy HALO instructors as they had to forfeit their training break to come up with a program. . . . We received a letter order issued by the US Army Special Forces Training Group (Abn) dated April 21,

1964, which stated in part that 1st Lt. Charles H. Fry and
MSG E-8 Richard Meadows "have successfully completed
the HALO Jumpmaster and Instructor Qualification Course
conducted by the Advanced Training Committee, Special
Forces Training Group (Abn), Fort Bragg, North Carolina,
during the period March 27 to April 16 1964."

We are led to believe that we were the first officially
trained HALO Jumpmaster/Instructors in the US Army.
We returned to Fort Gulick qualified to instruct HALO and
we got on with it.[6]

There is little wonder that free fall parachuting entranced Meadows. Few men (and women) who taste the sport do not enjoy it. No
matter how unathletic a person may be on the ground, up there, in
free fall, amazing physical agility can be experienced. Snap your
hands to your sides and adopt the "stand to attention" position and
you are suddenly diving head-first to the ground, building up to
speeds in excess of two hundred miles per hour. Flare your arms
and legs out and push the head back and you adopt the position
in the air of a floating feather as you slow down into a perfectly
stable position. Tuck in those arms and bend the legs and the speed
increases with no loss of stability. Push the arms back into a "delta"
wing position and you begin to noticeably track forward. Every minor move of the hands, arms, body, and legs gives a predictable and
finely controllable change of direction and momentum. It is also a
hugely enjoyable spectator sport, though there is always a feeling
among jumpers that a certain percentage of those who watch have a
morbid desire to see an accident occur. Free fall parachuting, however, does lose a little of its charm when, for military reasons, there
is a rucksack and weapon strapped to your body.

After the qualification course that he and Fry had attended at
Fort Bragg, Meadows became totally immersed in HALO training.
More and more of the MTTs and diplomatic visits to other Latin
American countries had a HALO element, whether just for demon-
stration purposes or to train other army contingents. These MTTs
typically lasted about two months. In Brazil they were required to
train the national team to take part in the world championships.
In the finals of the preceding year's competition they had been in
eighth position. After the SF training they came in third, behind
France and the United States.[7]

On July 21, 1964, Mark Richard Meadows was born in the Canal Zone, and there was no one more proud than Dick Meadows, who threw a party in true SF style to celebrate the event. Life continued along enjoyable lines, but there was a growing seriousness in the minds of all of the Special Forces soldiers. The situation in Vietnam made it certain that there was going to be an increasingly heavy commitment of SF troops.

Many governments held to the "domino" theory that had been developed during the Malayan Emergency of the 1950s, that should Vietnam fall then Laos, Cambodia, Thailand, and Malaya would also fall in quick succession, like collapsing dominoes. In 1965, the U.S. involvement in the war was escalated rapidly in response to the growing strength of the Viet Cong and the incapacity of the ARVN (Army of the Republic of Vietnam) to suppress it. The United States became more involved in the war not only to maintain the independence of South Vietnam but also to retain America's credibility with other allied nations who depended or might depend on its help to resist communist subversion. From the beginning it looked like it would be a long war, and when Meadows and his family left Panama in September 1965 he lost no time in doing what he considered his bounden duty as a soldier, and he volunteered for service in Vietnam.

7

Vietnam and RT Ohio

1965

After the mission described in the prologue of this book, Meadows was quietly satisfied with the results. He could not even begin to anticipate what far-reaching effects his irrefutable evidence of a large NVA presence in South Vietnam would have on the U.S. war effort and his own career. Neither did he know at the time that this mission was to earn him his first Silver Star.[1] The film he had taken was rushed to the Pentagon for a top security–level screening and accepted as proof that the NVA was indeed moving into South Vietnam, and Meadows was required to travel to Saigon and personally brief General Westmoreland. This was not the last time that he would be required to brief the general personally.

Meadows had volunteered for Vietnam duty within days of returning to Fort Bragg, and in November 1965 he received orders assigning him to the 5th SFG. He had hardly touched down when the now very familiar Colonel Bull Simons contacted him. Simons was then chief of Op 35 and working under Colonel Donald Blackburn, chief of SOG. It was not until Meadows took up his post as operations sergeant at Long Thanh that he was briefed on what SOG was all about. It was fascinating stuff. SOG, the Studies and Observation Group (formerly known as Special Operations Group), answered only to the Joint Chiefs of Staff. Though General William Westmoreland, the commander of Military Assistance Command, Vietnam (MACV), was briefed on the activities of SOG, he had no power of command over the organization.[2] Op 35 was the department covering ground studies, and as such it controlled all cross-border reconnaissance team activities. Within days Meadows made a direct approach to Simons: he wanted to lead a reconnaissance team (RT). He did not want to be the operations sergeant. He was given a leave of absence from the post for a period of two months. This only partially pleased Meadows, but he knew exactly what he needed to do to break away from his designated job. He had to build the best possible team, succeed on every mission, and try to make himself indispensable (he knew that was impossible, but it was a good aim). He also knew that there were some excellent RT leaders in SOG and that competition would be great.

With RT Ohio his reputation was quick to grow, and his secret lay in detailed training and planning, maintaining the physical fitness of his team, constant rehearsal of techniques and immediate action drills, and, of course, first-class leadership. The then-SFC "Billy" Antony[3] recalled his time with Meadows and RT Ohio with great fondness:

> Typically the "packet" with the orders for the next mission would come down and we'd study it before equipping and going into a local training phase. Teams rotated to take a break, but we'd often go out of sequence because of Dick's success with Ohio, but we'd always get some sort of break. Often teams just flopped out during their break, but Dick always kept something going on to hone our skills. He made a very big thing also about staying close and associating with our Nungs. We'd often go out of the compound to eat with them, and this gave the Nungs confidence and made them appreciate their importance to Ohio. This was really critical, as there were many losses in Vietnam recon teams due to "layback" after a mission and splitting from the Nungs during breaks.
>
> Dick's personality made you want to go with him. He'd place a challenge in front of you and get you psyched up (even over a beer). His mind was always actively finding new things and improving old tactics. Training was very detailed and we practiced all the time. You never had the time to get bored or stale. The missions really became little different to training. Dick made everything fun and no one ever wanted to leave his team. He could cut your ass up though and he'd leave no doubt in your mind of what he wanted. But he could do all that without ever giving offence. His mind was uncanny. He thought of everything and this gave us all a good feeling.
>
> In the jungle we talked with our hands. There was no unnecessary conversation. We became programmed robots but always 110 percent alert. If you didn't "cut the mustard"

you didn't work with Dick. He demanded and got and gave utter loyalty and took away all fear. Ohio enjoyed working together, often doing what other teams thought were chores. We stayed together all the time, even with the Nungs. While other teams might lie around doing nothing during a break, Ohio always had something to do each day. You were never asked to do anything Dick hadn't done or wouldn't do. You learned something from every conversation with him. He was knowledgeable but never pompous. You wanted to hang on every word he said. We were always trusted and always well briefed. You felt his presence when he entered a room. He was magnetic, and other people were drawn to him whether they liked him or not.

He was always quick to recognize good work and talent and just as quick to commend it. Mediocrity was not in his personal thesaurus. He didn't believe in "dry holes" either. If we had an uneventful mission, he'd request an extension in order to achieve something worthwhile. This was always in his mind at the mission planning stages and so we were ready for it. His theory was that the commanders would only commit another team and as we were on the ground and undetected then why risk others? In my opinion he was the best "One-Zero" in SOG, and there were a lot of good ones.

Not long after the filming episode, Meadows had to return to Saigon once more to make a presentation to General Westmoreland. RT Ohio had been on another mission alongside the Ho Chi Minh Trail when they suddenly arrived at a massive clearing. Meadows later said that it was like entering a shopping mall. The trees had been lashed together to provide a screen from the air. Backed off the trail and camouflaged to blend in with the jungle were four artillery pieces. There was not a lot that Ohio could do to destroy the weapons, as they did not carry any explosives. Meadows reckoned that the best they could do was remove the sighting gear from each piece and dump them into a river on their way out and then record the location for future air strikes and artillery barrages. However, Meadows did not dump all of the sights in the deep rivers. He took one back to give to a delighted General Westmoreland at the debrief in Saigon.

On a topic close to his heart, Meadows casually talked about prisoners of war as though it was the simplest thing in the world to take one. By the time he finished his tours in Vietnam he had established an all-time SOG record with a total of thirteen POWs taken from Laos and Vietnam. Ideally he would try to snatch a lone soldier who had strayed or dropped behind a marching column, but occasionally things didn't happen the way he had planned. Sometimes you just had to take advantage of the things Lady Luck put your way.

In January 1966, RT Ohio was on a mission in Laos and appeared to have had what Meadows referred to as a "dry hole." They had had no contact with the enemy and no sightings to report apart from some bomb damage assessment details that Meadows did not consider to be of great importance. Ohio had been following alongside a trail that did not seem to have been used recently. On hearing voices, the team stopped and took cover in an immediate ambush position, a tactic that was carried out in total silence due to painstaking rehearsal for just such an event. Along the trail, only a few feet from the totally still bodies of RT Ohio, walked five armed NVA soldiers. Meadows was about to initiate the ambush by opening fire when, to his amazement, the soldiers halted, placed their rifles on the ground, and took off their packs. It soon became obvious that they were taking a lunch break. With a grin of utter delight on his face Meadows told Ohio of his intentions by using hand signals. Taking great care, Meadows inched his way to within one pace of the five chattering men. Then in one flowing motion he stood up and sidestepped onto the track, effectively cutting off the field of view of his own men, who could not now provide cover for him. "Good morning, gentlemen. Don't move. You are now my prisoners." Three of the soldiers made a heroically fatal mistake and grabbed for their weapons. A burst from Meadows's submachine gun killed them instantly. The remaining two soldiers made no resistance as their hands were tied behind their backs. The bodies were searched, moved off the trail, and hastily covered with foliage. RT Ohio, having recovered from the "dry hole" situation, was now happy to exfiltrate back to Kontum.

Meadows probably got more enjoyment out of snatching prisoners than from any other type of operation. To him it was a fun tasking, and he made it fun for his team, too. Prisoner taking required very detailed planning. By the very nature of such missions there had to be physical contact with the enemy, which could lead to casualties (theirs, not Meadows's), and there was always the unexpected to cater for since it was impossible to predict what the actions of the intended victim would be. On one occasion Ohio ambushed a party of NVA on the bank of a river. The enemy resisted and were all killed with the exception of one wounded soldier who dove into the river. Meadows immediately dropped his own weapon and dove after the man, who was soon added to the growing list of prisoners. There was little security discipline in the NVA officers and NCOs. On capture they invariably were found to have notebooks with names and organizations and marked maps.

On one mission the Meadows luck almost gave out. RT Ohio was moving alongside a major trail looking for a good ambush position. They came to a place that had a rocky outcrop with a tree on top. From the rear it looked like a good observation position, so Meadows halted the team and went forward to take a better look. When he climbed onto the rock he found that he could not see the trail at all. It seemed a good idea at the time to climb the tree and take a look-see. It had a stout limb that grew out over the trail, so he shinned up and crawled out on the limb and got an immediate surprise. Six or seven NVA came around the corner and took a seat right under him. They only had to glance up and he was dead. His gun was slung over his shoulder and there was no way he could get to it. None of the team could see him, so he could not signal them to make an attack. If he made the slightest movement the leaves would begin to rustle and the soldiers would be sure to look up.

The soldiers did not seem to be in any hurry to move on and Meadows was beginning to get a painful cramp. He had no idea how long he would be there, and one of his biggest fears was that one of the Ohio team would come to look for him, in which case they would probably both die. It might have been his imagination, but it began to feel as though the branch was beginning to bend and he was getting closer and closer to the heads of the soldiers. Conscious that he would not be able to hang on much longer, he began to wonder if he would get away with falling on top of them and trying to get the drop on them. He would have had no chance, as he soon found out. Luckily the soldiers decided to go on their way. He gave them a few more minutes to get out of earshot, then tried to move, only to find that every muscle was locked into position. The painful move from the branch back to rock took a long time and he realized that if he had dropped onto the soldiers his body would have been useless. According to Meadows, he never climbed another tree in Vietnam.

Typical missions undertaken by the SOG RTs can be noted from the citations for decorations for Vietnamese members of RT Ohio as drafted by Meadows in August 1966:[4]

> During the period March 25 to August 1, 1966, LT Le Minh served in the capacity of team leader[5] to the combined US/ VN Reconnaissance Team Ohio Number Seven, of which I was the team's senior adviser. LT Minh distinguished himself by many courageous acts while in the performance of his duties. Due to his military experience and his aggressiveness LT Minh led his team on a series of four highly successful and classified missions against known Viet Cong installations. The following data is credited to Team Ohio during the above-mentioned period.
>
> April 25 to April 28, 1966. Team Ohio conducted a reconnaissance mission in an area believed to be used by the Viet Cong as a "Way Station," and a route of infiltration into friendly areas of operations. Upon entry into this area, we found that the area was not being used for these purposes at this time. However, it had been used some two months before with intent to be used again. The team captured two Montagnards who were believed to be keepers of the "Way Station," and destroyed the buffalo herd and banana trees at the site. The information from this mission resulted in the relocation of the other reconnaissance teams to other areas of operations.
>
> May 24 to May 28, 1966. While conducting operations against a large known Viet Cong controlled area, Team Ohio was credited with the destruction of three thousand bushels of rice and three villages of six houses each of which were used as "Way Stations." The capture of a local Montagnard supply agent and the locating of a North Vietnamese Battalion were credited to the team. An air strike was called in on the battalion and for a period of eight hours the team controlled and directed these strikes. At times the North Vietnamese would move into our area for protection against the bombs. Once one of the enemy soldiers came within ten

meters of the communication site and was killed by a team member. This action caused the team to move to another observation position. When in route the team came upon two North Vietnamese soldiers and captured them. After a very successful five days of operations the team was then exfiltrated. The information that was received from the North Vietnamese prisoners of war was of great value and resulted in additional air strikes to include heavy bomber strikes. On this mission LT Minh commanded his team in an expert manner and used tactics to protect the US advisor at all times, particularly during the contact with the FAC. He also made several bomb damage assessments with the American advisor.

June 18 to June 23, 1966. Team Ohio was infiltrated into an area to determine the activities and location of an unknown number of Viet Cong. In the accomplishment of this mission the team directed air strikes on the areas that had been positively identified as Viet Cong "Way Stations" and housing areas, killing an unknown number of Viet Cong. On one bomb damage assessment, members of the team located the bodies of three Viet Cong and secured one weapon. While in another action, members of the team made physical contact with an enemy outpost, killing two more Viet Cong and capturing another weapon. The success of this mission was credited largely to the sound judgement of LT Minh.

The following is part of the citation for Nguyen Canh Thach, RT Ohio's interpreter:[6]

August 6 to August 8, 1966. Team Ohio's mission was to infiltrate into an area, which contained numerous trails to seek out enemy installations for heavy bomb strikes. The primary mission was to capture a prisoner. The second day in the area we came upon the largest trail in our area. This trail was heavily used by a large force moving north. We observed small groups moving at random during the evening. On the morning of the third day we organized an ambush in order to capture the prisoner. We had been in position only ten minutes when a small group of Viet Cong came down the trail and were assaulted by Team Ohio. The plan was to capture the five soldiers without firing; however one did take offensive action to fire, but was stopped by Mr. Thach. This action possibly saved some of Team Ohio from becoming casualties. The team then withdrew, taking two prisoners and their equipment. Prior to exfiltration Mr. Thach conducted an interrogation that proved useful to the Command and Control Detachment. Mr. Thach has impressed me as one of the most dedicated individuals I have ever known. He has demonstrated professional skill, initiative, and experience and has a willing attitude. He contributed immeasurably to our successes. He has earned the high regard of both his US and VN associates. Mr. Thach's distinguished performance of duty throughout the previously mentioned periods represents outstanding achievements and reflects credit upon himself and his country. Signed: MSG Meadows. MSG E-8.

On October 29, 1966, Meadows received the following two letters:

Headquarters
United States Military Assistance Command, Vietnam
Office of the Commander
APO San Francisco 96243

MACJOO   Oct 19, 1966
SUBJECT: Outstanding Performance of Duty
TO: Chief
Studies and Observations Group
U.S. Military Assistance Command, Vietnam
APO U.S. Forces 96243

1. On October 16, 1966, your group was charged with direction of a combat operation of great importance to the United States. The team, which carried out this operation, was headed by MSG Richard J. Meadows.
2. This headquarters has received several reports, including two from officers of flag rank, commending the outstanding performance of duty of this team, its leader and the support personnel. The exemplary readiness and determination of all members of the team, their dedication and their responsiveness have been made a matter of

official record. In the words of one commander, the entire team demonstrated a complete professional competence and the utmost in personal courage.

3. Specifically to be commended is the unique performance of duty by MSG Meadows. His urgent request to lead his team in extremely hazardous circumstances and his superb performance under fire deep in enemy territory demonstrated the highest order of courage and devotion to duty. His superb professional conduct should be an inspiration to all of us serving in Vietnam.

4. Please extend my personal commendation and appreciation to all who participated in this operation. In particular, this letter should be made a part of the official record of MSG Meadows.

W.C. WESTMORELAND
General, United States Army
Commanding

The letter was forwarded to Meadows under the following cover:

MACSOG [Oct 19, 1966]
  SUBJECT: Outstanding Performance of Duty
  HEADQUARTERS, UNITED STATES MILITARY
ASSISTANCE COMMAND, VIETNAM, STUDIES AND
OBSERVATIONS GROUP, APO 96243, Oct 24, 1966.
TO: Master Sergeant Richard J. Meadows, Command and
Control Detachment, APO 96337.

1. I endorse this letter to you with great pride and personal satisfaction. The courage and competence, which you demonstrated in the performance of your duty, have been exemplary.

2. Your actions serve as an inspiration to all the members of the Studies and Observations Group, and are in keeping with the highest traditions of the military service.

3. This letter has been made a part of your official records.

JOHN K. SINGLAUB
Colonel, GS
Chief SOG

So, what was this "combat operation of great importance to the United States"?

On the evening of October 12, 1966, Colonel "Jack" Singlaub received a call direct from General William Westmoreland. The general had been contacted by Admiral Roy Johnson, Commander of the Seventh Fleet, on station in the South China Sea, and had been told that a naval lieutenant, Dean Woods, had ejected into North Vietnam from his burning A-1 Skyraider. A message from his survival radio informed the navy that Woods was uninjured. An attempt to extract him that day by Sea King helicopter had failed because the harness could not penetrate the tree canopy. The weather on the next day precluded flying. Could SOG provide a task force to rescue Woods? The problem was that Woods was only about fifteen miles from the garrison city of Thanh Hoa deep inside North Vietnam. To make it worse, Woods had had the misfortune to land between two major supply routes in an area where the NVA was very thick on the ground.

Operation Bright Light had been conceived some months prior to Woods's predicament, but the plan—to mount fast search and rescue operations after a pilot was downed—had yet to be used. Even though the plan was in existence, political clearance had to be sought from Washington before action could be taken. While clearance was being sought, Singlaub acted in preparation. Where was Meadows? His was the team for the job. A few hours later Meadows and his thirteen-man RT were winging their way by helicopter to the deck of the aircraft carrier USS *Intrepid* for briefing.

Meadows had been given only a rough outline of the problem. For the details he had to wait until he arrived on board *Intrepid.* Foul weather made for a rough journey, with an uncomfortable landing on the pitching deck. The navy information was excellent. They had a very precise location for the downed pilot. He was on a ridge that had a trail on it and he had found a hiding place twenty meters downhill from a point where a tree had fallen across the trail. There was no place to land a helicopter close to Woods, but Meadows found a spot on the air photographs that looked as though a helicopter might be able to hover while he and his team jumped off. It was only about eight hundred meters from Woods's position. It was not the best of situations, but if they could get in at that point it ought to be easy to locate the pilot. Then Meadows got the bad news.

Admiral Johnson called him personally on the ship's telephone and said that there had been an order passed through CINCPAC via MACV that there were to be no American soldiers on the task force. Johnson asked Meadows if his Vietnamese would go alone, and he replied that even though they were the best team in Vietnam they would not go without him. He was asked to try anyway. The men did not look at all happy when the situation was relayed to them. This was an American who had to be rescued after all. Then Meadows got a real surprise. They did not refuse to go but they looked extremely sad. Meadows actually pleaded with Johnson to let him go, so Johnson got in touch with General Westmoreland again and back came the order: "Go." He did not know if Westmoreland took that decision on his own shoulders or whether it came down from Washington, but Meadows did not care. RT Ohio was ready and eager. Woods had gone in three days earlier and time was critical. All that was needed was a short break in the weather.

The break came on the morning of day four. The team took off in two Sea Kings; Meadows, Antony, and half the Nungs in one and Chuck Kerns in the other with the rest of the team. Meadows later said that the flight in was horrendous. The team had never experienced flak before, and it seemed that the Vietnamese threw everything they had at the aircraft as they crossed the coastline. He was full of admiration for the calm, professional navy pilots who chatted away as though nothing was happening. They found the position quickly and the team jumped out into long grass and knew immediately that they were in trouble. All around them they could hear Vietnamese soldiers shouting directions to each other. The search for Woods was still going on. Of course, that was a very hopeful sign as far as Woods's survival was concerned, but it meant the enemy would certainly have heard the infiltration aircraft.

Moving as fast as they could and partially hidden by the long grass, they soon had the ridge in view and could see at once that it was a "hot" trail. As they closed with it a small NVA patrol came along. The point man was very alert, but the rest were chattering like school kids. Meadows had a grim choice to make. If Woods was where he should be, then they were very close to him. If the NVA found him first then he would have no chance and Ohio would probably never be able to rescue him. If Meadows opened fire on the NVA, Woods could take off and it would be impossible for them to find him. As fortune would have it, he did not have to make the choice. The point man spotted him and brought his gun up to fire. Meadows had his suppressed Swedish K into action immediately and took out the four NVA that he could see. He ran partway down the track shouting Woods's name, but it was by then obvious from all the NVA around that he had been taken. The patrol did a very rapid search of the bodies and took their weapons. (Meadows "liberated" a pistol from one of the dead men, who was obviously an officer.) They started to pull back along the entry line but had made so much noise in shouting Woods's name in English that the NVA were quickly on to them. They could now hear voices all around them and, curiously, the sound of bugles, which seemed to be used for some sort of signaling purpose. Ground to air contact was made on the move and it confirmed that Woods had been taken. Three helicopters were on call in the area. Meadows was using his favorite call sign, "Sugarfoot." As they got to an area with just lowish scrub and small trees Meadows vectored the first of the aircraft onto his marker panel. Chuck and his half of the task force started to get aboard. They were using a two-man hoist and it seemed to take forever. The aircraft then came under heavy fire, and just as the last two guys were about to be hoisted aboard Meadows saw a purplish haze around the helicopter. It had been hit, so he shouted, "Abort. Abort. Abort." Luckily, as it turned out later, the last two men who had been about to be hoisted aboard fell out of the harness.

RT Ohio now had a something of a problem. They were surrounded and all they could do for the moment was dive into a thick clump of bamboo. It was good visual cover but noisy as hell. Billy Antony looked at Meadows and asked, "Well Dai Uý, what do we do now?" "We go home" was the reply. The voices indicated that the NVA were in line above and coming down the side of the ridge toward the remnants of Ohio. It would take them no more than ten minutes to be upon them. If they made a move then that bamboo would start popping and cracking and they would be instantly located. There is simply no way that a man can travel through bamboo quietly, no matter how slowly he moves. The quick-thinking Meadows had an idea that just might work. He got on the ground-to-air radio and called for any aircraft in the area to respond. He received an immediate reply. There were two fixed-wing aircraft close to hand. He explained that he did not want any fire brought down, he just wanted as much noise as they could possibly make right overhead of his position. The pilots grasped the situation right away and promised to be there in less than five minutes. They were and they began to scream around the area at treetop level as RT Ohio made their run out. There was no way the Vietnamese could hear the movement. Meadows took a chance and moved fast using small tracks but roughly keeping to the line of their infiltration flight. They knew that their helicopter was standing by for instructions and they had to get out quickly. On a small ridge they found an area where the trees were so thin and weedy that the downdraft from the aircraft would probably separate them. They called it in and made one of the fastest hoist-aboards ever seen. Ground fire was heavy as they turned away to go home.

When Meadows and his party got back aboard the USS *Intrepid* they heard about Chuck Kerns's lucky escape. His helicopter had been seriously damaged by the ground fire and it only made it back to the sea by literally flying at treetop level. If the last two men to get on the hoist had stayed there they would almost certainly have been killed. As it was, almost everyone on board suffered minor wounds. Before they got over water Chuck had made all of the Nungs get into life preservers, and when the pilot said he was going in, Chuck literally threw them all out. When he got out himself there was so much shrapnel in his life preserver that he began to sink. The rescue boat had started moving as soon as they knew the helicopter was in trouble and it was with them in no time at all. It had been quite a trip. If only the weather had broken sooner the chances are that Woods would have been saved, and that would have been the perfect end to the mission.[7]

That first Bright Light mission of the Vietnam War, from which everyone returned, was to create the springboard to Meadows's third personal meeting with General Westmoreland. Colonel Singlaub was so impressed by RT Ohio's overall consistently high performance that he recommended that Meadows be granted a battlefield commission. This would be the first such award of the Vietnam War. Meadows was told of this in person by Westmoreland. In fact, he was offered a choice. He could have instant promotion to sergeant major E-9 or a commission direct to the rank of captain. Meadows unhesitatingly opted for the commission. In November 1966, his tour of duty in Vietnam came to an end and he was reassigned to the 6th SFG at Fort Bragg. Though obviously delighted to be reunited

with Pamela and young Mark, Meadows admitted that his tour in
Vietnam had unsettled him:

> It doesn't matter what we thought of the war then and it
> matters less what we might think of it now. We were sol-
> diers sent out to do a job and we did it to the best of our
> ability. I don't know anyone in SF who sold the army short.
> You don't live that kind of high-activity life with its heavy
> risk factor without getting hooked on it. How often in your
> soldiering days do you get to work with a bunch of guys of
> that quality? Of all the jobs that were going in Vietnam I be-
> lieve that being a "One-Zero" on a recon team was the finest
> of them all. I'm proud to have fulfilled one of my personal
> aims in Vietnam. I swore to myself that I'd do my best to
> make sure that I never lost a soldier. And you know what
> the key to that was? In my opinion it was detailed planning,
> training, and boldness. You've got to think boldly—plan
> boldly—and then go boldly. Boldness gives you surprise,
> and surprise is one of the best assets a soldier can have in
> combat. You've just got to be bold. When you've thought
> everything out, then start in on the "What if?" questions.
> Once you've "Whatiffed" the hell out of every situation,
> then you've got to come up with a solution and then train
> your men until all responses are automatic. But, you've got
> to be careful that you don't take their initiative and alertness
> away. I guess that one day the full story will be told and the
> U.S. will get to know about some of the bravery and dedica-
> tion that was shown by so many guys in SF in Vietnam. It
> will shock a lot of those guys and gals who used to line the
> streets to mock soldiers coming back from there.

8

Vietnam Through an Officer's Eyes

1966–1970

For the next five months Meadows was in limbo. The transition to officer status was not instant; there were procedures to be followed. There was no way to predict how long the commissioning process would take, and Meadows could not be given any positive assignment that he could get his teeth into. A precedent had been set with a battlefield commission direct to the rank of captain, and terms and conditions of future service had to be devised from scratch. At this point Meadows received a great deal of help from two old friends, Lieutenant Colonel Bud Sydnor and Lieutenant Colonel Jack Isler, who recognized that his expertise should not be lost to the army too quickly and that his retirement pension rights should be protected. They were able to advise and help to lay the groundwork in the hope that he would eventually be granted a ten-year commission despite his age. The alternative would have been forced retirement on the date that he would have left the army as an E-9. The joint effort was successful and the ten-year contract was eventually approved. On April 14, 1967, Master Sergeant Meadows became an officer. He was commissioned in Fort Bragg by a man who knew him exceptionally well. Pamela attended the ceremony at which Colonel Arthur "Bull" Simons awarded Meadows his captain's bars along with his third Army Commendation Medal.

Within days Captain Meadows was assigned to Fort Benning, where he would become the commander of a basic training company. He had always enjoyed training, and he found the work interesting, rewarding, and without pressure. The assignment allowed him time to reflect on his future as he settled into his new status as an officer. At the age of thirty-five, he was still extremely fit and he yearned to see more action. He knew that it would not be easy to foreshorten his assignment in Fort Benning, but as a Special Forces soldier he had an ace up his sleeve in the shape of Mrs. Billye Alexander[1] at the Assignment Branch of the U.S. Army. Through her good offices he managed to have himself placed on a Vietnamese language course; this made it easier for her to arrange another tour of duty in Vietnam for him.

He was not given a formal assignment before he traveled to Vietnam, but, as before, he was approached immediately on arrival and requested to take a specific job. This time it was Colonel Jack Singlaub (SOG) who sought out Meadows, and the meeting led to his being appointed as the operations officer of the STRATA program. STRATA was the acronym for Short-Term Roadwatch and Target Acquisition; Meadows was to be based at Monkey Mountain, near Da Nang. The STRATA teams of Vietnamese, Cambodian, and Nung origins were inserted for short periods of time, typically up to two weeks. In the early days some teams were accompanied by SF soldiers, but that ceased in October 1968, at the same time as President Lyndon Johnson ordered the cessation of all bombing in North Vietnam. Meadows's job consisted of the selection of teams to tasks, preparation of operations orders, and generally keeping an eye on training and motivation. On occasions he was able to fly reconnaissance missions, and he often acted as Covey Rider.[2] On one occasion Meadows's aircraft was shot down, but both he and the pilot escaped unscathed. The subsequent citation for a Vietnamese gallantry medal reads:

> A brave company grade officer of high staff and combat ability. As Combat Operations Advisor to the 11th Battle Group, Captain Meadows disregarded dangers and hardships while conducting frequent air missions to observe, maintain liaison with, provide guidance for, and drop and pick up combat teams behind enemy lines. In particular, during a military operation on October 2, 1968, in a mountainous area of Tuyen Duc Province, while providing guidance for operational teams, Captain Meadows's observation aircraft was attacked by hostile ground fire, but he and the pilot calmly landed in the jungle and, at the same time, he called in aircraft for accurate airstrikes against enemy targets, thus inflicting heavy personnel and weapon losses upon the Communists.

Meadows was later able to retrieve the propeller of the downed aircraft and use it to decorate his office. This was quite exciting stuff, and the fact that an SF man was "Covey Rider" was greatly appreciated by the recon teams on the ground—they knew they were dealing with a man "who'd been there" himself and this did a lot for their confidence in the support mechanism.

The work at STRATA was interesting, but after eight months Meadows was getting itchy feet. Apart from the occasional jaunt as a Covey Rider, there was none of the "buzz" of leading missions on the ground. His continual requests to lead missions fell on deaf ears. He was not refused the missions because of any doubts about his capabilities; far from it. As operations officer he had a very extensive knowledge of SOG activities, and the command structure was not about to risk a man with all that information being captured and probably tortured by the NVA.

But Meadows was a man who always kept his eyes open for opportunities, and his chance to escape from the office came in March 1969. A Marine force was in deep trouble in the Dewey Canyon area; the strike force that had gone in to assist them was also pinned down. He was told to assemble a task force that could go in and help out. Typically, he assembled the unit at high speed, planned the operation, briefed the force, and then assumed command. Now it was too late for another commander to be designated, and a delighted Meadows was back into action. The information from Lieutenant Colonel Smith (call sign Delmar), who was commanding the 3rd Battalion, 9th Marines, was scant. Communications were hampered both by enemy action and atmospheric conditions, but it seemed that the battalion had taken exceptionally heavy casualties. They appeared to be closed off on three flanks by the NVA and were taking heavy mortar fire.

Task Force Meadows was launched on March 7 to link up with call sign Delmar. Meadows initially calculated that the operation would take two to three days, but knew from experience that an accurate assessment was not possible. The aim that he stated for the mission was worded to give him the maximum flexibility: "TF Meadows will infiltrate into the enemy's rear area to kill, destroy and create confusion and to gather intelligence useful to the Dewey Canyon operation." Some of the names of the participants on the after action report were already well known to Meadows and respected by him: MSG Thomas Twomey, SFC Nathaniel Johnson,

SFC Jerry Shriver, SFC Fred Hochstrasser, SFC Joe Garner, and SSG Lawrence Hunt. The task force consisted of two full platoons, two reconnaissance teams, and the headquarters element. The majority of the other soldiers were drawn from the Special Commando Unit (SCU).[3]

Task Force Meadows was to be inserted in two airlifts on the afternoon of March 7. The first group on the ground immediately came into contact with the enemy. The incoming fire was not heavy. The attack had probably come from an outpost or a trail-watching patrol that was covering the possible LZ area as a matter of course, and it was easily suppressed. One man was wounded and evacuated by the insertion helicopters. Approaching darkness and the distance to the second LZ were the factors that decided that the second airlift would not take place that day, and the company moved south to establish a command post and send out RTs to check the area. The discovery of foodstuffs and campfire debris confirmed the suspicion that it was soldiers manning an observation post who had previously opened fire. Soon it became obvious from ground sign, markings on the trees, and the hard-packed earth that the area to which TF Meadows had moved was well used by the enemy, and signs indicated that an ambush had been laid. The fact that the task force had approached off the trail and on the same side as the waiting VC was probably the reason that the enemy, being outflanked and unable to successfully engage, had withdrawn to the east.

On March 8, TF Meadows moved east toward the LZ selected for the second insertion of troops. Passing through an old bunker area, they came under enemy small arms fire, which was quickly suppressed. After contact was broken it was found that two of the SCU troops had been wounded, and blood trails indicated that at least one of the enemy had been injured. The TF was unable to reach the second LZ on time, so Meadows gave the order that the infiltration should go ahead and used smoke to indicate his own position. The wounded SCU men were moved quickly forward for evacuation on the insert helicopters but could not make it in time. The TF on the ground was now seventy-seven strong, including ten Americans, two Vietnamese soldiers, and sixty-five SCU. When the area was secured, one helicopter returned for the wounded men. During the first attempt the pilot was hit in the helmet by a bullet but uninjured. The second attempt was under cover of escorting gunships, which put suppressive fire on the surrounding hills. All this had taken valuable time and Meadows was obliged to set up his command post for an overnight stay. During the night the enemy made a series of light probes that caused no problems.

The next day, March 9, was spent in patrolling outward from the command post. The area was in heavy use by the enemy and many stores of clothing, food, and ammunition were found. The bunkers and huts were burned and all the stores were destroyed. On hearing enemy activity to the south, Meadows called in artillery fire. During the reconnaissance phase, Lieutenant William O'Rorke's five-man patrol found a fresh trail and was following it south when O'Rorke spotted an enemy trail watcher who made the mistake of stepping into full view. O'Rorke shot him in the knee and was moving forward to capture him when one of his SCU decided that the wounded man had made an aggressive move and shot him dead. The dead man's clothing and equipment identified him as NVA. At this time Meadows took a call from Delmar via radio relay saying that he was receiving mortar fire from the TF's general area. Meadows adjusted artillery fire and the mortar fire ceased. During the night, which was spent at the same location, ambushes were set up.

At 0530 hours on March 10, Meadows got a message from the radio relay saying that Delmar wanted the two forces to link up by 1000 hours that day. Meadows said that it would not be possible to meet that time frame, but nonetheless he got the TF moving fast. The first contact with the enemy came quickly. They attacked using AK-47s, SKS carbines, and a light machine gun. The firefight lasted only about ten minutes and there were no casualties on either side.

At 1100 hours the TF entered an old enemy bunker complex and Meadows was able to make direct contact with Delmar for the first time. The Marines were under heavy mortar fire, and because Meadows could hear the rounds leaving the tubes, he was able to request an accurate air strike. Eight 500-pound bombs were dropped, silencing the mortars. The TF made fast time but constantly had to stop to destroy caches of food and ammunition. Meadows made contact with Delmar and requested a flare for a position fix. This showed Delmar's position to be about 2,500 meters away. Delmar was told that a link up before dark was not going to be possible and Meadows suggested that his TF should secure a nearby hill and remain there overnight while assisting in the location of enemy mortar positions. This was agreed. On searching the new position they discovered three graves approximately two days old. These were opened to ensure that they contained bodies and not munitions.[4]

The area was secured and ambushes were set up. One such ambush resulted in the capture of a wounded NVA soldier, who was given medical attention before being taken to Meadows's position for interrogation. Throughout the remainder of the day the enemy continued to harass with sniper fire, which was suppressed by the use of M79 grenade launcher rounds. Meadows put in a request over the radio relay for an immediate evacuation of the wounded POW. Although every effort was made to get him out, approaching darkness and thick fog made it impossible. Assessing the trail to the south to be the enemy's most likely line of approach for a night attack, Meadows called down an artillery strike. While all of this was going on, two SCU were attempting to prepare a tall tree for demolition to clear an LZ. One of them was hit in the arm and back by sniper fire. Delmar again called for assistance in locating a mortar, and the TF was able to suppress it with artillery. The remainder of the night was uneventful except that the POW died of his wounds.

March 11. The terrain was not conducive to fast movement. The hills were steep and heavily cratered, with a large amount of debris, unexploded munitions, and fallen trees. The situation was not helped by a thick fog that restricted visibility to one hundred meters. Meadows was now in constant communication with Delmar, and his TF took up a defensive position to the south of the Marines' location. Throughout the night the enemy maintained a series of probing attacks against the Marines and there was little the TF could do, as the fog thickened and visibility was down to fifty meters. By first light the fog had lifted a little and a green flare was seen to the south of the TF position. Fire was brought to bear on it, and the enemy responded with AK-47s and rocket-propelled grenades (RPGs). Meadows instructed the platoon under fire to discharge white parachute flares. According to information from a POW, a green cluster flare meant that the enemy could take the position without assistance; red meant that they could take it with difficulty; a white flare was an instruction to withdraw. Meadows hoped that his white flares would cause some confusion in the enemy ranks. There were only two U.S. casualties that night, as both O'Rorke and Shriver received light wounds from an RPG round.

March 12 was spent in the same position, with spasmodic fighting throughout the day. An unsuccessful attempt was made to resupply the Marine position, and as one of the TF patrols moved downhill to try to recover one of the bundles, they heard what they thought was the enemy moving a crew-served weapon. An artillery barrage was put into the area and nothing more was heard.

In the early morning of March 13, two Marine companies and TF Meadows began to march to the vicinity of the Marine battalion command post. The point of the column was ambushed four times, and during one of these ambushes the Marines wounded an NVA soldier. Meadows assumed responsibility for his interrogation, care, and transportation,[5] extracting the following information from the POW:

> Name: Dang Xanh Phu. Private. 18 years old. Unit: Nghe An Unit—3rd Plt, 25th Co, 18th Bn, 6th Regt, Div unknown. Co strength 60 men commanded by a 2nd Lt. En. Co arrived in area 1 month before capture. Co armed with AK47s and SKSs about half and half. 3 RPG per Co. Squads normally 6–7 men plus 2 engineers. Phu's mission for the day was to ambush part of route 922. Phu was sapper armed with SKS and 1 mine, claymore #7. His CP is 1½ hour walk from ambush site on azimuth of 320 degrees. Phu detonated mine that killed 1 Marine and wounded 2 others. While in Vietnam he has heard rumors of Chinese advisors, nothing of Caucasians. The end of intelligence from prisoner.

The heavy burden of dead and wounded soldiers made movement very slow, and when B Company of the Marines fell behind Meadows despatched his second platoon to supply flank and point security. It was not until late afternoon of March 14 that the two Marine companies and the TF took up positions on the battalion perimeter and the process of resupply could take place.

On March 15 Meadows was instructed to prepare the TF for extraction in order that it could be reinserted on a ridgeline to secure it for the Marine extraction operation to begin. By 1115 hours the TF was in position and took a resupply of ammunition, food, water, and clothing. At about 1800 hours Meadows was surprised and annoyed when he was then told to prepare the TF for extraction by three CH-56s, which would arrive in ten minutes! At 1825 hours, after a considerable and heated debate, TF Meadows was firmly ordered to board the helicopters and by 1910 hours the mission was completed.

The after action report on which this narrative was based is most interesting for what it omits. The Marine company had been savagely mauled and Meadows thought that casualties had been reported as approximately 50 percent, though this was never confirmed to him. It was largely Meadows's leadership that persuaded the Marine company commander to move back to the battalion HQ after the abortive attempt to resupply. Meadows was full of praise for the courage that had been shown by the Marines throughout. Many of the small skirmishes reported were extremely spirited actions, and the task force performed to an exceptionally high standard. Where the report states that "after considerable and heated debate, Meadows was ordered to board . . . " it refers to the fact that Meadows did not think that his mission had yet been completed and would not be until all the Marines had been evacuated. To his chagrin he was overruled. The Marines were, in fact, all extracted without further incident. Meadows was recommended for the award of the Distinguished Service Cross (though this was later downgraded to a Silver Star). It is probable that there would have been no complaints if Meadows had added the POW to his existing record score of thirteen. There is little doubt that he saved the prisoner's life. The most annoying thing of all to Meadows was the refusal of the staff at I Corps HQ to accept the identification of the NVA operating in the area.[6]

Meadows received a further benefit as a result of the highly successful mission. He was called in to speak with Colonel Isler and asked if he would be prepared to take on another assignment. He was redeployed to Marble Mountain to take over the command and training of a reconnaissance company. Always in his element in the training environment, this was much more to his liking. Toward the end of his life and reflecting on his career, Meadows was to say that of all the awards and honors he had been given, it was the commission that pleased him the most. This, he said, simply because it gave him a greater influence in training over a greater number of men. This change of employment extended his tour of duty in Vietnam, and he put body and soul into the mission and passed on much of his vast reconnaissance and surveillance experience to a new and younger breed of SF soldier. He had positive opinions on how the RTs should be used:

> I didn't always like the missions we were given for those
> teams. Sometimes it seemed that there was no good reason

to insert RTs. I think BDA[7] missions didn't always serve any useful purpose. Sometimes there'd be instructions to collect soil samples or make map corrections or try to do body counts. With those tasks we'd try to add them on to a convenient RT that already had a proper mission in the required area. Nobody was about to risk lives for unimportant missions.

It was okay when a ground commander had asked for a mission. He usually had a good idea of what he was looking for. Commanders would apply for a mission and clearance would be given by the Pentagon and the "packet" or "frag" [fragmentary order] would come to us from Saigon. We'd turn the one- or two-page document into a workable operations order with a definable mission and then brief the RT leader. The Vietnamese Army was privy to the highest level of information and the system lent itself to leaks and penetration by the enemy. After they would insert, the RTs usually had an option to establish radio contact once or twice per day, morning and evening. If three contacts were missed then we'd get an aircraft up to try to establish communications. Typically an RT would have two or three U.S. advisors, the team leader and the commo man at least, and a Vietnamese and four, five, or six Nungs. It all varied a bit though, depending on the missions.

The Nungs were straightforward mercenaries getting about US$60 per month, with extra for parachute pay. They were essentially Cholon Chinese and many of them were new to the jungle. They were tough little guys and they learned fast, had a big capacity for hard work, and would do what they were ordered to do without question. The fact that the SF guys had the communications gave them total control of course. But the teams who took the time to get to know and understand their Nungs got excellent loyalty in return.

The extension of duty caused Meadows to miss the birth of his daughter, Michele, in Miami. In June 1969, he was assigned to Fort Benning as the operations officer to the Patrolling Committee of the Ranger Department. At the same time he was told that he had been successful in his application and that the Secretary of the Army had granted him a ten-year contract as an officer, with a retirement date of April 30, 1977. In his own mind Meadows acknowledged the assistance of his two good friends Sydnor and Isler in pushing this through. He enjoyed his time with the Ranger Department. He had enjoyed earning his own Ranger Tab (he had been an honor graduate on his course). His enthusiasm for soldiering and absolute mastery of the crafts of the profession showed in every lecture and every field training exercise (FTX) that he planned. He thought that the Ranger course was probably the best in the world for young men and he tried to make learning fun. His door was always open to any student at any time. But there was that little piece of Meadows that still yearned for action, and he was about to get it.

9

They'll Know We Cared

Son Tay, 1970

The regular "thwack-thwack" of the HH-53's rotor blades was strangely hypnotic in the darkened interior of the helicopter; the assault force soldiers appeared to doze.[1] Meadows looked at his watch for the umpteenth time. 0115 hours. About one hour to touchdown. "Touchdown"? He grinned. That was amusing because when they hit the deck there would be none of the gentle landing of which the big bird was capable. They would be going in hard, probably harder than any pilot before had ever deliberately grounded his aircraft.

This was the big one. The one he had dreamed about for years. Even an hour out from the target his body was tingling with anticipation. He was not surprised that the soldiers under his command seemed to be dozing. Soldiers have that knack of switching off until the moment before action. Maybe it was the body's defense mechanism carefully husbanding the store of adrenalin that would surge around the bloodstream when the moment came. Some really would be sleeping, but many would be pretending as they coped with their own private thoughts. No one knew what awaited him. None of them knew whether they would return from this high adventure for which they had trained so hard for the last few months. Despite their secret fears, there was an air of calmness about the team—almost serenity—the aura that comes from a group of men that knows that it is ready for anything. "These guys will give it their best shot," Meadows thought to himself, "and the POWs—well at least they'll know that we care—that their country really cares." He looked again at the hard floor of the HH-53. Somebody, he forgot who, had suggested using mattresses to cushion the shock of a hard landing but this had been vetoed. Keeping the payload weight down was critical and mattresses also carried the danger of causing the fast-exiting troops to snag a boot and trip. They were heading to

107

within thirty miles of the North Vietnamese capital, Hanoi, possibly the most heavily defended city in the history of modern warfare. He cast his mind back again to the events that had brought him on this journey, to this helicopter flitting only feet above the jungle canopy of North Vietnam.

In late July 1970, Meadows was sitting at his desk in Fort Benning. His official title was operations officer to the Patrolling Committee of the Ranger Department. He had been pleased to get the notification from the Secretary of the Army granting him the ten-year contract as an officer. With time already served, that gave him a retirement date of April 1977. His job with the Ranger Department was interesting and he had always enjoyed working with young potential leaders. He firmly believed that the Ranger course was the best in the world for giving young soldiers a sense of purpose and unity. Interest, however, did not totally replace excitement, and Meadows occasionally longed for the old days in SOG. Life changed with the next telephone call. An action officer at the Pentagon asked him to authenticate his identity. After that he was very surprised to be told to cut an order assigning himself to a joint planning team with the Joint Chiefs of Staff. He had, he was told, been personally selected by the new Office of the Special Assistant for Counterinsurgency and Special Activities, Pentagon (SACSA) chief, Brigadier General Don Blackburn. There were no further details.

The journey to Washington, D.C., was a long one as Meadows tried to figure out what was happening. None other than his old commanding officer, Colonel "Bull" Simons, greeted his arrival. Meadows grinned as he looked at the squat, powerful form of his old friend and he took pleasure in again hearing the harsh, grating tones of Simons's voice. If the Bull was in on this mission as well as Don Blackburn, then it had to be good. The last he had heard of Simons was that the legendary soldier had suffered a stroke. "How are you, sir?" Meadows inquired. "Pretty damned good, Dick. Come with me." As he followed Simons into the office block, Meadows thought about the two men. "Headhunter" Blackburn had earned his nickname during World War II when he had brilliantly led his "regiment" of Igorot headhunters against the Japanese Army on the island of Luzon in the Philippines campaign. He had ended the war as a twenty-nine-year-old full colonel. In 1960, during his tenure of command of the 77th SFG at Fort Bragg, Blackburn had been the man given the responsibility to form and organize White Star. He was later to command SOG (1965), and it was there that he had realized the true value of Meadows. Blackburn and Simons had met as soldiers in the Pacific when Simons had been a part of the 6th Rangers, with a reputation for courage, ingenuity, and aggressiveness. And it was Simons that Blackburn had selected to run the White Star program. Blackburn and Simons were both well-known exponents of unconventional warfare. "Yes," thought Meadows again, "this has got to be good." And so he became a member of the planning team for Operation Ivory Coast.

Even though he suspected a mission of some importance, Meadows was staggered when Simons confided in him that they were going to make an attempt to snatch all the prisoners from the Son Tay prison camp just a score of miles away from Hanoi. Simons outlined the now well-known story of how intelligence sources had determined that at that point in time there were sixty-one POWs in Son Tay. The rough plan had been slowly maturing under conditions of the strictest secrecy since early May and now was the time to refine it, start recruiting, training the personnel, and perfecting new operating techniques. Meadows immediately grasped the magnitude of the task. He had been to North Vietnam before, and the attempt to rescue Dean Woods had taken place within a hundred miles or so of Son Tay on the first Bright Light mission. Still, with this team and the massive cooperation from all quarters of the armed forces—if there was a way to do it, that way would be found. Meadows was curious about one factor:

At first sight this seemed to be a mission that should have gone straight to SOG in Vietnam. When he queried this with Simons he was told that Blackburn had thought that it would have been impossible to maintain security out there. A lot of the SOG base's training activity was monitored closely by North Vietnamese intelligence agents. It was possible that any changes in the type of training or absence of any of the normal people might be noticed and reported. The North Vietnamese had suspected in the past that operations might be mounted against POW camps, and it was decided that it would be much safer to use Special Forces personnel from CONUS (the Continent of the United States) and set up training facilities that could be strictly controlled. This appears to have been the correct decision, as many years after the war was over it became common knowledge just how effective the North Vietnamese intelligence penetration had been.

Yet another old friend of Meadows was to become a key member of the planning nucleus, and it would be Meadows who got him the job. One rainy Sunday morning Lieutenant Colonel Elliott P. "Bud" Sydnor was sitting quietly in his house at Fort Benning when he received a surprise call. He later recalled the situation:

Well, he [Dick] got me the job. It was in a roundabout way because Colonel Simons had contacted one officer that I know who had turned the mission down because he didn't know what it was and apart from having small children, he was running the Florida Ranger Camp. So, Dick mentioned me by name to Simons. These are Dick's words. Colonel Simons said, "Well. Where is he?" Dick said that I'd just arrived at Fort Benning about a month ago. Well Simons called me one Sunday afternoon at Benning. He asked what I was doing and I said that I was heading up the tactics committee at the infantry school. A great job. He said, "No. No. What are you really doing?" And I said well, I've told you all I can tell you. I've just got here and I'm just getting my feet on the ground and I've got one of the best jobs. A sought-after job here in Benning. He said that he needed to see me.

My wife and I knew that Dick had gone to Washington, but we didn't know why and we didn't know that Simons was involved in anything. So he came down and we talked for about an hour in the parking lot. We sat in the rain like a couple of CIA agents. At least that's the way I tell the story now. All he asked me was if I was interested in a job (I think seriously that he came to see if I was still fit). I had worked for him directly in Laos on White Star after we'd been east and got replaced. We superimposed ourselves on my old operations center and then two or three months later Laos went neutral and we were out of a job. That's where I knew him. Anyway, to get back to the point, all he told me was, "You know there's something going on that's good for the U.S.A., good for the army, and good for Special Forces. Do you want to be a part of it? Without me telling you what it is?" I said, "Yes."

Simons said that was good and told me to go back to my HQ where I'd be given some orders. I was told to follow them exactly. Well, I almost never got out of there. When the orders came down every guy on the post that outranked me questioned me. They asked me if I knew what I was doing. You see, War College graduates are supposed to be the cream of the crop in terms of assignment officers passing out everybody's share of the good guys. I had just come from the War College and all of a sudden I, this prime piece of meat, was leaving and couldn't tell them where I was going. And I didn't know where I was going! That's how Dick got me there. He just mentioned my name. That stood as the recommendation and it was enough for Bull.

I went to Washington around the last week in August and found out that we were primed to report to Eglin Air Force Base on about September 3rd or 4th. Colonel Simons told me what they were fixing to do. He just gave me a quick brief. He said there is a camp; here's a model of it; here is the operations order that you'll be involved in. You're going to be the ground force commander. He told me that he was task force commander but he was not going to stay in the air, that he also was going to be on the ground. Colonel Simons had gotten us a room; we were bunking together down in Crystal City, which is right on the edge of Washington. That night as we were talking he said, "Okay. I'm the task force commander and I have a command and control ship, which is one of those biggies, like a converted 707. But I do not plan to put people on the ground without being there myself. That's your problem." I thought, "Wow," but then he assured me—you just did not have long conversations with Bull, you just didn't because he was such a positive person. If you wanted to keep your job, you did it—so he said, "You work it out. I will not interfere with your operation." And I knew he wouldn't. So, there it was. My second in command on the ground was my boss.

I read the operations order and I was amazed at how small it was and what a neat package had been produced. It was probably as clear an operation order as I'd ever read. As far as I can remember, it was no more than ten pages to cover an operation that was scheduled at that point to last no more than thirty minutes. And that operation order was the work of Dick and a couple of others.

Meadows was modest about his input in the planning and writing of the operation order:

> As a mission it was clinically simple on the ground. It had to be. If you're dealing with a plan that had to have at least three stages of possible change if things went wrong, then it was a case of KISS [Keep It Simple Stupid]. It was great working with people like Don Blackburn, Bull Simons, and Bud Sydnor, but I was lucky enough to also get to know such people as Warner Britton and Larry Ropka. What those guys didn't know about air planning wasn't worth knowing. And later, when we got guys like Herbie Zehnder and Marty Donohue, and I'm mentioning only a few, you just had to have a real good feeling about the whole mission. Later on General Leroy Manor came into the picture in a big way. He was a great guy. The big thing about the guys at the top was that they had all worked together in the past, some in World War II and certainly in Vietnam. I'd worked with Blackburn and Simons before, but I'd never worked in Vietnam with Bud. We seemed to be there at different times, but he had a great reputation. The trust didn't have to be earned in that team, it was already there. The command relationship was going to be very good. The plan that Bud Sydnor saw was the first draft to demonstrate feasibility. Later, after Bud joined us, a formal planning team was set up and I guess there were about thirty-five guys on it. We had army, navy, air force, and intelligence guys from each of the services and the CIA. We still kept the plan simple though. An early major decision that had to be made was where to train. Security was always going to be one of the biggest headaches: that and keeping the teams motivated when we couldn't tell them where they were going.

It was General Leroy Manor, commander of the Special Operations Force (U.S. Air Force), who came up with the solution. Now designated as the overall commander of the mission, his suggestion that they use Auxiliary Field No. 3 at Eglin Air Force Base, Florida, was a good one. The ROTC had only recently vacated the site, and so a little base exchange, mess hall, theater, and lecturing facilities already existed along with recently refurbished accommodations more than adequate for their needs. There was sufficient helicopter maneuvering space and firing ranges within the area, which was set in vaguely similar ground conditions to the Son Tay prison. It lacked the physical security of a formal gate and guardhouse at the entrance, but such things were easily taken care of. It had the thing that was most necessary, anonymity. The site was big enough to swallow up all the physical requirements of the training phase of the mission and it had been in constant use until about six weeks previously, so no undue attention would be attracted when the troops moved in. The normal sounds of an active air base meant that the helicopter work would cause no comment.

The manner of Bull Simons's recruiting has now passed into Special Forces legend. To an audience of some five hundred Green Berets at the JFK Center at Fort Bragg he made the statement that he was looking for "a few good men" for a special and important mission. It would, he said, be relatively hazardous. It would take a few months to prepare for and carry out the mission, but everybody should be home by Christmas. Simons's reputation had a double effect. A very few knew that it would be somewhat more than "relatively hazardous" and opted out. Most of the others for the same reason decided to try out for a place. Simons was to personally interview all of the 125 volunteers he initially chose. These included all the administrative personnel. He was later to select fifty-six officers and NCOs to form the assault force. Except for five, all had seen combat. Even though they were given no mission details, all of the soldiers were sworn to secrecy and ordered to report to Auxiliary Field No. 3 at Eglin on September 3. They would have no mail facilities, no incoming telephone calls, and no visitors. There would be no movement permitted outside of the designated training area.

Intelligence resources had succeeded in putting together a finely detailed scale model of the Son Tay compound (code-named Barbara), and from this was devised a life-size mock-up constructed of "two by fours" and heavy target cloth. It had been decided that due to the orbit of a Russian spy satellite that passed over Eglin Air Force Base twice daily, whatever mock-up was used had to be designed so that it could be disassembled prior to the passage of the satellite. The cover story put to the troops was that a number of American hostages were being held in a walled compound patrolled by twenty or so guards and that there were probably many more guards in a barracks quite close. They were given no intimation at all about which country this compound was in.

With satirical humor, the Son Tay Raiders later designed a patch to show a pair of mystified eyes peering around the stem of a mushroom and mounted it on the motto KITD/FOHS (Kept In The Dark / Fed On Horse Shit). In the opinion of the two seasoned officers Bud Sydnor and Dick Meadows, the part of the mission that put leadership to its most severe test was the training phase. Consider the situation when experienced soldiers, ignorant of the true purpose of their mission, were asked to work with a greater intensity than had ever been demanded of them before. When Bud Sydnor was asked about this he gave a candid statement:

> There was a lot of bitching. These were seasoned soldiers who felt that we showed a lack of trust in them by not briefing them. They would bitch about the weight they were carrying and how many times a day we were doing the practice. We were doing it six times a day then, three in the afternoon and three at night. I'll tell you when all that bitching stopped. It was when we started shooting in CONUS at night, less than three feet behind somebody's heels in the dark. That's when most of it stopped. That's when they knew that whatever it was that was scheduled to happen really was going to happen. The bitching didn't stop completely. You know what soldiers are, but it was no longer serious bitching. Shooting like that in training's against all the rules and it's dangerous and that's when the prudent ones and the mature ones came around and 90 percent of our people were very mature.
>
> Colonel Simons hand-picked them and then he let me and Dick sort out among them because they brought in some extras. It was decided that each one of those groups, however small, and they ranged from fourteen initially to twenty, would have extra men running with them even when we were shooting. Of course, when we did get round to actually shooting we could only put one-third of the force on the ground at a time because there were no brick walls to separate the Blue Force on the inside from the Red and Green Forces on the outside. We had a few accidents, one grenade

accident that was fortunately not serious. We had to fire a couple of guys. One soldier came back after a rehearsal and I asked him where his acetylene torch was. Well, he said he'd left it by the compound gate because we were going back in thirty minutes to do it all again. So, we just said okay, you can't be one of us anymore if you can't do what you're told. One guy turned himself in. He said that he couldn't keep up, so we substituted one of the extras for him.

At Eglin I had to use a leadership ploy I'd never used before. You see, I was the new guy on the block to those people. It was Dick who told me this story. Somebody had gone to him and asked, "Who is this guy, Sydnor?" This was after I'd called everybody together and told them that if somebody was not doing what they were supposed to do and they didn't get rid of him, I'd hold them responsible. And I said if they were holding somebody back who did know what he was doing just because they didn't like him, then I'd hold them responsible for that, too. So that's when they went to Dick and said, "Who the hell is this?" All Dick said to them was, "He's a professional." And that's the best compliment I've had in my life.

There's another story about Dick as well. Along about the second month (we trained all of September and all of October) Dick came to me and said that a deer was going to be run over that night and that he'd like to have a barbecue with his team. And I had to tell him that because he was knowledgeable about what was going on and as a consequence of that and the fact that he had a more extensive background than the other leaders, his team was a little ahead. I told him that we didn't want one force to get so far ahead of the others that it created bad feeling and so I would like for him not to have this barbecue. He settled for that because that's the kind of guy he was.

At a reunion some years later one of the raiders observed:

You know I don't recall much bitching. There probably was because what soldier doesn't bitch? It's part of a soldier's natural instinct. But deep down we all knew that something major was definitely going to happen. You just didn't get guys like Bull Simons, Bud Sydnor, Dick Meadows, and all those high-quality flying guys all involved in the same mission unless it was very serious. And when those guys are right down there with you training, rehearsing, and shooting and not just standing back watching and criticizing, then there's a real sense of purpose. You don't get all that serious money being spent on ammunition and aircraft time unless it's for real.

That comment reinforced Meadows's own statements:

As a leader you had to try to not just do what the soldiers did but more if you could. You had to try to be a better shot. You had to try to be fitter. You had to have the new ideas and you had to show real faith in the mission. It was difficult to cope sometimes with the questions. All those guys were experienced senior NCOs and were used to being in the picture. They were used to their own guys asking them for details and being able to provide answers. It hurt them not to know. What was worse, it was clear to them that Bull, Bud, and I did know and they thought we didn't trust them. When the odd guy had to leave, the security probably began to make more sense to the others. There weren't many that left. I can only remember personally getting rid of one man. He'd had a few drinks in the canteen and I told him to lay off it and get to bed. When I went back to the rooms later on he wasn't there, and sure enough he'd sneaked back into the canteen again. He had to go.

I'd have been pretty disappointed if those guys hadn't kept asking what was going on. I sure as heck would've wanted to know if the situation had been reversed. You know, I read somewhere that we'd done 167 rehearsals. Now, I'd say that we probably did only about thirty of each of the three contingency plans. We must have fired over ten thousand rounds of ammunition each though.

In this way the teams accepted the large degree of physical training that was part of the syllabus. They may have to carry sick or wounded men over a variety of obstacles. A big emphasis was put on the shooting skills that they practiced twice daily in daylight and dark. Although the intelligence agencies were able to give first-class details of the compound, there were many important ingredients they could not supply. Were the prisoners chained at night? What was the construction of the internal doors? What would be the fastest way to eliminate the NVA guard force? How would they enter the compound? Would they use ladders or use explosives to breach the walls? These and many other questions tested the fertile brains of the SF soldiers as the plan slowly matured.

In an attempt to improve night shooting, the "Singlepoint"[2] sight was trialed. This clever but simple device required the rifleman to keep both eyes open and line up a red dot on his target. Even without proper mounts and simply taped to the rifles, the device was a dramatic aid to night shooting effectiveness. It was Meadows himself who brought the device to the attention of Simons. He had attended a small arms conference in June 1970 and had been impressed by the sight that was being advertized by the U.S. distributors, ArmaLite, Inc., of Costa Mesa, California. Simons instructed Meadows to obtain two or three sights from the manufacturers. In Meadows's words, "The results were unbelievable." Many other experiments were conducted with acetylene torches, bolt cutters, and custom-made explosive charges to breach the walls. This remained the biggest single problem until it was ascertained that a helicopter could actually land in the compound—just barely—provided that it was accepted that it would never take off again. Once this concept was approved, then the focus of training for Meadows's assault team, the Blue Force, became how to get out of the helicopter and close with the buildings and let the prisoners know what was going on before the enemy could bring effective fire down on them. The estimated maximum time that could be allowed for this was thirty seconds.

Seemingly no expense was to be spared. From Fort Belvoir, a research facility housing part of the Army Development Command, came prototype night vision goggles to assist the helicopter crews and some of the ground forces in getting early warning of approaching enemy. These aids were to prove invaluable in at least one small part of the action to come. Back in 1972 you would not have needed two hands to count the number of aircraft fitted with FLIR,[3] yet some of these were to be loaned to the raider force for the duration of the mission. Meadows had his own comments on the air element of the mission:

I don't think the world had ever seen, and maybe still hasn't seen, so much air-planning and flying expertise gathered under one command. Say what you will about the ground force's mission, but to me it was the infiltration and exfiltration that was the key. If we got in undetected, then surprise would carry the ground forces along for the critical period, and once we got those POWs on board the choppers we didn't want them going back at any cost. I used to listen to the planners and pilots discussing and sometimes arguing about ways and means, and I was always amazed at the enthusiasm and knowledge. When you talked to people like Marty [Donohue], Larry [Ropka], and Warner [Britton] and all the others without exception, you just felt comfortable; they really wanted to do it. Regardless of his role, everybody was working to the success of the mission. I remember one of the air force guys very well. His name was Keith Grimes and he was the task force weather man. He came up with a cute little idea for using gridded air photographs as a means of quickly identifying locations between the ground forces and the aircraft. Poor guy, he was later killed in an air crash in New Mexico. I think the air force named something in his honor at Hurlburt Field. You get a team like that and that's what SF is all about. Somebody should wave a great big hat for those guys. None of us ever doubted their commitment and ability.

How many men in those aircraft heading through the night sky toward Son Tay were recalling the now famous briefing given by Bull Simons to his task force. At 1800 hours on November 20, 1970, at Takhli, Thailand, he made the following statement:

We are going to rescue 70 American prisoners, maybe more from a camp called Son Tay. This is something American prisoners have a right to expect from their fellow soldiers. The target is 23 miles West of Hanoi.

You are to let nothing, nothing, interfere with the operation. Our mission is to rescue prisoners, not take prisoners. And if it turns out that they know we're coming, don't dream about walking out of North Vietnam unless you've got wings on your feet. We'll be 100 miles from Laos; it's the wrong part of the world for a big retrograde movement. If there's been a leak we'll know it as soon as the second or third chopper sets down; that's when they'll cream us. If that happens, I want to keep this force together. We will back up to the Song-Con River and, by Christ, let them come across that God damned open ground. We'll make them pay for every foot across the son-of-a-bitch.[4]

Would the raiders have guessed where they were going? Meadows had his own ideas on that subject:

Well, we were dealing with some very experienced soldiers. The cover that Americans were being held hostage was a bit thin. There were no news reports of such an event. The style of the mock-up did suggest a prison rather than an embassy, and I guess that some of the guys worked out that we would be heading to Southeast Asia. But did they guess at the location? I'd say probably not. Not many of them would have heard of Son Tay. They may have thought of Laos or Cambodia as probables and they would have sure thought of Vietnam, but when Bull made his announcement that night at Takhli, I do not believe that anyone had guessed at Son Tay as the target. There was a short silence after Bull spoke while his words sunk in. I guess it only lasted for a few seconds but it seemed a long time. Then the walls nearly came down with the applause. That was a good moment. That was another confirmation of success.

All had not gone smoothly for the commanders and planners of Ivory Coast. The requirements for a night operation with cloudless skies and at least a quarter moon allowed them to select a first window of opportunity between October 21 and 25. The plan was approved but not given the necessary presidential blessing due to Nixon's absence from the White House. Though not desirable for security reasons in the eyes of the planners, this extra time was not wasted: more rehearsals were carried out and even more refinements were made (it was during this phase that FLIR was fitted). The next available window of opportunity was November 21 and presidential approval was granted. The problems were not over, however, for even as the raiders were preparing to launch, intelligence was produced to suggest that Son Tay was a dry hole. The prisoners, according to an intelligence agent in North Vietnam, had been removed. Faced with conflicting information as to whether the prisoners were there or not, the Joint Staff had to make a hard decision. The whereabouts of the source of the intelligence meant that the information had to be taken seriously. But had the prisoners been moved because the North Vietnamese had learned of the attack, or was the source misinformed. The information had not been actively sought by the CIA. To make such a request would have been a serious breach of security. The evidence in support of the prisoners not being in Son Tay was more or less uniformly matched to the evidence that indicated they were still there. If the raid was called off and the prisoners were in Son Tay, then apart from the raiders, the world would know nothing of the plan and the whole effect of the effort would have been lost. If the prisoners were not there, there would be embarrassing accusations of "warmongering." The decision to go ahead was a brave one under the circumstances.

Even that was not the end of the matter, for the typhoon season was fast approaching and General Leroy Manor was advised that November 21 was likely to be subjected to inclement weather. He was advised that November 20 would be his best opportunity. Thus, a further decision had to be taken and Manor made what proved to be the correct choice by advancing the operation by twenty-four hours. After advising all the supporting commanders of his decision, Manor moved to Monkey Mountain, which had been selected as the command post. It was while he was at that location that Manor received photo reconnaissance intelligence reports that Son Tay still showed signs of occupation.

The results of the raid have passed into the annals of Special Forces history. It was an unqualified success in terms of execution. The extremes of planning, training, and rehearsing were justified; the air infiltration methods and the expertise of the pilots earned them admiration throughout the world of professional soldiers. The coordination of supporting forces, including the mock attacks on Hanoi and Haiphong, was impeccable. When things initially went wrong at Son Tay and Bull Simons's helicopter landed in the wrong place, Bud Sydnor coolly switched plans to cater for this eventuality. Just as coolly he switched back to the original plan when Bull rectified the error. Neither of these switches caused a moment's hesitation or misunderstanding in the minds of the troops. The reactions were smooth and fluid as they instantly adjusted tactics. The courage of all participants is undisputed. The fact that the camp was unoccupied does not change the military perception of success. Every man performed to perfection, and had the prisoners been there then there is little doubt that they would have been rescued.[5]

Those newsmen who detracted from the raiders' efforts had to eat their words long after the event, and in Meadows's opinion it was largely due to the efforts of one man. For a considerable time there was conjecture as to how the raid may have affected the POWs still incarcerated. Meadows had something to say about that:

> Let me get my thoughts in order because I want to mention Ross Perot here. He'd had a very active role in the Vietnam War. He showed a great concern for the POWs and MIAs, sympathy and compassion for the families, and he had his own sort of liaison with North Vietnam. I guess some guys had permission to go in and represent Ross. They used to fly over, talk about things, and come back out. A bit like Henry Kissinger did for the president. It got to a point where they agreed that he could take in a planeload of presents for the POWs one year. Ross was pretty excited about that and he coordinated with the families to have special presents brought in and loaded onto a 707 that was going to fly out there. I gather that he had the plane flown to Thailand but something went wrong and he didn't get the final permission to go into North Vietnam. There was a lot of publicity about that. The whole world locked onto him because of his effort and was very sympathetic that he couldn't get the mission accomplished. Anyway, at the end of the war when the POWs were released, Ross had someone in the reception line talking to them and asking what he, Perot, could do for them. A lot of them said that they'd like to meet the raiders of Son Tay because it was through them that many of the POWs had survived.
>
> I'll return to Ross in a minute. The normal reaction after the raid, as we found out later, was that the North Vietnamese panicked and began to bring in all the prisoners from those little camps like Son Tay and consolidate them in Hanoi because they felt they could hold them safely there. The Son Tay raid made them realize that we had the intent and

the ability to go right in there and hit them. I had a friend, Sergeant Thompson [Special Forces], captured at Long Bay and held for five years in solitary. He was kept in one little room and he didn't talk to anyone after the interrogation was finished. He actually heard the choppers come in and the planes overhead and, of course, he thought maybe they were coming for him. Soon after that he was taken to Hanoi and for the first time the POWs could talk to each other and look after each other. Pilots that were later captured were also able to spread the word about the raid, and in some cases the Vietnamese guards told the POWs what had happened. They said that there had been a raid but the Yankees had failed. It boosted morale everywhere. It made them think, "My God, our nation hasn't forgotten us. They tried it. It's not likely that they'll try it again, but it might speed things up for the eventual release."

Now, back to Ross Perot. When those guys came out they knew what Ross had tried to do to get the airlift in and they already had a strong appreciation of him. So when he got to know that the POWs would like to meet the raiders, Ross dreamed up the idea of going to see the Secretary of Defense to get his permission to allow all of us to come together under his financial arrangements. Well, I was stationed in Okinawa with my family out there and the message went through the DOD trying to locate everybody by order of the Secretary of Defense, who had said that they must all be released from duty for this period of time if they wanted to attend.

Well, I looked at it and thought, well, it looks like it may be one big drunk and I decided not to go. Then I looked again and thought that maybe there was something underneath it all and that we should go. So, Pam and I went. You've got to remember that at that time most of the raiders, including myself, weren't really sure whether we'd done the POWs some real damage. Had we caused people to be killed or tortured in reprisal? We just didn't know. Sure, we felt good about the "good part" because we all believed in what we did. We believed in the right of one soldier to try to rescue another even at the risk of death. Yes, we felt good about that part, but we didn't know how they felt. The night that Pam and I got there they held a big reception and there were hundreds of people there. Ross had rented two whole hotels in San Francisco and had all kinds of good programs worked out. That evening there wasn't much mingling between raiders and POWs because we didn't know each other. Also, we were in civilian clothes with nothing to identify us. It was kind of like POWs getting together and raiders getting together and talking to their own groups. The big thing was the next day.

Everybody had to go off to a big auditorium in town where they had Nancy Reagan, who was representing the governor of California. Ronald had some big meeting downtown. There were other important people there that Ross had got along and they had a general called Robbie Riesner. He was already an ace from the Korean War and they didn't have many aces in that war. He flew missions during the Vietnam War and *Time* magazine had done an article on him. So, what happened? When he was shot down and captured the North Vietnamese knew all about him. He was tortured beyond most men's capacity to absorb it—but he did—and he was going to be the guy to open the show. Robbie's got a kind of a sad-looking face and he got up as the first speaker.

He spoke very well. He stood up, in uniform, and said, "We ex-POWs understand that there is some doubt in the minds of you Son Tay Raiders as to whether your mission was successful or not. I can tell you that we looked at it as the greatest success of the Vietnam War. We're standing and sitting here because of you. You saved our lives. You did that. You didn't rush to us but you certainly saved our lives by forcing the North Vietnamese to consolidate us in Hanoi, where we could begin to look after each other, to talk to each other. Some of us hadn't talked in five years. Erase any doubts from your minds. You saved us."

Well, because of that our heads came up a little higher and our chests came out a little more and we began, for the first time, to really feel good about it. We all needed that. Now that's what I wanted to say. Ross Perot had sensed that and did something about it, and that's where he surfaced in my mind as being a great man. It was his view that the

get-together was necessary to get some sort of cohesive-
ness back into the system again. No politician that I know
of would have gone to those lengths and not inconsiderable
expense to do something that he just knew in his heart was
the right thing to do.

An astute battle analysis of the Son Tay raid was written in November 1991 by a young army captain. He will recognize his own
words, but I will not embarrass him.

Col Simons's HH-53 had landed outside of a secondary
school 400 yards from Son Tay. The mistake was immediately recognized and the pilot returned to pick up Col Simons and his security element. This mistake proved to be
fortunate; Col Simons and his team killed over 200 enemy
soldiers in the few minutes they were there.[6] This sizeable
force was not foreseen during the planning stage and could
have possibly been able to reinforce the Son Tay compound
before the raiders could exfiltrate. Col Simons and his security force landed at Son Tay at H+8 minutes and the contingency plan Green was canceled without missing a beat (Maj
Meadows).

The rest of the mission was executed as planned. The
entire enemy were either killed or had run away. The assault element finished clearing the prison cells; however, no
prisoners were found. Cpt Meadows radioed to LTC Sydnor, "Negative items found." On hearing this, Col Simons
asked Cpt Meadows to repeat his transmission. Again, Cpt
Meadows confirmed "Negative items found." At H+17 minutes, the order to begin the extraction was given. By H+27
minutes, all raiders had been extracted and the mission was
over (LTC Sydnor).

Although no prisoners were found in Son Tay on November 21, 1970, the raid was very much a success. Never did
the North Vietnamese think the US would try an operation
so deep in their northern territory. The planners and raiders
used the element of surprise along with the synchronization
of effort to attack the enemy at their most heavily defended
area and be successful.

Of all the characteristics the raid on Son Tay possesses,

surprise is the most important. Without surprise, the rescue force would never have made it inside North Vietnamese borders. The planners painstakingly compartmentalized information to prevent any leaks. They even withheld the real mission from the raiders until they were already inside Thailand, only eight hours before the mission was to take place. The shock effect on the North Vietnamese was effective. This was evident by the fact that after the raid, they were never able to react to find the rescue force before it was well outside North Vietnamese borders. Tactical surprise was achieved with the aid of the Navy's deception strike, a flight route that avoided enemy radar, and a smooth, aggressive synchronized assault on the objective.

The synchronization of all the assets involved in the raid was paramount to the operation. Every man, weapon, aircraft, and decision point had to be perfect. The Naval diversion was timed perfectly even though the pilots flying the simulated assault over Haiphong harbour never knew the real reason. Fuel consumption and flight times for the air force had to be calculated perfectly. A slight error in any calculation could result in any aircraft running out of fuel or the rescue force not being on target in time. Most impressive were the contingency plans. When Col Simons's aircraft was not in the right place, LTC Sydnor quickly activated contingency Green with no delay in the timing of the operation.

The raid on Son Tay prison camp, by military definition, failed. To accomplish a mission the leader must succeed in his task. The task of the raid was to rescue American prisoners. This did not happen. However, to ask any Prisoner of War in Vietnam if the raid was a success he will say without a doubt it was one of the most important events that had happened in his life (Col Dutton). Conditions for the prisoners changed within four days following the raid. Men that had been in solitary confinement for four and five years were immediately taken out and put in cells with other prisoners. The routine torture stopped. They received medical treatment, something they had not had very much of since they were captured. They were fed better food and they were given new clothing. The single most important psychological relief that kept them from losing touch with reality was that they were grouped together. They could talk to each other (Col Dutton). The POWs survived captivity in North Vietnam through their determination and the belief that their country would never forget them. Before November 21, 1970, they were living on determination. After November 21, they knew they were going to stay alive.

Meadows's contribution to the Son Tay raid is clearly obvious, but a look at the man through the eyes of someone who did not serve with him, but had every reason to observe him closely, is interesting:

How do you get into a man's mind? Where or what is the button that makes him react, and how or why does he think the way he does? To study people you do not need to be a psychologist, just interested. Let's take this guy Captain Meadows for example and look at a segment of his life. The curiosity—what is the motivation behind his actions?

He's been isolated from his family and friends for four months. He lives in a single room billet where he stays most of the time if he's not training or conducting business with his unit. The hours are long by the standards of a normal garrison. But not here, to work well into the evening is a normal and even a welcomed routine, for boredom quickly becomes the enemy. Being a leader of this unit keeps him busy; he has been planning an air assault raid in his head for quite a while. Now the training is in full swing and planning continues. He's gone over the rehearsals in his head time after time. He knows exactly what's needed to execute the mission without incident. He quietly and calmly gives the orders, guiding his unit in the right direction. His intuition is brilliant; a smooth decision making process that leaves others confused while he meticulously and methodically matures the plan. He sees and thinks the "what ifs" that no one else sees. He consults with his peers and subordinates periodically but only to research something he has been thinking about. And without disclosing his ideas, he eases out of the conversation to return to the drawing board in his head where the real plan has been written.

During training he checks on his soldiers and his young leaders. Watching their skills in both combat and leadership development. He allows the small expected mistakes within his parameters of the direction he intends to lead the unit. Like a sheep herder, he watches over his responsibility, the men. His training philosophy: take care of the men and train them the right way that allows personal and professional growth. By doing this a leader secures the success of the mission as well as the survival of the men. "Mission first, men always." And when the training is done for the day and the soldier has been put to rest, he's thinking and planning for tomorrow. He's studying the drawing board, making the necessary notes. A quick thought of his wife and he drifts off to sleep.

And why, why all the selfless devotion, sacrifice of his time to painfully make sure everything is right? Who can answer this question? I can. And simply put, the common denominator of everything he does is honor. He has honor. I know this to be true. I've studied it for fifteen plus years, watched, listened and practiced. This Captain Meadows is unusual and I know it, I know it all too well. He's my mentor, role model. He's my Dad. And in 1970 he had a small part in an air assault raid. He's the most unusual man I've ever known and has taught me without teaching. I continue to chase his reputation and I don't mind, it's the best goal I could have.

The greatest reward I've ever received was at a private dinner; just the two of us. I was told by my mentor that he was proud of me and pleased that I had learned the common denominator—honor. That night he gave me something very important. He gave me his unquestionable trust. Something he has never given to any other man. Now I'm Captain Meadows and I'm planning the missions; I've learned the secret.

This astute piece of writing by Mark Meadows pinpoints Dick Meadows's sense of honor as the focus of all his actions, and that is probably true. However, it left Meadows with a weakness. If a soldier, acquaintance, or friend breached the Meadows code of conduct by not acting honorably, then he stood the risk of being coldly and dispassionately cut out of Meadows's life forever. It was not in Meadows to ask why the code had been broken—the mere fact that it had was enough. The rule was not just applied during his military days—it remained in force to the end of his life. This was an odd facet in the character of a man who otherwise was so generous, hospitable, and charitable. These acts of excision sometimes led to criticisms that were not justly founded, and he was to suffer occasional commercial damage because of them.

This code was a little at odds with how Meadows viewed his duties to his soldiers. Like all military men who have experienced combat, Meadows had his private inhibitions, prejudices, and weaknesses, and he knew the meaning of fear. He managed to accept them and keep them all in perspective. This is demonstrated in one of his training philosophies:

> If you examine a man exclusively for his weaknesses and his faults, you will be in danger of neither liking him nor trusting him. Look for his strengths. As a leader encourage him to build on them. Do this properly and from that he'll recognize and correct his own shortcomings. If you have a difficult man with whom you think it is worth persevering, then don't ever get angry with him. Especially don't go to bed angry with him, because that's when the little maggots eat at your brain and you wake up still angry with him and you've lost your objectivity. Worse—you might have adversely affected a good man's career.

Meadows, age ten. (Courtesy Shirley Meadows Harvery and Grace Meadows)

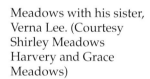

Meadows with his sister, Verna Lee. (Courtesy Shirley Meadows Harvery and Grace Meadows)

Unless otherwise noted, photographs are from the Meadows family collection.

Preparing for
Korea.

Canoe training with the 22nd SAS Regiment in England on the River Wye, with
Sergeant John Cann, in 1960.

(*Above*) Fort Bragg, 1965. Dick Meadows and Chuck Fry were the first two qualified HALO Jumpmaster/Instructors in the U.S. Army. (*Below*) Meadows and Fry
ascending for a high-altitude jump in the Canal Zone.

Hey, free fall's fun!
Canal Zone, 1965.

RT Ohio in Dak To in early 1966. Meadows is standing third from the left and carrying his Swedish K submachine gun.

Meadows, Borek, Golden, and Wilson in Dak To in 1966.

Billy Antony of RT Ohio giving M79 lessons in Kontum in 1967.

Paul Darcy and the RT Ohio Nungs in Kontum in 1966.

On the Ho Chi Minh
Trail with RT Ohio in
September 1966.

There is time for a
smile even on the
Ho Chi Minh Trail.

Richard J. Meadows is commissioned by Colonel Arthur D. "Bull" Simons at Fort Bragg, North Carolina, on April 24, 1967. With him is his wife, Pamela. At the same time Meadows was awarded his third Army Commendation Medal.

Time to write home.

Training near Da Nang in late 1968.

Meadows standing on the wreckage of the aircraft in which he, as "Covey Rider," and the pilot, Major Mason, had been shot down two weeks earlier, near Da Lat.

Interrogating an NVA POW taken during the Dewey Canyon operation on March 13, 1969. The POW had killed one Marine and wounded two others.

Meadows is awarded the Legion of Merit by Major General Orwin C. Talbott at Fort Benning on July 27, 1971.

Vietnamese photograph of helicopter "Banana 1" in the Son Tay POW camp. (Courtesy Wayne Rich and Ron McKown)

Vietnamese photograph taken in the Son Tay POW compound after the raid. Note Zehnder's helmet and Meadows's bullhorn. (Courtesy Wayne Rich and Ron McKown)

Three legendary Special Forces characters: Colonel Arthur D. "Bull" Simons (right), Lieutenant Colonel Elliott "Bud" Sydnor (center), and Captain Richard J. "Dick" Meadows (left). The photograph was taken during the Son Tay planning and training phase at Eglin Air Force Base in September 1970.

Meadows and his Son Tay assault group.

Meadows's SOG identity card.

Medical training for the ORUS guard force in the Upper Huallaga Valley, Peru.

Reviewing the troops in the Upper Huallaga Valley, Peru.

Dick and Pamela with their good friend Ross Perot.

Dick on his boat on the Alaqua River.

Michele, Lisa, Mark, and Pamela with General Wayne Downing receiving the Presidential Citizens Medal on behalf of the late Richard J. Meadows on July 29, 1993.

(*Left*) The author at the newly unveiled statue of Richard J. Meadows at Fort Bragg, North Carolina, on June 6, 1997. (Author's collection)

(*Right*) Pamela Meadows speaks at the unveiling ceremony. (Author's collection)

(*Below*) Pamela Meadows accepts the medallion as Richard J. Meadows is inducted into the Ranger Hall of Fame

The look of
a soldier.

Final preparations for Son Tay.

En route to Son Tay.

10

The Rangers, Mr. Meadows, and Delta Force

1970–1980

The Son Tay raid was treated by much of the media in the expected fashion. There were accusations of military ineptitude and of President Nixon trying to find a means to escalate the Vietnam War after President Johnson had stopped the bombing in 1968. There was, however, no question in any soldier's mind that the raid had been a clinical success, and in later years it became a model study for the Special Forces of many countries. The Raiders were frustratingly sworn to secrecy and only scant details were released. Simons, Sydnor, and Meadows found themselves in demand to give such briefings as they were allowed, and the writing up of the after action report took about four weeks. (The refusal by the U.S. government to give a full report on the raid lasted for about five years.) Eventually life settled down to normal again, and in January 1971 Meadows found himself back with the Rangers at Fort Benning.

Even though it looked as though his Special Forces soldiering days were over, Meadows had no deep regrets:

> I liked the Rangers. I was active in the evolvement of new training techniques and also responsible for the development of young leaders. At that time of my life I reckoned that I'd done enough to justify the responsibilities I'd been given, and it's the finest school for young soldiers anywhere in the world. We were able to take a good look at some long-standing training maneuvers and FTXs and modify them to suit the needs of Vietnam and other places. I also enjoyed my time with the basic training company, though I never thought that I would. There's a great satisfaction in taking young men, some of who could be described as "hippies,"

and watching them mature into good soldiers. It was also a
time when we had something of a color problem, and when
you can get black and white mixing and working in har-
mony to a common cause, that's also satisfying. It's at the
age of those young guys that you can really start to instill
the meaning of honor and commitment.

Meadows's assignment at Fort Benning gave him more time
with his family, and with a son then coming up to eight years of age
there was a lot of fun to be had. Meadows had decided that his boy
should learn to care for and respect weapons at an early age, and
young Mark soon became a crack shot. However, one of the hunting
trips with his son did not have quite the outcome that he expected.
Out in the woods and armed with the .410 shotgun his father had
bought for him, Mark was quite at home. He had his list of things
that he could shoot (along with the things that he could not shoot)
firmly locked in his mind. On this particular patrol he made either
an error of judgment or a simple misidentification. He shot a red-
headed woodpecker. Now, this beautiful little bird was a protected
species and the young Meadows was overcome by remorse.

Meadows Senior, thinking no doubt to enforce the lesson of cor-
rectly identifying the target, cajoled his son repeatedly into looking
at the pretty little thing and saying what a great shame its death
was. Mark would not be parted from his tragic trophy and on returning home insisted to his mother that the bird be wrapped in
plastic and put into deep freeze. The bird stayed in the freezer for
a couple of months before agreement was reached to bury it. Mark
never went hunting again.

Meadows was to gain a further military commendation from the
Rangers, but his time with them was relatively short. In March 1972
he was ordered to 1st SFG in Okinawa. He was expecting a fairly
low-grade job as a comparatively junior captain at that time, but he
was pleasantly surprised to discover that he had been chosen, over
the heads of twenty majors, to be the operations officer for 1st SFG.

The operations officer had a busy life; his area of interest covered Japan, East and West Malaysia, the Philippines, and Indonesia.
The continual round of briefings, the constant need to update contingency plans, the organization of MTTs, and the immense amount
of reading necessary to stay current meant that though he was accompanied by his family, he was not able to spend much time with

them. As usual, he impressed all who served with him. His briefings never contained wasted words and he rarely had to use notes. His confidence, planning abilities, and bearing led to him being selected in June 1974 to become the advisor to the defense attaché in Jakarta, Indonesia. This post was rarely given to an officer beneath the rank of major.

The time came in January 1975 for Meadows to be given his last military assignment. He knew that his post was to be with the Florida Ranger Division and it seemed logical to buy a home in the area. He had fairly fixed ideas on what that home should consist of, apart from being within commuting distance of Eglin AFB. The priorities were to have something with a reasonable plot of land, some privacy, and, dear to his heart, be close to the water so that he could enjoy his fishing. Having made all the necessary arrangements with the realtor, he left the selection of a suitable property to Pamela. Not surprisingly, the prospect was daunting to Pamela. She had been born into a military environment. As a daughter of a military family, much of her life had been spent in the enclaves of military bases. The ordered surroundings, the immediate availability of shops, and the camaraderie of military families were a way of life to her. It was a situation within which she felt secure. She toured the area with the realtor to find that those houses for sale within the townships were not acceptable against their needs and that those properties that were more rural seemed very isolated. They were almost on the point of changing their minds and accepting military quarters again when a house came on the market on the outskirts of Crestview. It was perfect in every sense except one. There was no fishing. They decided to accept the compromise—after all, it was only for two years. When Meadows finally retired they would decide where to settle.

Sydnor later commented on this:

I had some part to play in getting him assigned there [Eglin Air Force Base] because it was going to be his last assignment and he wanted to be in Florida, which is where he planned to live. He did yeoman work at the Florida Ranger Division and anyone who knew him would say that. For instance, just before I took over the Ranger School from my predecessor in June, there had been two deaths, and more recently they'd had four more in the same area. Dick was responsible in a large part for reorganizing those exercises, and on one occasion when two Central Americans who were students on the course went missing and the others were just giving up, he just got out there and found them. That's his reputation and his MO. It's an example of how he showed people early on what to do and then never let them get out of their depth.

The transition to civilian life was not initially easy for Pamela. She had those traits of the British character that could find life in the southern states of America a little overwhelming. The British are comparatively reserved by nature and can take a long time to make friends, and the custom of dropping in unexpectedly on neighbors is not common in Britain until a rapport has been established. In the United States, Southern hospitality is legendary and Crestview had this in abundance. Pamela found herself inundated by well-wishers bringing food and welcome gifts, and she soon came to realize the genuine warmth of her new environment. Crestview was (and is) a city with a true community spirit shared by all its inhabitants, and the Meadows family was soon immersed in this atmosphere.

So, what happens when a family that has been living in military quarters with restricted open space suddenly finds itself with a few acres of ground that belongs only to them? To Dick Meadows (now Major Meadows) it represented a golden opportunity to allow his children to share his own love and understanding of animals. First on the scene in the three-and-one-half-acre yard at Crestview was the horse. Three pigs closely followed this. The pigs were part of an agreement with neighbors whereby they would be purchased for food when slaughtering time came around. Another seemingly good idea was a brace of ducks; ducks need water—no problem, dig a hole, line it with a plastic membrane, and there you have it, a pond. Ducks are also vulnerable to predators, so like the pigs they had to have their own compound. Horse, pigs, and ducks were closely followed by an assortment of dogs and cats.

Dick, of course, coming home in the evenings or after spending days out in the boondocks on FTX, was able to enjoy his "farm" with minimum effort. As is the way of things with children, after a couple of weeks they tired of the feeding, grooming, and cleaning chores that interfered with their own growing commitments to the extracurricular activities of school. ROTC, band, and club memberships all demanded time. Pamela found herself with an ever-increasing workload as mother, housewife, chauffeur, and farmer. Small wonder then that when Dick came home proudly bearing a pair of goats, she said, "Enough." Dick's explanation that the goats would actually reduce the amount of work in the yard by keeping the grass cropped fell on deaf ears.

The "farm" experiment was successful in that both children did grow up with a love and understanding of animals. Time marched on and in June 1977 the day arrived that Meadows had not been looking forward to. Retirement. No more soldiering. For a time he was at a loose end. In Crestview his wife, Pamela, had become a respected person in her own right. Through her work on the organizing staff of the county educational system she met and impressed a wide range of people from all walks of life. The job was demanding but she enjoyed the many and varied challenges that came her way. Mark and Michele, themselves now an integral part of the community, considered Crestview to be home. When Meadows sat them all down to discuss where they should look for a house in which to settle, he was greeted by blank looks. They were already at home. Where else was there to go?

Meadows's reputation was then unknown in Crestview, and when he and Pamela appeared in public it was a case of people saying, "Look, there's Pamela and her husband," and not, "Hey, there's Dick Meadows." Every retired Special Forces soldier will understand what emotions Meadows felt at that time. Skill in the arts of war and the mastery of the profession of arms does not mean a great deal to a civilian employer. There is probably a greater fear engendered by the thought of retirement than in facing a combat situation. The U.S. Army is an institution whether a man serves in the Special Forces, the infantry, or a logistics corps; things which the army has taken care of for many years suddenly become a personal responsibility. The civilian contractual laws are a mystery; how does an old soldier set about securing his family; there are medical insurances and a host of other things to consider. How does he assess his own skills and abilities in order to define what he has to offer a potential civilian employer?

Meadows, having undergone this process, was about to take a post at a military school in Georgia when out of the blue another voice from his past spoke out. General Samuel V. Wilson contacted him with an exciting offer. A new unit was to be created and Wilson was very keen to have Meadows take part in the formative stages. Meadows fell prey to Wilson's persuasive powers and gave a positive commitment even before he learned who was to command the organization. Colonel Charlie A. Beckwith had been selected to raise and train SFOD-D, the Delta Force.[1] The volunteers for the unit had to be selected from within Special Forces and trained to operate principally within the spectrum of counterterrorism. Wilson was inviting Meadows to take civilian employment as the principal training advisor for a projected period of two years. The job was nonexecutive, in that he would have no command powers, but Wilson made it clear to Meadows that the respect he had earned during his military career, along with his mission charter, would ensure him a voice in all matters of training and planning. The project was highly classified and not for general discussion.

While listening to Wilson, Meadows had quickly mulled over a number of factors that he had to consider. A commitment to the mission would lead to further separations from his family, as he would have to base himself at Fort Bragg, a considerable distance from Crestview. His days in the Special Forces had given him huge experience in covert operations, but the work that he envisaged that Delta would be engaged in was completely different. Was he still physically fit enough for the challenging task? How would soldiers many years his junior take to a retired civilian training advisor? Would he be capable of sustaining a good working relationship with Beckwith, who had many philosophies and characteristics in conflict with his own? After accusing himself of negative thinking, Meadows adopted a more analytical attitude. He had, after all, made the decision to take the job and he had shaken General Wilson's hand, and he felt unable to retract it. He recalled the point at which he had made up his mind:

> I knew that what was being put together at Fort Bragg was going to be something really different in my experience and there was a great pleasure in being invited to participate in something new. I knew many of the names that had been related to me and I had a lot of respect for them. It was also an honor for me to be asked, as a civilian, to play a part in building up the new force. Pam was reasonably happy. I would be in the U.S.A. and not working in any hot spots and she knew it would be a fulfilling job.

Meadows had plenty of time to apply his mind to the task, as the security curtain on the initial Delta operation required him to be screened once again up to Top Secret level. The unusual circumstances of a civilian being employed in such a role meant that the army had to formulate a special contract, and he was paid as a major with proper seniority. Wilson put as much pressure on the system as he could, but it was not until November of that year that Meadows was able to formally take up his post. The job was certainly not a sinecure. The scope was wide-ranging and demanding.

Meadows would be required to serve as a special assistant to the commanding officer of SFOD-D and act as a focal point for all matters of current intelligence that would affect the development of training directives. He would also be the linchpin for the formulation of individual training programs, monitoring state-of-the-art technology and assessing environmental changes. He would plan, develop, and assist in the administration of the operational readiness testing program. Additionally, he would be the liaison officer responsible for receiving and delivering briefings up to National Command Authority level. Should that not be enough to keep him occupied, the final sentence of his job description read: "Perform other duties as assigned."[2]

As Beckwith told him, "Dick, it's one helluva job for just one man."

It is worth looking back to the point in time when the concept of the Delta Force gained U.S. political and military blessing. In 1977 there were four countries with well-known counterterrorist capabilities: the United Kingdom, France, Germany, and Israel. All were benefiting from these capabilities. First, they were able to commit training teams to approved countries and thus gain influence and deep knowledge of senior military officers and politicians. Each country was also able to gain a financial return from such training teams. Third, such organizations made dramatic improvements to the security of their home nations and those nations with whom they had strategic or political alliances. They all had terrorism on their doorsteps, and so the teams served practical purposes. In 1977, all four countries were very active in the international arena. Their teams' skills had been proven in actual counterterrorist operations and they presented formidable competition within the marketplace. With the exception perhaps of the liaison between the United States and the United Kingdom, new techniques, new equipment, and up-to-date intelligence on the opposition was jealously guarded.

A soldier enters a different world when he passes through the doors into the realms of counterterrorist operations. He has to learn many skills that are not usually relevant to his more conventional counterpart. He may be asked to operate in civilian clothes under deep or temporary cover. There is an emphasis in this role on the use of weapons of a type that he has rarely used in the past. He may be asked to master skills more generally associated with the criminal than the soldier as he trains to pick locks and blow down doors. He will certainly have to master new communications skills. Perhaps more relevant to the degree of change to which he must adapt is that he may find himself operating alone with no support for prolonged periods. He also has to commit himself to the deep study and subsequent understanding of a differently motivated kind of enemy who will use tactics that the conventional soldier would despise. He will have to become more clinical in his military thinking. All of these factors place a different kind of stress on the chosen soldier. Therefore, a special sort of selection system had to be devised.

Meadows was instrumental in helping to plan the selection course. The system which evolved was a very demanding physical and psychological assessment that has now stood the test of time. He and Beckwith spent many hours at the Meadows home in Crestview hammering out possible methods of selection and tactics for getting the various military clearances to meet their needs. Meadows need not have worried about his fitness, as he was still an outstanding athlete, and this stood him in good stead as all the routes of the selection course had to be walked and timed in order to set the standards. This meant carrying the same loads as the volunteers would be burdened with (in the region of sixty pounds). It was a period that he enjoyed immensely. He was also working with many old friends, like Walt Shumate and "Country" Grimes, who was to become the first sergeant major of Delta.

The techniques for the various requirements of Delta gave the team a lot of scope for experimentation with new weapons, new explosives, and new tactics. Meadows was able to liaise with the British SAS, the French GIGN, and the German Bundesgrenzschutz Gruppe 9 (GSG9) at a time when the charismatic Colonel Ulrich Wegener was still in command. Meadows, though enjoying all aspects of his mission, will probably be best remembered by the early Delta Force men for his innovative planning of hostage rescue exercises.

When the team was called out one day and briefed for a mission that was to take place in another country, they could hardly believe their ears. They had not yet been validated and yet they were going into action. The Canadian government had a crisis situation on their hands and had requested their assistance. In a blacked-out C-130 the team was flown to Quebec, Canada, where they were joined by their commander, "Pete,"[3] who had been dispatched from Washington, D.C., where he was studying at the time. They were met by officials of the Canadian armed forces and politicians and briefed on the situation. A number of hostages, two of them U.S. citizens, were being held in a building by a group of armed men; one hostage had already been shot. It was suspected that there were only three or four terrorists, but they were in a good tactical position. The negotiation process was under way, but it was not proceeding well and the terrorists had threatened to shoot another hostage if their demands for money and transport were not quickly met. Political clearance had not yet been granted for Delta to go into action.

As intelligence was fed to Delta the picture of what was happening became clear. The terrorists and hostages were in an old three-bedroom detached house set in open ground. Every time a policeman showed his face shots would be fired at him. Periodically one of the terrorists could be seen passing a window, but sniping was out of the question unless all could be hit at the same time. That option was clearly not going to be feasible. The photographs taken during the fleeting appearances of the terrorists were not high quality and not acceptable for positive identification purposes. The team began to plan its assault options while listening to impassioned pleas in French over the telephone as the various officials requested permission for Delta to go into action. They managed to get a couple of men into a position where they could observe the scene, and plans of the house were obtained from a local realtor's office. The waiting seemed interminable and the stress became even greater.

Then the negotiations seemed to break down completely. The terrorists gave a deadline of thirty minutes before the next hostage would be executed. Permission was immediately granted for Delta to go into action. They now had less than half an hour to take control of the situation.

When the assault went in over the open ground, a fusillade of shots was fired from within the building. Luckily, they all seemed to pass over the heads of the assaulters. The team burst into the building and in a few seconds realized that they had been duped. The "terrorists" were rubberized dummies already shredded by the attackers' bullets. But where had the shots fired at Delta come from? That mystery was soon cleared up when it was discovered that trapdoors covered holes in the ground which Meadows and his assistants had previously dug to take cover in at the last second.

Meadows had been told to make the exercise as realistic as possible, and that was certainly achieved. The CIA did an excellent job in putting up English and French signs and in supplying the incoming intelligence, background briefings on the terrorist group, and "actors" with Canadian and French accents. Vehicles with Canadian license plates were parked around the area and everything was covered by hidden cameras. Meadows wanted bullets flying, as that was the only way that he thought the soldiers would be totally convinced. Of course, the whole exercise took place in the United States, but Meadows had the C-130 fly for the right amount of time for a flight to Canada and it made slow, flat turns that wouldn't be noticed by the passengers. "Pete" proved himself to be a well-chosen leader. He was totally calm the whole time. Once the soldiers found out that they had been fooled there was a mixture of emotions. Some got very, very angry and the situation had to be diffused by separating them until they cooled down. Their anger was understandable because the planners had prolonged the waiting time as long as they could to let the tension build up. In itself, this was an important lesson for the men of Delta Force. That was the time that worried Meadows the most. The longer the men had to wait, the greater the risk that they'd spot something amiss and realize that the situation was not for real. They were from a wide variety of backgrounds and it was always possible that someone would recognize that they were not in Canada. But they were lucky. Everyone thought that they were in Quebec. The unit did a magnificent job with their planning and the assault, and Meadows later said that it had been an honor and pleasure to work with such dedicated soldiers.

Meadows recalled that in many ways he had been influenced by the training during the work-up to the Son Tay raid, as he remembered that it was not until the raiders started shooting in close proximity to each other on a U.S. Army range that they really believed that they were going into action. The only real danger in the Quebec scenario was to the men in the building who had to get into their holes at the last moment and hope that no one blasted bullets through the trapdoors. Even though the directing staff called an end to the exercise as the Delta soldiers burst through the doors, there was no way of knowing what effect the adrenalin would have on them. These were men who had just heard shots zipping over their heads on the way in. They truly thought that a hostage had been killed, because they'd seen the "body." The planners knew they would be all fired up and totally mission oriented. It was worth it though. Most of the hidden cameras worked well and the films made excellent training aids.

So, Meadows made a solid contribution to the now fully formed SFOD-D, which was called forward to take part in its validation mission on November 3, 1979.

11

"Agent" Meadows in Tehran

1980

It all began in Iran on November 4, 1979, with a surprise action by disciples of the Ayatollah Khomeini. Brushing aside the U.S. Marine guards, fanatical followers of the Ayatollah occupied the sprawling U.S. embassy in Tehran and took nearly one hundred hostages comprised of Marines and male and female embassy staff. The action followed a student protest against the United States for having made the decision to allow the former Shah of Iran freedom of movement in America. The Shah had fled his country on January 16, 1979. The architect of the downfall of the "Peacock Throne," the Ayatollah Khomeini, had left Paris to make his victorious return to Tehran on February 1. The resultant protest from the Kurds was brutally and quickly quelled, leaving the way ahead free for the Ayatollah.

From that point on, his verbal attacks against the United States and the West in general became more vociferous as he began to tighten his grip on Iran. His economic and foreign minister, Abol Hassan Bani-Sadr, was equally verbose in his support of Islam. Initially the Ayatollah took no action regarding the embassy siege and simply stated that the attackers were only students exercising their right to protest. Between November 17 and 20, he ordered the release of all female and black hostages from the embassy, leaving a probable figure of fifty-three persons still imprisoned. The world waited expectantly. Earlier in the year the Iranian Revolutionary Guard had occupied the U.S. embassy and the Ayatollah had immediately ordered them out. Not so this time.

On November 21, the tension heightened when he made a threat to kill all the remaining hostages if the United States attacked Iran in any way. Within the embassy compound some of the bound and blindfolded prisoners were paraded before a hostile public. The noisy crowd promised death to the Shah if President Jimmy Carter would give in to their demands to send him back to Iran.

Two American flags were burned in front of television cameras and a placard proclaimed "When Khomeini fights, Carter trembles." A gallows was constructed in front of the embassy's main building.

On the same day an anti-American Islamic mob stormed the U.S. embassy in Islamabad, Pakistan. Although President Muhammad Zia-ul-Haq quickly sorted out the situation, many U.S. buildings were attacked along with the British library in Rawalpindi. Although the Americans were accused of sparking the incidents by supporting an earlier seizure of the Grand Mosque in Mecca, there was no truth in this and the actions were thought to be an overt demonstration of support for the Ayatollah Khomeini. On November 23, Bani-Sadr declared void all Iranian foreign debts (the United States was by far the biggest creditor). On December 4, Khomeini was confirmed as the absolute ruler of Iran. When the former Shah left the United States to seek refuge in Panama (after being refused entry to Mexico), it went almost unremarked in the Iranian press; certainly it did nothing to affect the possible fate of the hostages in the U.S. embassy.

The tit for tat of diplomatic posturing took a predictable course. The United States protested vigorously through all international political channels. A UN Commission was formed to retrieve the hostages. The western press attacked Khomeini and Bani-Sadr. The UN Secretary-General, Kurt Waldheim, cut short his mission to Iran when he was refused permission to see any of the hostages. Bani-Sadr, who had taken a leading role in this, was appointed as premier. Six American diplomats, who had been hiding in the Canadian embassy ever since their own had been occupied, escaped with CIA assistance on January 29. This infuriated the new Iranian foreign minister, Sadegh Ghotbzadeh, who made threats against the Canadian government but said little about the United States. On February 4, Bani-Sadr was confirmed as Iran's first prime minister, and three days later he was given increased powers from Khomeini and told to deal with the U.S. hostage situation in any way he saw fit.

On March 10, Dr. Waldheim ordered the rest of the UN Commission to leave Iran. The Ayatollah had proclaimed that the only way that any member of the UN Commission would be allowed to see anyone was if all the hostages first expressed their disapproval for the crimes of the Shah and the "Great Satan," the United States. This stand by the Ayatollah was perhaps the turning point in the negotiations. Until then he had firmly insisted that the hostages were being held by "students" and not by the Iranian government. This new and serious turn of events was reflected in increased disillusionment in U.S. political circles, placing even more pressure on President Carter (who had just lost to Edward Kennedy in the Massachusetts primary on March 4). Carter's press secretary showed the mood when she said, "The Iranian government's ability to function as a government and fulfill the commitments it has made is now seriously in doubt." The growing anger culminated on April 17, when President Carter stated that military action would be his only choice if Iran failed to free the U.S. hostages.

Turning now to Colonel "Charlie" Beckwith, commanding officer of the SFOD-D (Delta Force), will serve to show that things were already happening behind the scenes. Indeed, there was some concern in military circles at what was considered to be a rash statement by Carter. The reasons for this can be well imagined.

The day before the Iranians occupied the American embassy in Tehran coincided with Delta's long-awaited validation mission. This very demanding test was observed not only by the senior U.S. military officials concerned with Delta's future but by key figures from the Special Forces of other nations. The team was presented with a very realistic hostage rescue mission about which they had no prior information. They had to perform under the eyes of some of the most experienced counterterrorist officers in the world. They knew that their future was at stake. The mission was an unqualified success. Even as Beckwith and his team began to relax after the harrowing experience, they received unofficial word that the embassy in Tehran had "gone down." The date was Sunday, November 4, 1979. It was on Monday, November 5, that the army's Special Operations Division made contact with Beckwith and requested that a Delta liaison team be sent immediately to Washington. Major Richard J. Meadows, USA (Ret.), formed part of that team.

From that point onward an intelligence nightmare began. Against all logical expectations, it appeared that the CIA no longer had a physical presence in the city of Tehran. Additionally, the Delta liaison team was getting firsthand experience of a common Special Forces problem. All the planners were "experts" and were producing some quite ridiculous notions for the rescue of the hostages. This is not surprising, given that Delta, rightly, had been formed and raised under a cloak of secrecy; their capabilities were grossly underestimated by some and equally overestimated by others. There were also a few senior officers who had gotten a whiff of something big and wanted to be a part of it in any capacity. It has been offered as a criticism that Meadows was sometimes too quick to give his agreement to go along with some of the more way-out suggestions and that he was too keen to adopt the "Who Dares Wins" attitude suggested by some high-ranking planners. In his defense, it has to be remembered that he had no executive rank to give him formal powers of argument or agreement.

The scope of the mission was awesome. Mount a rescue operation for fifty or more Americans imprisoned in a building in the heart of the capital city of a hostile nation. The city of Tehran is deep into the hinterland and flanked by inhospitable mountains to the north and wind-swept deserts to the south. The embassy building was large and sprawling and there was no information as to where the hostages were being held or even if they were in fact together. Bad maps supported by good air photography gave Beckwith's team the ability to begin to formulate a number of plans. During this phase much time was wasted in having to convince the senior officers of the futility of the many hare-brained suggestions that were proposed, but eventually the nucleus of a plan evolved.

In outline, the idea was to launch the task force personnel and all the supporting stores and fuel for Operation Rice Bowl from a staging post in Egypt to the Omani island of Masirah in the Arabian Sea. From there the Joint Task Force (JTF) would head to a landing strip deep in Iran code-named Desert One. To effect this move a total of eight C-130 Hercules aircraft with staggered take-off times would be used. The JTF was a mixed bag; the Delta assault and rescue force would be accompanied by a small Ranger group that would provide ground security at Desert One, which would in fact become a small airport as the operation progressed. This part of the mission would be under the command of U.S. Air Force colonel Jim Kyle. The first task of the Delta Force would be to organize the airstrip for the reception and refueling of eight Sea Stallion helicopters that would launch from the aircraft carrier USS *Nimitz,* which was already on station in the Arabian Sea. Additionally, they would prepare all the equipment they needed to carry out the hostage rescue and have it ready for reloading into the helicopters.

Desert One was some three hundred miles southeast of the city of Tehran. It had been necessarily chosen from satellite photographs. The CIA and a member of the ground control team had already covertly checked out the suitability of the sand for the landing of heavy aircraft. The team had also planted a number of remotely controlled landing lights. Once the Sea Stallions had refueled and been reloaded with the necessary men and equipment, they would take off for the next staging post, Desert Two. Of the eight helicopters that would arrive at Desert One, six would be the required minimum for the extraction of the task force and the hostages. Desert Two, which had also been selected from satellite photographs, did not require soil analysis since only helicopters were to land there. Situated in hilly ground about sixty miles southeast of Tehran, this site, which was an abandoned salt mine near Garmsar, would be where the task force would conceal themselves and the helicopters throughout the daylight hours of Day One.

During the night, two prepositioned vehicles would collect the assault force from Desert Two and take them into Tehran and to the eastern aspect of the embassy. The assault would be mounted against the Roosevelt Avenue wall. Separate Delta groups would release the three hostages known to be in a different location at the Foreign Ministry and secure the soccer stadium, which was adjacent to Roosevelt Avenue. From the stadium the hostages, the task force, and the Americans who had provided the ground vehicular support would be extracted by the six Sea Stallions. Fighter and ground-attack aircraft would be on stand-by to neutralize any hostile actions by the Iranian fighter aircraft based at Mehrabad International Airport just a few miles from the city. This may appear to be a simple plan, outlined as it is in three paragraphs. It was in fact enormously complex.

The "icing on the cake" that would settle a number of unknown factors would be to have someone in Tehran with an intimate knowledge of the plan who could assess its effectiveness with a professional eye. The CIA staunchly declared that they had no assets within the country that could take on this sort of role. Furthermore, they would not send anyone specifically for the task, nor did they consider that they had the time to train any of the many volunteers from Delta's ranks. Meadows, who had been a member of the planning team from its inception, proposed his own solution. "I'll go to Tehran." Was this the "big one" that Meadows had always dreamed about?

No. After all, my mission was to be totally covert, and if the operation worked it would probably never be mentioned again. I had no command responsibilities. Don't forget, I wasn't the only American to be going in there. I was just the focal point. The man that Charlie [Beckwith], Pete [Schoomaker], Bucky [Burruss], and Logan [Fitch] and the others knew. I would be the man who could give certain code words to indicate that our part of the preparations was in place and that the plan was feasible. At the time that I said I'd go, I didn't think about the details of cover and all that. That hit me later.

Sure we'd had intelligence of good quality about a lot of the details. We knew the makeup of all the physical barriers, but there was a lot we had to leave to chance. What was the guard disposition? What weapon access did they have? How alert were they? Was Desert Two a good enough place to hide six helos and all our men throughout the day? How long would it really take to drive from there to the embassy? Would the trucks even work? Was the warehouse where the trucks were going to be hidden under surveillance? Was there any reason why the choppers couldn't land in the soccer stadium? Was there an effective system of roadblocks that could disrupt the plan? Would any existing curfews affect our movements? Was there any pattern of civilian movement during the planned time of the mission? Did we seem to have got our timings right? There was a whole bunch of things that would be good to know. There's no doubt that the mission could've gone ahead without me in Tehran, but there's a sort of comfort factor in knowing you've got it right and there's not too many surprises waiting for you.

If I'm to be real honest, I did know that when the operation finally mounted there would be no action slot for me to fill. I was a civilian and this would be one way of helping out the guys I'd been working with for two years and for whom I had the highest regard. I want to put it on record, though, that I didn't volunteer until the CIA had rejected, for whatever reasons, the Delta guys who had already asked to do the job. I was a civilian, remember. A soldier had to accept it if he was told that he couldn't take part, but I had the freedom to argue.

The CIA did not support Meadows's proposal. They did not see how a man untrained in the tradecraft of their own agents could survive in an alien environment such as Tehran. He was unmistakably an American, knew nothing about the culture of Iran, and had no professional base of experience in deep cover—"amateurish with only poor cover, no backup, no training and no aptitude for training" were the words used to reject him. The response to this was vintage Meadows: "If you won't assist me then I'll go anyway. I'll go as Richard J. Meadows if I have to." The CIA reluctantly decided to cooperate with some basic training and produce the required false passport when the time came.

This cooperation did not come easily. Ross Perot had gotten himself closely involved with the situation, and it was his intervention that led to personal meetings between Meadows, Stansfield Turner (CIA director at the time), and the chairman of the Joint Chiefs of Staff. At these meetings Meadows was able to demonstrate his commitment to the mission. Perot had also taken another personal initiative in sending an agent of his own into Tehran to seek intelligence. He offered this asset to Meadows should he require it.

The reservations of the CIA were well-founded from a purely clinical point of view. Here was a man with an immense reputation of being totally mission-oriented, but all of his undoubted successes had been conducted as a uniformed soldier operating within the parameters of military operations. Even as a civilian his experiences had been completely within the military sphere of Delta. He looked every inch the military man, and his bearing, manner of speech, and mental reactions screamed the word "soldier." He was also privy to every aspect of the mission. What if he was arrested and interrogated. But look at the situation from the perspective of Beckwith and his subordinate officers. They would take responsibility for the rescue and, as has been said, they had excellent intelligence on the physical aspects of the U.S. embassy in Tehran. This had been gleaned from solid sources, such as retired military attachés and other embassy personnel. But answers to all the little "unknowns" could make the difference between smooth sailing and a rough passage.

Meadows's initial instinct, with some grudging agreement from the CIA, was to try to develop a character with an English/Portuguese background. His supposition was that he had sufficient British contacts through which to put together a passable background. His first action was to visit a town in Portugal in which he had spent a little time some years earlier. He chose Lagos on the south coast. He would not be remembered there after so long. His brief time in the town then had been a simple holiday with no incidents, but at least he would be able to answer basic questions about the area.

In Lagos he began a search of the local cemeteries to locate a gravestone with dates which supported the cover that was beginning to form in his mind. The date was important. He found what he was looking for on the headstone marking the burial of one Senor Reyes who had died in 1949. The grave was unkempt and it appeared unlikely that any family still visited it. Taking a room in a small hotel, Meadows set out to be noticed. He wanted to have some person who would remember him if there were ever an investigation to check out his story. He chose an attractive waitress who spoke English and tried out his story on her. His lack of Portuguese was easily explained.

Meadows used the Anglicized version of Miguel (Michael) and explained that his father, Bernardo Reyes, had met his British mother, Hattie Booth, on a visit to England back in 1928. They had, Mike said, fallen in love. Following a brief period of correspondence after Bernardo returned to Portugal, Hattie had joined him out there and they married in 1929. Mike's father had given Hattie an assurance that they would eventually return to England. However, after Mike's birth in 1931, Bernardo showed no signs of moving, so Hattie returned to Cheltenham with her baby son. Except for one short visit to Hattie in 1936, Mike's father remained in Portugal until his death in 1949. Hattie died in 1959. She never remarried. Mike took on the surname of his "father."

Mike went on to explain his childhood in Cheltenham and his employment during World War II and his subsequent work as an aircraft parts salesman and then as a mining equipment salesman. His work had taken him to South America, where he remained for a number of years gaining a working knowledge of Spanish but forgetting almost all of his Portuguese. Throughout his story there were interwoven many names from his past visits to Britain—men he had known in the SAS and members of his wife's family.

Meadows was almost childishly pleased when the pretty waitress asked no fundamental questions about his story; indeed, her only observation had been to express sorrow at the lonely childhood he must have had. Thereafter he made a point of only using the dining room when she was on duty and tipping her far above the normal rate in the hope that he would be remembered. The return to Washington made his pleasure brief.[1]

The CIA refused to accept his paper-thin cover and openly stated that Meadows had proved their initial assessment of his lack of capabilities as an agent. In an effort to stay at least with the bare bones of the story Meadows had concocted there was an attempt to teach him some basic Portuguese that failed dismally. As a last resort it was suggested that he try to pass himself off as an Irishman, as there was a chance that he could master the Irish brogue sufficiently to deter curious Iranians from reaching the obvious conclusion that he was American. So Meadows officially became Richard Keith (after the late cousin who was his namesake)—a much more Irish sounding name.

He stayed with a similar cover but began to put positive names to the story. He would be an ex-representative of Dowty Mining Equipment, a company based just outside Cheltenham, England, with affiliations to a corporation in Washington, D.C. Persons to vouch for the authenticity of his background would be John Cann and John Spreull, ex-SAS colleagues, and his sister-in-law's husband, Bob Lloyd, then a manager with Dowty UK. He used the Cheltenham address of his sister-in-law, Pat, as his British home. "I was thinking of the possibility of capture and interrogation using modern drugs. I felt that if I kept as many familiar names like Bernardo, Hattie, Lloyd, Spreull, and Cann in my mind along with dates which were correct, then there was a chance that it may be enough to just get by. I would explain Bernardo's name as a family joke. At that stage I guessed that the critical points would be entering the country and making a close inspection of the embassy buildings. I was wrong, but we'll come to that."

With some reluctance the CIA finally endorsed the Meadows venture. Code-named "Esquire," and issued with an Irish passport in the name of Richard Keith, he was despatched to Britain to work on his accent and the finer points of his new identity. He elected to stay with Pat and Bob Lloyd. Apart from the need to practice his Irish accent, there were a number of British idiosyncrasies Meadows had to master. The British manner of using both knife and fork when eating and apparently using the fork upside down was noticeable.

In the minds of Pat and Bob, it was the manner of his dress that gave out the strong "I am an American" signal. The Lloyds did not know what Meadows's mission was. They suspected that he was part of a sophisticated counterterrorist field training exercise, as befitted his employment with the Special Forces. They entered into the spirit of the game willingly. A complete new wardrobe was bought in Cheltenham—from the skin outward Meadows became British. He bought trousers slightly longer than was the custom in the States. Formal polished brogues replaced the leather loafers he favored. His ties were chosen to look as though they vaguely represented a school or gentleman's club. He grew his hair longer. He modified his manners slightly—the "Sir" and "Ma'am" so commonly used in the United States were dropped and "Hi" was replaced by "How do you do." He had to adopt a more reserved behavior. Because letters might be censored, he had to learn to avoid American spellings.

Pat and Bob chose his business suits and originally were going to opt for shades of brown. As Pat was to say later, "There's something about browns which seem to blend into the surroundings and make a person unremarkable." In the end they chose navy blue, as it seemed to be a common color worn by businessmen. Meadows later commented: "They [Pat and Bob] were of great help. They corrected me on all sorts of small details. I'm afraid I wasn't a great student, especially when it came to my Irish accent. All I could manage was to take the edge off my American pronunciation. Having a Brit wife, having Pam's dad staying with us, and spending time with the Brit Army helped with using Brit-type sayings, but there's no way I'd win an Oscar for acting."

He also had to commit to memory the codes that Delta would use during the mission and to familiarize himself with the PRC-25 and PRC-66 radio equipment he would have to rely on.

It is worth at this point looking again at the intelligence picture of Tehran. Though the imprisonment of the hostages had left the CIA with no means of contacting their local agent network, they were still able to achieve quite a lot. In December 1979 an agent was infiltrated into Iran; he has become known as "Bob." Bob had been flying in and out of Tehran for some years and became responsible for checking out aspects of ground intelligence. In early January he was joined by an Iranian exile, "Mohammed," and preparations began in earnest, albeit slowly. Vehicles were purchased under the guise of a construction company's requirements and stored in a rented warehouse away from the city center and close to the road to Desert Two. Here they were mechanically checked and fuel, oil, and water levels and batteries maintained. The construction cover was enhanced by the purchase of various building materials that would be obvious from the backs of the vehicles and would also serve to give some physical cover to the rescue team on its journey to the embassy. These preparations were vital to the plan, of course, but what Bob and Mohammed could not do was provide positive intelligence as to the precise whereabouts of the hostages.

Some people have said that Beckwith had a dislike of Bob, but there is no evidence to bear this out and, after all, Bob was critical to the plan. It is much more likely that his concern was that Bob did not fit easily into the scheme of things purely because Beckwith did not know him. This was the prime factor in Beckwith's demand to have someone on the ground who was known both to him and the whole team. That he did not have a complete trust in Mohammed is quite understandable. Delta had been working for so long under conditions of extreme security that it would have been difficult indeed to place faith in the late appearance of a man of the same nationality as the country into which they were about to infiltrate.[2]

Along with Meadows there were other Americans who would illegally enter Tehran: there were members of a Special Forces team based in Berlin and a young air force sergeant who had been born in Iran. The latter person, "Fred," would work closely with Meadows. He had volunteered his services after a check of records showed that he spoke Farsi. In Fred's own words: "What people didn't realize was that I had left Iran when I was eleven years old and my Farsi vocabulary was that of a child. A lot of the time when I was talking, people must have just thought that I was dumb or a bit slow."

At the very last minute, at Frankfurt airport, Richard Keith became Bryan McCarthy of British/Irish extraction. Meadows could not remember the full reasons for the last-minute switch of identity. He thought it had something to do with expiration dates on the Keith passport. "I was still being 'cleaned' by the CIA a matter of a few hours before leaving Frankfurt. I don't know for certain, but all the fuss about the passport and the change of identity led me to suspect that the security before the mission was not good. Delta kept their end tight, but there were just too many other people who knew what was going on."

The infiltration of the undercover team into Tehran went without incident. Meadows chose to stay at the Arya-Sheraton, where he registered under the name of Bryan McCarthy. The hotel was large, with a cosmopolitan range of guests. There were a number of entry and exit points. Communications in the rooms were good. At reception there was no undue interest in the arrival of Mr. McCarthy.

Meadows covered all the streets around the embassy on a number of occasions. Sometimes he would be dressed in a smart business suit and carrying a briefcase, striding purposefully as though on his way to a meeting; sometimes he would be more casually dressed and take time out to chat to reporters and even give a friendly wave to the guards. Sometimes he would use a car. His findings never varied. The guards, part of the untrained and ill-disciplined militia, were ineffective. Some slept; others just slouched and chatted to their comrades. Invariably their weapons were propped up against the walls of the towers. They would not be a problem. They would probably be paralyzed with fear when the assault went in. Taking these strolls around the target area, however, gave Meadows cause for concern.

He had to try to take a look at the place at as many different times as possible. He had to make sure that the guards were as sloppy by night as they were by day. He had to try to find out if there were different commanders who kept their men alert. There was a curfew at night, so it just wasn't possible to check every hour of the day. There were only a limited number of times that he could break curfew without risking compromising the mission. The view was limited by car, as it wasn't the sort of area where you could stop and take a close look. He did use the car a few times, but it was much better to go on foot. He tried to take routes that gave him the longest possible head-on view of the embassy, but that limited him to just one road. He felt more vulnerable during those walks than at any other time. He felt that he really stood out and it was difficult not to give in to the urge to walk more quickly. There was a big temptation to look out of the corner of his eyes at the embassy, but he reckoned it was less suspicious to show some open curiosity. That part of Tehran is symmetrical in layout, so it was easy to memorize a route before he took a walk. The only change of appearance that he could realistically make was to wear a hat and spectacles with plain glass when he was a businessman. He tried to slouch more when wearing casual gear. It was not just the embassy that had to be checked. The whole of the inside team had to be familiar with the departure airport in case they did not extract with Delta.

Meadows was very matter of fact when he related the nature of his reconnaissance walks. It can have been no mean feat to force himself onto similar routes day after day in the heart of a hostile city. On occasions he must have suspected that he was being followed, and with a cover so thin the question of interrogation and torture must have been constantly in his mind. If he was "blown," then there was no way that he would be able to disappear and hide in Tehran. He made light of those suggestions:

> I just tried to look confident, as if I had every right in the world to be there. Checking out the embassy, though, was not the most difficult mission. We also had to drive the routes between Desert Two and the assault launch point. We had to make sure that the men and the helicopters could be hidden. We had to establish accurate timings; check that the trucks were in good shape and look at traffic patterns. During those drives we really were exposed. We did the drives together, me and the other guys, because they would be helping out with the driving when the mission went ahead. On one drive back we had problems. They had a strange traffic system in Tehran. To cater for rush hour traffic, road travel directions would be changed. In the morning one part of the highway would be for incoming cars and in the evening another part would be used. Well, we were in a hurry to get back to beat the curfew and we made a mistake and got into the wrong traffic lane and bumped a police vehicle. An angry policeman came over to us. Our driver (an SF guy) was asked for his passport. Well, it was in his briefcase in the trunk along with the radio gear and pistols and the car was covered in desert sand! Our guy was great. He stepped out and began giving the traffic cop a hard time in fluent German, shouting and waving his arms about. He opened the trunk and in seconds had his passport out while the cop was still wondering what the hell was going on. Those other SF guys were good. They were real quiet professionals. I don't want to give you their names or where they came from; they're still angry at things that could have identified them written in books and articles. Anyway, the cop let us go after cussing us out for a while.

In the hotel Meadows behaved in the manner he thought a businessman would. He scattered papers and trade journals around his room that demonstrated his work in mining and quarrying. He expressed an interest in the results of the British football and rugby

matches. He made careful notes of his expenses and left them neatly
tabulated on his desk as though they would be used in his claims
later. He inquired regularly at reception whether there were any
messages or faxes for him from Ireland and made occasional dis-
paraging remarks about his boss's failure to maintain contact and
appreciate his efforts. He made extensive inquiries about the sorts
of goods that visitors could buy and the customs restrictions. He
showed a particular interest in carpets. He made a point of sitting
in the lobby and restaurants for extended periods in the evenings
rather than allowing himself to be thought of as a recluse who kept
to his room.

Most of his work was done with "Fred" as his driver and interpreter. Meadows was full of praise for Fred. "That young guy had
never been on a special mission in his life. He was great. He's what
the American soldier is all about. He volunteered for a hazardous
mission without knowing any of the fine detail. If we'd been caught
then he'd have suffered more than any of us because they would
claim that he was Iranian. We'd have been spies, but he'd probably
have been called a traitor to his country and tortured and then executed. He gave a hundred percent effort all of the way."

Fred also had a number of memories about the way that Meadows performed his mission in Tehran:[3]

> When we first went to the warehouse where the trucks were
> hidden, we had to start them all up and do whatever checks
> we could to make sure they were okay. "Mohammed" and
> an old man met us, and Dick seemed to be suspicious of Mo-
> hammed. When all the trucks were started up and running,
> Mohammed and the old man walked away from us. Dick
> told me to follow them. I didn't feel good about that because
> it seemed that they didn't want to be overheard. He told me
> to go outside and move the jeep and keep an eye on them.
> They circled the building and I stuck with them trying to
> pick up what they were saying. When we all got back inside
> Dick told them that their mission was to stay and provide
> some security at the warehouse and refused their request
> for guns.
>
> We went back to the hotel and Dick went in first in case
> we'd been burned. When he came out he said, "Bad news,
> Fred. I've got to go to Rome to check in and report. It's all

down to you now." I said there was no way that I could do it. Dick said, "The United States, Delta, and all those departments in the Pentagon are all depending on you. You can do it. Believe me, Fred, your life will never be the same again when all this is over." That guy could make you believe in anything. I was under his wing the whole time and to me, he was ten feet tall. I had to do some reconnaissance while Dick was away and sort out some codes for roadblocks.

We'd had some little incidents which Dick just sort of took as they came. He never got flustered and if he was worried then he never showed it. My passport data didn't match my driver's license and I remember that Dick just shrugged it off and told me to dirty it up by rubbing it. He made me feel that it was just an unimportant little detail. The day after that, thirty-five people were knifed in riots. We were driving along a street and we saw this young lady with long hair standing under one of the religious posters and this big guy with a bushy moustache said something to her and poleaxed her with a punch. I stepped on the gas and was going to charge at him. Dick quietly stopped me and without a single word of criticism he just said that we had another mission to attend to.

When Dick returned from his trip to Rome, shortly before we were due to move up to Desert Two and set up the radio, we went back to the warehouse for a final check to find that Mohammed had gone. The old man was there and along the whole front of the warehouse there was a deep trench and there was no way we'd have been able to get the trucks out.

Apparently the old man had been questioned by the laborers who dug the trench and said that he did not know either Fred or the "European." The men, he said, had dug the trench so that communications cables could be laid. Meadows was in a dilemma. Had the mission been blown? Was the warehouse under observation and were they about to be arrested? Why had the contract laborers even asked about Fred and the "European"? The dominant factor was the mission. They had to go ahead and take their chances. Without the trucks Delta would fail. In order to get the trucks out the trench had to be filled. There was no alternative. The old man refused to help. Fred remembered Meadows's cool actions.

Outside and just a little way along the road there was a crowd of children gazing at a truckload of fruit. Meadows took a handful of oranges, looking steadily at the children. Their unfathomable eyes met his without blinking. The too-mature expressions of the Arab urchins told their own story of early hardship, a mistrustful wisdom brought on by the constant search for food and "baksheesh." The clean but tattered clothes showed the youths' origins as being the shanty areas that formed the loosely defined boundaries of the city of Tehran. The large brown eyes of the kids now began to flicker with interest, as they moved between the blue eyes of the "European" and the oranges he had begun to juggle. He tossed the juicy, golden fruits from hand to hand. He put them down and began to peel one. He tossed it to one of the boys and also gave him some money and told him to buy some cokes. Would this do the trick?

He paused, cocked his head, and looked pointedly at the three-foot-deep trench running the full width of the warehouse. Casually he nudged a football-sized rock into the channel and considered it carefully before beginning the amateur juggling of oranges again. Behind him, Fred's thoughts were on deadlines and the potential disaster if they were unable to move the trucks from the shed when needed. Timing was all-important on this phase of the mission. He continued to push rocks into the trench, aware that filling it was going to take a long time. A noise distracted him. He looked up and to his pleasure and surprise saw that the street urchins had moved to the edge of the trench and were now heaving and straining to push the boulders and rubble into the void. Meadows regarded Fred's amazement with a smile. "Kids," he said, "Kids are great, you know."

The youngsters made short work of filling in the trench and were rewarded for their efforts. The old man made a comment about the European having more money than you could shake a stick at. Meadows was annoyed at having been forced to draw attention to the trucks and the need to get them out. He had filled in the trench and he had given money to the children. Both of those actions were noteworthy to any casual observer, let alone the military if the site was under surveillance. It was April 25, and he and Fred were due to leave the city and set up the radio to monitor the progress of the task force. They would be away for less than twenty-four hours and they just had to hope that the cable layers, if that is what they were, did not come back to the site. No one really knew the capabilities of the Iranian police. Would the absence of the trucks be an indicator to them of a rescue attempt? Smuggling was rife in the country and it might be in that direction that suspicions would fall.

On April 22, the day after Delta had landed at Wadi Qena in Egypt, Meadows mailed an interesting letter to Pat and Bob Lloyd in England:[4]

04.22.80

Dear Pat & Bob,

Arrived yesterday in good order. Have made several business meetings and things appear in good order. The weather is hot and dry but cool at night, so unlike England.

Tomorrow hopefully, I will meet with a gentleman who will escort me to a salt mine where we shall determine if Dowty mining equipment will be considered for future use. I will keep you informed.

I went to the stadium yesterday and saw a good game, not quite up to English standards, but good.

Pat, I hope to bring a rug back for you, as I understand it, a person can export one only on departure.

Well, as I told you on the phone prior to my departure this past Sunday, I hope to see you some time next week. Perhaps I will be required to go to Stockholm first. Keep my room for me. Love to the children and pass on to Pam & M&M also my love.

Bryan

That Meadows chose to refer to the football stadium and the salt mine was not a breach of security but common sense. He was working against the possibility that his mail might be read, and this would cover the visit he had made to the stadium, the meetings he had already had with Mohammed and other members of the team, and his projected final trip to Desert Two the next day. It is interesting to note his one small slip in using the American rather than the English method of dating his letter.

On April 23 Meadows had sent his message to Washington confirming that all arrangements were in order. Now, two days later, the time had come for him and Fred to complete the next part of their mission. They would set up their radio in the vicinity of Garmsar and prepare to meet the incoming Joint Task Force. The task force was bringing its own drivers along, and Meadows and Fred would take them to the Tehran warehouse and then guide them back, with the trucks, to Garmsar so that they could deliver the force into the city the next night. Fred takes up the story:

> We set up on the slopes of a small hill and began to listen out on the task force frequency. At the appropriate time Dick sent out the call that we and everything else were in place. He then told me that he was going to sleep for a while. How could anybody sleep? I felt that an enormous trust had been placed in me and I was very proud. After a while I heard a helicopter and it seemed to be headed our way, so I shook Dick awake and told him. "Let's get moving," he said and he took off up the hill. What he forgot was that he was carrying the radio but the headset was on my head, so there we were with me trying like hell to keep up with him and us connected by the radio cable. Dick was really fit and he just about hauled me up the hill by the cable. It must have looked real funny and we had a laugh about it much later on. It turned out that the "helicopter" noise was actually a train on a nearby track. Up to that point we'd not known the track was there. We had a great laugh about that.

For Meadows and Fred the wait was a long one. Radio silence was imposed and they could not make a call to check the progress of the JTF. They had arrived early in order to check once again for the presence of unexpected locals. Though the train had come as something of a surprise, it seemed to offer no threat unless it chose to travel at the same time that the helicopters were landing, but as this would take place in darkness it was an acceptable risk. At 1200 hours Meadows was able to give his final "All clear" message to the now airborne JTF. Then the waiting began again. As the heat of the day turned into the bitter cold of an Iranian night, the two men shivered as they sat it out. At this point there was no way that they could light fires to make coffee or heat food. Time crawled on and Meadows noted that it was now well past the hour when he had expected to be told that the helicopters had landed at Desert One. The timing for the JTF arrival at Desert Two was critical; the helicopters had to be camouflaged and all troops hidden before dawn broke.

The scheduled take-off time to begin the journey to Desert Two was 2030 hours. It was now well past that and no signal had come in.

Unknown to Meadows and Fred, dramatic events were rapidly unfolding at Desert One. The C-130s had landed almost on schedule and an anxious Delta Force was ready and waiting to transfer fuel and equipment to the Sea Stallions. They were unaware that an unexpected sandstorm and mechanical problems were taking their toll on the approaching helicopters. It was 2045 hours before the first two limped in under the control of exhausted pilots. One pilot reported hydraulic problems. At that time Beckwith did not know that one Sea Stallion had gone down and another, after getting lost in the sandstorm, had returned to the *Nimitz*. Two more helicopters arrived and Delta began the urgent process of loading stores. So, four aircraft were in but the mission required six. The deadline was gone and Beckwith calculated that an extension to the takeoff time of 2130 hours would still be feasible even if a little tight. The fifth and sixth birds arrived and the Delta Force men were delighted.

The anger and acute disappointment of the team can only be imagined when Beckwith, after having been told that only five choppers were airworthy, had to give the order to abort the mission. Though devastating news, it was not the end of the world. The mission could be remounted in a few days time because the validity of the flight in had been proven. What happened next was to ruin any chances of a mission remount forever. One of the Sea Stallions, moving to a C-130 to take on more fuel, crashed into it and caused an immediate inferno. Eight men died, and only desperately heroic actions by all the JTF personnel enabled so many other lives to be saved. It was a thoroughly despondent Delta that limped back to Masirah en route for Egypt.

An attempt to get a message to Meadows from Desert Two failed due to atmospheric interference on the satellite communication system, and it was not until just before daybreak that he received the information "Unable to deliver the auto parts." He was still completely unaware of the disaster that had caused the abort. Until he got instructions to the contrary, Meadows believed that the abort was a temporary situation and that the mission would be rescheduled in a few days. He and Fred carefully cleaned up all signs of their vigil and decided to return to the city. They were dirty and unkempt and their vehicles showed all the signs of cross-country movement. Their excuse, if questioned, would be that they had broken down and had been forced to spend the night under the stars before making the repairs in daylight. Their return to Tehran was uneventful and Meadows headed straight to his room to clean up. He was disappointed but not unduly worried. The time would surely come to remount and he would carry on as normal. His main point of concern was the fact that they had filled in the trench outside the warehouse. How long would it be before the workers returned to finish their job. The matter was out of his control, so there was nothing to be gained by worrying. His complacence lasted only minutes. The telephone rang.

To Meadows's surprise the caller was Ross Perot. Immediately he was perturbed by the fact that Perot had called him and risked a breach of security, but as he listened he made a silent offer of sincere thanks. Perot was able to tell him of the disaster at Desert One and to inquire if he needed assistance. Meadows was shattered but worse was to come. Perot informed him that in the cockpit of one of the abandoned Sea Stallions was the pilot's map and operational notes. He was able to tell Meadows that the location of the warehouse was clearly indicated on a city map of Tehran and that the code name "Esquire" would indicate to Iranian intelligence that there was at least one agent in the city. Meadows thanked Perot for the information and declined, for the time being, the offer of help. A quick look at the television, which was showing footage of Desert One, confirmed his worst fears and his heart went out to the soldiers of Delta. He knew what had gone into mounting the operation and he knew exactly how they would be feeling. He had to move fast. The rest of the team had to be informed immediately and instructed to get out of the country. The SF men had their own plans that Meadows had no requirement to know. He guessed that they would fly out from Mehrabad International Airport. He had urgent personal considerations to make, but first he had to brief Fred.

Only Meadows and Fred were likely to be tied to the warehouse, as they had been the only regular and overt visitors. Meadows now regretted his actions in enlisting the support of the children to fill in the trench. They would surely remember and be able to describe both men if questioned. There was another problem that arose when he talked to Fred. There was no way that Fred could exit through immigration at the airport due to the discrepancies in his passport and other documentation. He would have no choice but to go overland. Fred later made the remark: "When Dick realized that we were going to have to separate and that I would be left to my own arrangements there was real pain showing on his face."

With Fred on his way, Meadows had to consider his own options. He could have joined Fred, but the police would probably already have linked the two of them as partners. Fred with his family connections actually had a better chance alone. Meadows could opt to go overland himself and try to cross into either Iraq or Turkey, but with not even a few words of the language that would be an immensely difficult journey. He could lie low in Tehran for a few days and then try to slip out through the airport. No. He would never be able to hide in Tehran, where every eye would be open for him once the pilot's documents had been analyzed. His main concern about using the airport was accidentally betraying the other SF men, who would undoubtedly be using that route out. They were all professional enough to avoid eye contact, but what if one of them should have problems. It was in the nature of SF soldiers to go to the assistance of their comrades. He was the one most likely to have problems and he didn't want to bring others down with him. He thought it likely that they were already at the airport, and if he delayed his own departure for a while they might avoid each other. How long could he wait. He decided to act normally and without haste.

Though he did not relish the thought of being captured and tortured, he was far more concerned about the possibility of being paraded through the streets and put on television as a killer working for the "Great Satan." He remembered far too well the treatment of the prisoners of war in Vietnam. He decided that he would rather force the enemy to kill him than face the indignity of such treatment. He brushed away the morbid ideas and set about thinking the situation through. In the last analysis the airport offered the best chances of success. The dangers in that route out were far less than any alternative. If he was picked up at the airport he could make sure that there was a fuss that caught the attention of any foreigners who were passing through. Over the open telephone he spoke to the airlines and finally selected a flight to Ankara, Turkey. He packed his few possessions and for one last time scrutinized his room for any tell-tale items even though he knew this was a waste of time.

At reception he checked out in an unhurried, relaxed manner. After paying his bill he spent a few minutes chatting with the receptionist about his visit to Turkey, where he was going to select a town and hotel for his forthcoming honeymoon. He was lucky in finding a cab with an English-speaking driver that he had used before. On the way to the airport he asked the driver to divert to a street in which there was a shop where he said that he had been haggling over the price of two carpets. He pointed out the shop (into which he had never set foot) to the driver and asked him to remember it. As they drove to the airport Meadows repeated the story of the honeymoon to the driver and asked if he knew Turkey. Then he negotiated a sum of money which would ensure that the driver would visit the shop the next week and try to get the best price for the carpets, which Meadows wanted to present to his bride to be. He also paid a deposit for the services of the taxi to meet him off the flight from Ankara in seven days time.

As he walked into the airport lobby he noticed that there seemed to be more policemen and military around than when he had last made a reconnaissance of the place. Of course, they were all looking at him. Shrugging off his paranoia, he calmly made his way to join the emigration queue. An unkempt and unshaven soldier took up station to his right. He avoided Meadows's eyes but stayed close enough for the smell of his sweat-stained uniform to be highly unpleasant. As Meadows progressed down the line, so the soldier kept pace. Handing over his passport, he was disturbed to see the emigration officer's eyes flicker back and forth between the passport and something under his desk. Giving Meadows a cold, uninformative look, he went into an office at the back. Meadows tried to look unconcerned and let his eyes wander around the building in what he hoped was a normal manner. Through the glass partition, which divided immigration from the departure lounge, he spotted two of the SF men. They had probably noted his presence, as their seats faced emigration. Good. If he were taken then there would be firsthand knowledge of the event that would be quickly and accurately passed on. He wondered about the passport. It looked good to him. Another consideration that went through his mind was the stories he had heard about certain countries in the Middle East and Africa where corrupt immigration officials would pretend to find fault with documents. They would imply that a "tip" would be sufficient for the clerk in the back room to clear up the problem. If the unfortunate traveler chose to pay then there was a good chance that he would be immediately arrested and charged with attempted bribery. Meadows forced himself not to glance at the security camera that he knew covered the emigration station.

The policeman nudged Meadows none too gently and he thought that this was the moment of truth. Despite his prior planning, the thought of making a run for it still crossed his mind. Drawing on every vestige of self-control, he looked at the soldier, who had a cigarette dangling from his lips and was making the clicking motions which showed that all he wanted was a light. Drawing on his best Irish accent, Meadows said that he did not smoke. With a grunt the soldier left to find a more civilized person. The passport was brought back, stamped, and handed over, and without a further glance the official indicated that Meadows should pass through into the departure lounge. Trying not to show his relief, he walked slowly through and took a seat with his back to his two comrades without giving either of them a glance. He was not surprised to find his armpits and waist awash with perspiration.

From Ankara, Meadows was able to get a flight to Frankfurt, which had been his initial launch point. He was debriefed by CIA agents, who were less than forthcoming in giving him any details of events at Desert One. Fred was weighing heavily on his mind. It was the first time in his military career that he had left a team member behind. He had one strange memory of Frankfurt:

> I think it was in Frankfurt that we went for a meal after the debrief, and I'm sure it was to a Mexican restaurant. There was plenty of wine and beer flowing but I didn't drink a lot. I wasn't in the mood. I was thinking about how those guys in Delta would be feeling and wondering where Fred had got to. I slept like a log that night and had a strong hangover when I woke up the next day. All the clothes I'd had with me in Tehran were missing—right down to the skivvies. All I got was shrugs when I asked about them. I still have the feeling that I was drugged deliberately so that my room could be cleaned out. I can't think why the CIA or anybody else would want to do that. The only remark I'd made which caused a ripple was when I said how strange it was that it had taken Ross Perot to get the news of my possible compromise to me and not any official person. My worries over Fred weren't necessary. Some four weeks or so after I got back to the U.S., I got news that he had turned up at Frankfurt airport. It had taken him about all that time to get out. I'm not going to talk about how he did it. Of course he

had help, but there are long memories in Iran and it would be wrong to give information that could identify Fred's helpers.

This was the second major operation in which Meadows had played a leading role but where factors outside the control of the military had caused the mission to fail. In both cases (Son Tay and Tehran) there had been public criticism of events. Meadows was angered by the apparent inability of the media to understand the circumstances:

> The outcome of the mission was a huge disappointment. The details don't matter. It's been analyzed and criticized in *Newsweek*,[5] every newspaper in the U.S., some newspapers in Europe, Charlie's book, and everywhere that soldiers meet for a beer. It's been called a debacle. Now my English isn't that good, but I'd prefer to call it a tragedy. Every soldier gets his fair share of things going wrong, and that's when you have to get professional and look to see what can be learned from them. Those guys in Delta were big enough to get over a setback. There's been a heck of a lot of water under the bridge since then and they've put all that sort of stuff behind them. Let's leave them to get on with it.

In September 1980, Meadows's contract with SFOD-Delta came to an end.[6] He was fully retired and seeking new trails. There is no doubt that it was a unique post that was created for Meadows with Delta. A civilian, he was given a sensitive mission with an organization being selected, trained, and brought to operational readiness under a blanket of strict security. Once more he had to confront the future. Pamela was now very firmly ensconced in her career; his daughter, Michele, was now twelve years old and his son, Mark, was sixteen. Crestview was definitely to be home for the Meadows family. Unlike many former Special Forces men, he did not turn to the CIA for employment. He wanted more personal control over his own life, and in any event some aspects of his Iranian venture still rankled.

A follow-on to the Tehran mission occurred in July 1982 when *Newsweek* made Meadows their "Man of the Week." He was never happy with this sort of publicity, but he went along with it in the

hope that fair treatment by the media might lead to a better public understanding of the many intangibles facing those involved in
special operations. At the insistence of the *Newsweek* team he spoke
a little of his childhood and agreed to meet his father for the first
time since shortly after he had enlisted in the army. It was a meeting without much warmth and Dick Meadows never saw his father
again. The article appeared in the July 12, 1982, issue of *Newsweek.*

12

Footloose

1980–1984

Meadows's old friend Ross Perot gave him breathing space by hiring him for his proven analytical and planning talents. At first he was set to work organizing the security of Perot's properties and family, but this soon became monotonous work to a man of Meadows's character. Through Perot, who was chairman of the Texas War on Drugs at that time, he became interested in the overall drug problem of his country. In cooperation with U.S. Customs he put together some very innovative plans to take positive action against the narcotics traffickers. As part of his contribution he was quite prepared to infiltrate the drug cartels and set up an aircraft refueling strip in Latin America to sabotage drug-running aircraft and feed information on flights and routes from that point. The Meadows plan turned out to be too rich for the blood of government and was filed away, unused. The study of the drug problem did, however, leave Meadows with a lasting hatred for the drug cartels of Latin America, and he was to turn his attention to them again in later years.

For a period of about two years Meadows underwent some acute frustrations. He could plainly see areas of crime and terrorism that could be influenced, but he was impotent to carry out most of his ideas. "No one seemed to accept that if you can call something a 'war'—like we called it the 'Drug War'—then it should be approached like a war and settled by warlike actions. We had men with the skills to do something about it either covertly or overtly, but no one in authority could be persuaded to support us. It wasn't just the drug cartels. There was the international illegal arms trade that was screaming out for attention. We did have a very small success in that area though."

Meadows was referring to a period of high adventure when, with two Texas police officers, and acting in cooperation with U.S.

Customs, he masterminded a sting operation. He had by then accepted the presidency of Peregrine International Associates, a company specializing in security operations across a wide spectrum. They had, in tandem with U.S. Customs, already been highly successful in running a sting operation against a South African arms smuggler. This success gave Meadows the confidence to take on, again at the request of U.S. Customs, a much more complex and potentially risky mission.

This time the target was an international arms dealer said at the time to be one of the top traders in the world. The trader had succeeded in putting together a deal with the Iranian government to sell them surplus tanks from America. At that time the Iran-Iraq war was raging and both countries were barred from any arms purchases in the United States. The problem the dealer had was that smuggling several dozen tanks out of the States was not an easy task. The purchase and subsequent exportation of the tanks had to appear to be legitimate. Meadows and his two partners were inserted into the equation to pose as smugglers with the wherewithal to obtain falsified end-user and export certification.

With the trader supplying the documentation and the "smugglers" offering the means of transport and inspection access to the tanks, the scene was set. The original intention was to play out the charade up to the point of having the tanks rendezvous with Israeli ships at the Texas port of Beaumont. Meadows wanted to finesse the whole situation and create a scenario through which the trader, the suppliers of the phoney documents, the high-ranking Iranian officers (with false passports and visas), and the fee of $40 million could all be taken together. With his Texan partners he threw himself wholeheartedly into playing the part of a gunrunner. He let his hair grow long, adopted a "cowboy" image complete with boots, giant belt buckle, a gold bracelet, and a Stetson hat. Money was no object, as the dealer paid up front whatever was asked of him. The operation was scheduled to last only a few weeks, but it turned into a whole year.

After a few months a new factor came into play. An Iraqi contingent almost accidentally stumbled into the network. They were looking to purchase (illegally) $30 to $40 million worth of TOW anti-tank missiles. Now the team had both opposing factions in the same war slowly getting entangled in the same web of deceit. Meadows had no hesitation in telling the Iraqis that they were welcome and that he could meet their requirements. The TOWs would be flown out of Longview when all certification was in place. Should this be successful, then both operations would be raided at the point of departure, with a personal message from Meadows to both Saddam Hussein and the Ayatollah Khomeini. To support the operation Meadows put together a team of former SF men, with all expenses being funded from the sting itself. Whenever cash was needed Meadows would meet with the trader and get up front money.

The trader financed a private Learjet, and all international travel was first class. On a visit to London there were furtive meetings with both Iranians and Iraqis.[1] Meadows and his companion on that occasion were certain that they were followed from time to time, but their total disregard for money and extravagant lifestyle probably removed most of the opposition's suspicions. What government agency would supply that amount of money to its operatives? One of Meadows's companions at the time recalled the visit:

> One of the more enjoyable and interesting trips was going to London with Dick in the Concorde. A lot of what happened on that trip is a blur after all these years, but I do recollect meetings with an Iranian spy purporting to seek help in overthrowing the Khomeini regime. Also, we were occasionally followed around by types that must have come out of central casting in the Moscow equivalent to Hollywood: bushy eyebrows, five o'clock shadows, large overcoats, and all that goes with that type.
>
> We also visited the London Special Forces Club, an institution of great tradition in the British way of things, composed of kindred souls who have dedicated themselves to special operations in the defense of their country. It's the place to spend hours at the bar listening to stories of night parachute drops into occupied France and lightning strikes against Rommel's Afrika Korps. Dick was a welcome figure there and a center of attention, as he had a lot of contact with Special Forces in Britain. For starters, he was one of the first Americans to go through the British Special Air Service course and he certainly left a lasting impression.
>
> When we returned to New York from London, we thought the moment was finally arriving. Of course, things had changed again, just like the weather. This time the sce-

nario was for several Iranian generals to arrive with phony
passports. We would accompany them to a bank on Wall
Street. There we would pick up the tens of millions of dollars for the purchase of the tanks. This act would be followed
by the arrests. I think there were about ten of us involved at
that stage.

However, there seemed to be some foot-dragging, and
the date kept slipping in increments of 1 to 2 days each time.
Fortunately, during this time, our target was footing the
bill for our expenses in New York. Dick decided we needed to put some pressure on and passed the word to spend
money. He didn't have to give that order twice. I remember
lounging in the penthouse of the Helmsley Palace, where
we called room service for cheeseburgers and six packs of
Dom Pérignon. The tab was in the neighborhood of $12,000
for that one evening. In a few days we had racked up a bill
around $80,000, but you'll have to ask others to confirm that
figure. Our targets still did not appear. However, the mid-
dleman finally cried "ouch," and we returned to Texas to
await the next chapter.

During the seemingly interminable waiting period of the sting,
Meadows was not idle. Another ex-SF companion of his at the time
remembered an incident:

I remember leaving New York at dawn on a Learjet bound
for Honduras to assist Dick in handling a skyjacking. He had
an old friend, Chuck Fry,[2] who was advising the Honduran
military at the time, and he had the Honduran command
sanction bringing in Dick. He got to work immediately, getting information and putting together options and contingency plans. It was a first for me and I got another education.

Sometime later, I think the next day, a darkened Hercules
arrived with a group of advisors from Delta Force. There
were some old friends among them. Remember that Dick
had put most of these guys through the selection course and
training and there was a lot of history between them. Jaws
dropped when they came down the ramp and saw Dick already on the tarmac to greet them. The surprise turned to
awe when they saw the bus we'd arrived on. The Learjet

was nearby. I think Dick enjoyed the mystery all this conjured up, and I don't know if he ever gave an explanation to them.

This side event ended a day or so later when the skyjackers gave themselves up through some adept negotiations and the wearing down process. However, in the middle of the previous night, all of the foreign hostages on the aircraft, eleven I think, managed to escape in a sudden rush for an emergency exit. The story is not clear on how that one was pulled off, and Dick will know more.

We returned to New York to keep up the pressure [on the sting]. However, all of this intense foreplay didn't produce a climax. The whole thing went out, not with a bang, but with a whimper. Support gradually disappeared and the Iranians and Iraqis became more distant and elusive than ever. Eventually ATF got involved and arrested our arms smuggler on very minor charges.

I'm not an insider as to what happened in those later days to know how such an enormous undertaking got off-track. I do have my suspicions, for what they're worth. End-user certificates, the documents required for purchasing and exporting the tanks, were bribed from allied countries in the Middle East. In the need to give credibility to the sting, these were real bribed documents. My guess is the signatures on those documents would cause considerable political embarrassment if they were to surface during the sensation that would surely follow a successful operation of this magnitude. I suspect the project was leaked, and the targets consequently faded into the shadows. To me this is the only logical hypothesis that fits the events, but I must stress this is only my suspicion and I have absolutely no substantiation.

There are many anecdotes about adventures in which Meadows played a leading role; some no doubt are apocryphal. He had apparently been responsible for tracking down a consignment of stolen uranium. He was credited with the discovery of an IRA arms cache on U.S. soil. In support of Operation Just Cause[3] he carried out early reconnaissance and preparatory visits into Panama and Nicaragua. Meadows was a key advisor to the FBI in the early days of the development of their Hostage Rescue Team (HRT). In that capacity he was able to draw heavily on some of the techniques and experiences of SFOD-Delta. On one drugs-related mission he managed the recovery of a stolen aircraft; these and many more such stories will slowly be forgotten.

In November 1982 Meadows took stock of his life and decided that he was not really happy within a corporate environment, but after his separation from Peregrine he was at a loose end. Now in his fifty-second year but still hard and fit, Meadows was unsettled and disillusioned with the security industry. The market was totally money orientated and there seemed to be no sense of honor. Anyone who wished could call himself a "security consultant," and there were no international standards or qualifications with any real meaning. Third-rate solutions and third-rate equipment were being sold at premium prices for huge profits; untrained escorts and bodyguards were being supplied with no contractual comeback on the suppliers if something went wrong. High prices were being paid for security surveys that scratched only the surface of the client's problems, and the whole business was riddled with commissions to ensure that friends got the follow-on contracts whether they were qualified or not. It crossed his mind to set up his own security company in the United States, but that needed more money than he had available. To borrow would mean ownership by a third party, and he wanted to skipper his own ship.

During his time with Peregrine, Meadows had met a good cross section of entrepreneurs and he remembered that there had been hints of a market in Peru for army surplus equipment. He had spent time in that country when he had served with the 8th SFG, and a good friend of his was now working in the U.S. embassy in Lima. He liked Latin America and he had studied the political problems of both Peru and Colombia when he was trying to get action off the ground against the drug cartels. He decided to pay a visit and assess the business potential.

13

Entrepreneur in Peru

1984–1989

Meadows called on his friend at the U.S. embassy in Lima and spoke to the few businessmen to whom he had been given introductions. The situation was much worse than he had imagined.[1] Under President Fernando Belaunde corruption was rife. The cocaine trade was booming. The activities of the two principal guerrilla movements, the Movimiento Revolucionario Tupac Amaru (MRTA) and the Sendero Luminoso (SL), had grown to such a level of violence that rich families were either living in cocoons of self-imposed security or fleeing the country. Often they left their affairs and estates in the hands of corrupt or inefficient management. Meadows studied the newspapers and chatted with the local taxi drivers and shop and restaurant owners. Not everyone was willing to talk openly. So concerned was Meadows that in his own inimitable manner he forgot the fact that he was supposed to be there to investigate the army surplus business and he began to talk long and loud to anyone who would listen about what he saw as "the coming storm." Before long he was invited to make formal presentations to groups of businessmen and even to his own embassy:

> I guess that I didn't tell the guys at the embassy anything that they didn't already know. They were probably checking me out to see if I was some sort of renegade. I made a lot of senior business contacts during that short stay in Lima and they eventually asked me why I didn't talk to President Belaunde himself. I said that if they could get me to him I would be pleased to give him my views. Well, they did. I met him and a bunch of his ministers and went through my act. At the end I suggested that he take some rapid and serious action to resolve his problem. Guess what his answer was? "What problem?" I suppose that was typical of

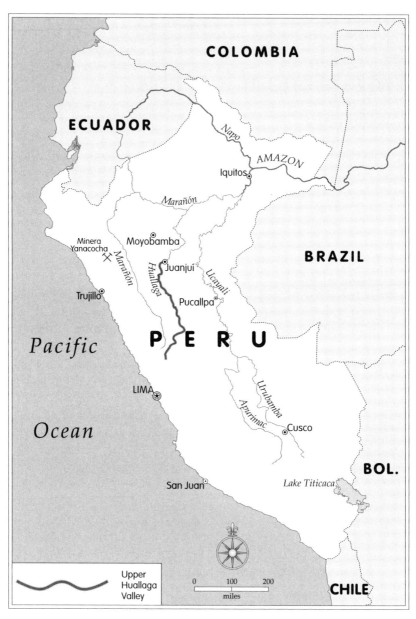

Peru's Upper Huallaga Valley, an area that benefited from Meadows's security expertise.

official attitudes in Peru at that time. The government was coining in the money and didn't believe that either the SL or the MRTA would ever present a personal threat to them. The campesinos and the rest of the population could go to hell on a raft for all they cared. I heard afterwards that he [Belaunde] was angry that a *gringo* had the nerve to speak to him about interior matters.

Meadows returned home to Crestview in an optimistic mood. He was very interested in the prospects offered in Peru. He had a great sympathy with the underdog, but what could he do for them? The first thing, of course, was to give them a cause, but how was he to do that? He also had to make a living. If security was such a problem in Peru, then why not start right there in Lima. The cost of living was acceptable; he had a nucleus of contacts which had been strengthened by his recent visit; he had a basic grasp of the language and understood the culture. In Pamela, who must have been looking forward to having him spend more time at home, he found only solid support. He decided to move to Lima for a limited amount of time and try to set himself up as a security consultant. If it didn't work then he would only be out of pocket by a couple thousand dollars.

Initially he rented a modest apartment in Miraflores. He soon found out that the businessmen who had been so keen to get him to expound his theories to Belaunde were not so anxious to lay bare their own secrets. Nevertheless, his conversations gave him access to gossip that was denied to the staff of the embassy, and where possible and ethical he passed this on. In turn this led to his becoming properly, if somewhat covertly, accredited as a privately contracted civil servant for the provision of intelligence and security advice. This secured him an income with which to support his mission. Conditions in Peru at the time will give a feeling for the problems faced by Peruvians and expatriates alike in 1984.

In July 1980 the military handed power back to President Fernando Belaunde, who had been deposed twelve years earlier in a coup led by General Juan Velasco Alvarado. Left-of-center military reforms had included large-scale nationalization of private industry and affiliations with eastern bloc countries, and a nationalistic stance that was hypercritical of U.S. policies in Peru prevailed. Running out of steam with reform policies, the military came under pressure to allow the country to return to civilian rule. They accepted the elections that put Belaunde back into power with seeming good grace, but now, in 1984, it was becoming apparent that their support for him was waning once again.

The army was the most politically powerful service within the armed forces. The concept of social conditions as a crucial factor in national security had been the motivation for the coup of 1968. It was also evident that though the military vigorously pursued the counterguerrilla campaign because of the threat to national security, many senior officers felt that the guerrillas were morally right in their goals while wrong in their methods. Many saw carefully controlled intervention from above as a viable means of forestalling violent revolution from the peasant classes.

The Peruvian army has little connection with the traditional ruling class; most senior officers come from lower- or middle-class backgrounds and so there is no affiliation between the officer corps and the ruling echelon. The military officers have few links to local or foreign business, so their actions are not influenced by considerations of personal profit. In this context, and at that time, the Falklands crisis served to reinforce the armed forces' traditionally intense nationalism and its antipathy to foreign influence, particularly that of the United States.

Washington could bring its influence to bear in international financial circles, and the reluctance within the military to assume responsibility for the current economic situation seemed to preclude a further coup. Nonetheless, the military's growing anger and frustration over the escalation of guerrilla violence and the government's lack of performance did suggest that military intervention before the end of Belaunde's term of presidency in 1985 was a distinct possibility.

Belaunde talked about a minor guerrilla problem, but in fact it was a full-scale insurgency. The SL controlled huge tracts of land. They had infiltrated the police, whose corruption and brutality had already made them enemies of the campesinos. They ruled by fear in some areas. Castrations and tongue slittings were common punishments for informers. In some villages, though, the peasants likened them to a sort of Robin Hood organization when they doled out the food they'd stolen in supermarket raids. They funded themselves through bank robberies and attacks on vehicles carrying wages, taxes on the narco organizations, "war taxes" imposed on businesses, and sometimes kidnappings for ransom. Embassies, foreign businesses, and international hotels were all targeted. There were huge amounts of dynamite available in Peru, where slack security meant it was easy to steal from the mining operations. All public utilities were targets. During the two years or so before Meadows arrived there had been about one thousand attacks against the electricity business alone. All in all, about four thousand attacks had taken place since Belaunde was put back into office and about twelve hundred people had been killed. There was no doubt in Meadows's mind that if action wasn't taken soon the SL could take over the country.

Meadows talked long and hard to businessmen and executives of various projects, and though they accepted what he had to say, they were not going to pay for security. They preferred to keep their heads down or get out of the country and run their businesses by remote control. Meadows did not know how to move ahead, though he could see great business potential. He knew that the overall political and economic situation could be changed if some backbone could be injected into the owners of these businesses to keep them in Peru. The only way to do that was to make them feel secure. Peru was in a critical state, and nowadays it is difficult to appreciate how close the country came to falling apart in the mid-1980s. There was practically no international press coverage. The SL and the MRTA were virtually unknown outside the country except in intelligence circles; narcotics trafficking corrupted the highest levels of the military, police, and government. But it was not that the guerrillas were gaining; rather, it was that the country was losing. Both guerrilla movements were out of time and synchronization with the rest of the world, and they could never have reached such powerful positions without the ineptitude of the government.

The idea that Meadows had was to help the private sector hold together until such time as the state could handle the threat itself. The factories, mines, and export-producing facilities of Peru had to stay in business or the situation would surely be lost. Not only democracy but also the economy was ready to slip over the edge. Whichever went first would take the other with it. He could see a good market for his expertise, but he simply could not find a way to break into it.

Then he had a stroke of good fortune. Control Risks, a large British security consultancy company, was rapidly establishing itself throughout South America. As part of their business they provided a professional response to cases of kidnap where the family or corporation was insured through Lloyds of London. At that time kidnappings in Peru were becoming more frequent and often violent. The hierarchy of the company then was comprised of former British SAS officers, and Meadows was a well-known name in SAS circles. His reputation was bolstered by common contacts within the CIA in Washington, D.C. They sought to meet with him.

They were interested in him because he lived more or less permanently in Lima, had a good working relationship with the U.S. embassy, had good business contacts, and had no allegiance to anyone but himself and his family. They wanted a man on the spot who could respond to any kidnap case they might have to deal with. Meadows became a retained consultant. At that time he was given to believe that he might eventually become their head of operations in Peru. When that showed no signs of happening he left the company, but not before he had gained experience in the art of kidnap negotiations. This expertise led to his becoming involved in a case that was to dramatically alter his business future.

The Romero family is counted among the wealthiest in Peru, and when a family member was kidnapped it was Meadows who took on the challenge of advising and steering the family through the crisis. There are a number of misconceptions about the men who become consultants during kidnap negotiations. In the media they are commonly called "negotiators." That is a misnomer. Their task is to provide the family with sound advice on how to proceed in the manner that is most likely to ensure the safety of the victim. It is the family that makes the decisions after listening to the advice. The consultants are not paid huge amounts of money, nor do they receive any cash that is related to the size of the ransom or the insurance policy.

The consultant, through knowledge and experience, can guide the family through the situation and ensure that no mistakes are made in the delicate process of negotiation. There is often a question raised about the ethics of negotiation toward a cash ransom, which in the last analysis will help an illegal cause. Does the act of saving one life justify money being paid that may go toward guerrilla operations that will take more lives? There are too many differences in the way of life in those countries where kidnap is endemic and the United States and Europe to give a clear-cut answer. In the latter we are used to a very high standard of law enforcement and access to the best of technology. Even so, the prime aim in the minds of the law enforcement agencies is the safety of the victim. Even the FBI will agree to the payment of a ransom provided that they believe that not to do so would put the victim's life at greater risk.

In parts of South America the situation is not so clear-cut. The causes of the guerrillas who conduct the kidnappings are often close to the heart of the local populace, who give them shelter. Life is cheap and there is little doubt that in some countries, if the victim were found to have little or no monetary value, then he or she would be killed. Skilled negotiation can achieve a number of things. It enhances the prospects of the victim being returned safely. It reduces the amount of money paid as a ransom. It produces good intelligence for the authorities. And it improves the future security of the affected family.

The consultant can get very close to the key members of the victim's family. He may often take on the role of counselor to wives and children. Part of his duties require him to discuss family security and advise on improvements. The Romero family patriarch discussed his security concerns freely with Meadows, and he was impressed by his knowledge, his foresight, and his understanding of Peru's long-term problems. The family owned huge tracts of land in the Upper Huallaga Valley, where the MRTA to the north and the SL to the south threatened one particular palm oil plantation. Meadows was asked if he could improve the security of these holdings. He promised to look at the problem once the kidnap had been resolved.

The case was long and fraught, but it was eventually brought to a successful conclusion. Meadows, now used to having his sales pitch for security surveys and management being politely listened to and then turned down, was pleasantly surprised when he was asked by the Romero family to fulfill his agreement to look at their rural problems. He was impressed by the integrity of the family and their openness, but he was still surprised that they elected him to carry out a complete survey. He had made a lot of noise in Lima about the shortfall in government, and though many people shared his views, they were not keen to overtly show any sort of association with him. If the Romeros were just expressing gratitude for the kidnap case, Meadows did not want to be thought to be capitalizing on the misery of a kidnap situation. He put the project on hold for a while.

But it was not just an expression of gratitude on the part of the family. For some time Romero had been able to study Meadows at close quarters. The former soldier's opinions on the development of the guerrilla war were obviously close to his heart, and Romero had utter confidence in his predictions. Meadows was equally persuasive about the measures that could be taken to combat the SL and the newly emergent MRTA. The fact that he cared about the country was also very clear. Any frustrations he expressed in conversation hinged around the reluctance of the wealthy and politically effective members of Peruvian society, who appeared to have given up the struggle. He was able to talk about the ideology of the SL and the MRTA with great eloquence. He did not appear to despise their aims, only their methods. This charismatic *gringo* was certainly cut from different cloth than those Romero was used to dealing with. Some weeks later Meadows did go back to look at Romero's problem in detail.

The Huallaga Valley was bandit country. It was ideal for growing coca, and so the narcos were heavy on the ground. They paid bribes to secure their export routes and would kill informers at the drop of a hat. The SL was beginning to attack agricultural facilities as well as the mines, power stations, and police posts; it was active in the southern half of the valley. The MRTA was expanding its operations; it was active in the north. Right in the center of the valley, in the upper reaches, were the palm oil plantations—slap-bang in the middle of a potential battleground. Meadows spent some time looking at the problem. What security there was could only be described as totally inadequate. Certainly some of the men had weapons, but they were badly maintained and they could never have been used effectively. The army was in the area but it was impotent. They were no better equipped than the opposition and very poorly paid. Many of their leaders were known to be corrupt and were rarely seen in forward areas. There were some good, honest officers, but many of them were forced to ignore things that their soldiering instincts told them were wrong. It was a bad situation, and the biggest problem was deciding whether he wanted to take the project on. If it turned sour (and there was every ingredient for disaster) then he would be finished in Peru. Meadows rose to the challenge and returned to Lima to construct a plan and a budget.

He needed a force that was well armed with the appropriate weapons and trained in defense as the first priority. Their efficiency and discipline needed to be apparent to the enemy observer. That alone would be a deterrent. They should have basic training in liaison with the locals and be able to gather working intelligence. They should be cooperative with the army and, though better paid, trained, armed, and equipped, should never look down on them. Making a plan for that was not particularly difficult; the training of indigenous forces is second nature to a Green Beret. Meadows's problems lay in other quarters.

There were two aspects of the business that he had to struggle with. Where was he going to get the weapons and equipment? The last thing he wanted to get involved in was the importation of firearms. That would bring too much official scrutiny. His other concern was a lack of experience in business budgeting. He knew that his plan could only work if it was constantly supervised. There was no point in training a force and then kissing it goodbye. A standard had to be set and validated regularly. He would need to assess any intelligence the men were able to obtain and act on it. Good relations with the military commanders in the area would be critical, and he would also want to keep the U.S. embassy informed of the situation. He would need help from some of his former SF colleagues to get the project off the ground. That would have been easy to do covertly, but he wanted to be in Peru for a long time and did not want to start out with the reputation of being someone who specialized in training private armies behind the government's back.

The Meadows budget for the operation was clever. He decided that the direct costs of all the equipment should be handled by the client. He would help to identify credible equipment sources and draft the specifications for each item. Then he would suggest a wages scale for the force and a simple career structure. As a separate item he would give the projected costs for his own services and those of anyone drafted in to help him. He would declare his profit margins from the start and state that there was no way he was going to get involved in "kickbacks." Then he had another thought. If the client was going to bear all the costs of equipment, then it made sense for him to form a proper company and give Meadows the contract for training, maintaining standards, and making regular threat assessments.

In that way he would be the man who set and enforced the standards. That would be done in two ways: on a regular preplanned basis of which everyone was aware and then some surprise inspections thrown in. To his knowledge this was the first time an operation like this had been set up in Peru and he wanted it to be a success, but even more he wanted the men to be proud of what they would achieve. He realized that one problem would be harnessing the guards' natural aggression and keeping them in defense mode. He was well aware of the situation in Colombia, where paramilitary organizations were out of control and acting as though they were law enforcement agencies.

He put the proposal to Dionisio Romero and there were no objections to the costs, but he was asked why a private company should be formed. Meadows answered with four words: "Time, cost, and quality." It would be faster and easier to import the necessary equipment to a formally approved company; a number of middlemen could be cut out; a proper career structure could be formulated; and Romero would have total control over the quality of the individuals employed. Romero agreed and ORUS, Peru's first private security force, was under way.

The ORUS project was an outstanding success. Within three months there was a well-trained, well-equipped, and loyal security force patrolling and defending the thousands of hectares making up the estate of Palmas del Ospinas in the Upper Huallaga Valley. There was, however, one aspect of this success story that was to cause Meadows difficulties in the years to come. The members of the force were so taken by his charisma that in their hearts they would have admitted that their loyalty was to him. They were in solid employment for the first time in their lives, with a decent wage, accommodations, and a career. The man who came to inspect them regularly was never feared. He was fair but uncompromising if the high standards were not met. He talked to them about their families, their ambitions, and their grievances and generally made them feel that he was a friend as well as a boss. He displayed all the old talents that had made his Nungs in Laos and Vietnam revere him. For Meadows there was the great satisfaction not only of a job well done but also of having achieved solid employment and a generous retainer for himself.

Two spin-offs were to emerge as a result of the ORUS project. First, such was the high esteem in which the Romero family was held that doors which had previously been politely closed now began to open in two dimensions. First, the showpiece, ORUS, became so highly respected that other businesses wanted their security matters attended to by the man who had set it up. Second, Meadows was beginning to be invited into the high-society circles of Lima. Both of these dimensions were to prove the mainstay of his business in Peru. Obviously, from the first point of view, Meadows began to benefit from more and more security work of widely divergent natures, and this was welcome, but it is initially interesting to look at the second dimension: entry into Lima's society circles.

A common quote is that the sprawling city of Lima is a small village when it comes to gossip. Upper and lower classes have both developed it into a fine art. A common saying in the city, which encapsulates this aspect nicely, is: "If you fart in San Isidro, it will be heard in Miraflores." At the domestic end of the scale, servants would tell each other of the telephone conversations of their employers based, as they had to be, on hearing only one end of a conversation. With great imagination they would conjecture the other half of the chat and pass it on to other servants. At the upper end of the society, dinner parties and drinks were frequent and politics and intrigue were never far below the surface. Exaggeration followed, as everyone was anxious to impress with the depth and accuracy of their personal knowledge. Extramarital affairs are almost a hobby in Lima, and the quiet American was an attractive and somewhat mysterious target.

This aspect of Lima society is hardly surprising. The city, as experienced by the wealthy, is very confining. Few people of substance were willing to drive out of town at night to venture through the violent slum areas that encircle it. It was commonplace for the windows of cars stopped by heavy traffic to be smashed with a club as attempts were made to snatch handbags or jewelry from the occupants. Outside the city limits it was not unusual for rocks or even bodies to be placed on the road in an attempt to force cars to stop so that the driver could be robbed or worse. Across bridges one could encounter stones strung across the road at windshield height. In the eyes of the wealthy it was simply not worth the risk to leave the city during the week.

For three months of each year Lima is blanketed in a cold, damp fog. During this period those who are not lucky enough to be able to retire to the country for long periods increase their social excesses. Meadows was quick to assess the potential of the "gossip market" and build up an excellent network of informants. Many of these were women. He had the attributes to make this work: He was utterly charming and made individual women feel as though they were the most important persons on earth when he was talking to them. He was certainly handsome enough for those women to make a beeline for him at social occasions, and he was absolutely discreet. His old-world courtesy engendered an immediate trust. He never repeated gossip. There were many open attempts at seduction. The end result of the matter is that he had the best political and economic intelligence network in Peru and it was based purely on charm and charisma—never payment. A quote from a letter to Meadows gives an idea of the emotions he could stir: "Where are the men who we women can trust implicitly and totally, knowing that in the pinch you would always be there? Where are our fine shining examples of simple rectitude, fair play, straightforwardness, and courage? All those 'down home' qualities, which are really the standard for our American dream. I learned a lot from you, Dick, you made me believe goodness still has a chance and that gentlemen still exist—with good humor to boot."

Meadows used his knowledge wisely, and within closed circles he would explain his philosophy:

> There's a saying that knowledge is power. Where it helped me was to avoid business scenarios that were morally wrong and to access situations through being able to tailor a proposal to highlight weaknesses that I had learned of from third parties. I was always careful to make it appear that I was putting hypothetical cases together when I was briefing potential clients. There is one example when Tom Smith [more of him later] and I were asked to react real fast for Faucett Airlines. That would have been early in 1988 I guess. Faucett's one of the two really big international carriers of Peru. The request came direct from the president and owner of the company. It seems he had some security concerns about a ranch that he owned in Pucallpa, which is up near the Amazon and in SL country. He wanted an immediate assessment and some recommendations to put into action the same night. We were pretty excited by the deal. Faucett would be a high-prestige client. Tom went up immediately to the area, and when he returned we put together an emergency defense plan for Faucett. The meeting was held in the president's home and went on into the small morning hours.

The next day Tom and I got together to review the situation. Tom expressed a lot of reservations about the people who had been at the meeting, and this pretty well supported my own feelings. I was able to make some very fast and discreet inquiries about those gentlemen and we were able to take a decision not to go any further. It didn't matter that the information I got may have been exaggerated. We were going to stay squeaky clean in everything we did. That's what I considered to be the power of information in Lima—the ability to avoid the unpleasant and dishonorable.

Meadows added to this with a twinkle in his eyes:

Of course it was always easy to deliberately start a piece of gossip. If my visa time was up and I had to leave Lima to take care of something else for a while, I could always make a fake telephone call. I knew my housemaid would listen. I would then have gone off to Australia, Africa or wherever I wanted people to think I'd gone. Little Maria could pass the word around the housemaid network quicker than you could blink. It wasn't just the women who gossiped, the men were just the same and you just had to soak up everything you heard and then analyze it later based against what you knew was fact.

You've also got to remember that in those days there was a great profusion, maybe I should say confusion, of covert operations going on. The police might be working on a money laundering operation; the DEA may be carrying out a drug mission; CIA handlers would be running their agents. You name it and it was happening in Peru. But none of it was really secret. I used to be given all sorts of information, and even if it seemed to be total fiction there had to be a basis for the rumor somewhere, so I just kept my eyes and ears open.

The U.S. embassy knew that Meadows was a straight player and through them he met a number of key personnel from Peruvian military circles. In particular he got close to the naval hierarchy. To Meadows it seemed that they were the most professional and far-seeing service, and to them he was a true military professional whose views were always interesting to hear. He was not flustered by senior rank and could be guaranteed to give an honest analysis of any situation. His early views on the spread of the guerrilla war had filtered through to the ears of the senior military officers, and much of what he had predicted only a short time ago was beginning to happen. By 1988, Meadows was in an enviable position. He had virtually cornered the security consultancy market in Lima. A lot of basic work was backing up and he never seemed to have the time to clear the logjam. In all honesty, much of the work was basic survey programs—the bread and butter of the security consultant, but not Meadows's favorite pastime. He preferred to exercise his talents up-country, where the threat was most visible, rather than poke around factories and private homes and write detailed reports that were made boring by their necessary similarities.

To show the scale of the work, in early 1988 I got a message asking if I would go to Lima and help him clear the backlog. Dick met me at the airport and took me to his apartment. He had moved from Miraflores to San Isidro and had a fine view of the golf course where he took his morning runs. We had supper and I got a good feel for the intensity of his work. He had to make a visit to the Upper Huallaga Valley and he asked me to take on about ten surveys of both private and commercial premises in and around the city. I managed to get the surveys completed within a couple weeks and on his return Meadows took me out to dinner.

"Spike, let's go for some pisco sours and ceviche. There's a saying in Lima that one pisco isn't enough but two's too many. We might have three tonight though."

Over the drinks in a little open café in Miraflores he told me that one of his ambitions was to open a Mexican restaurant in the area. He contended that though he didn't know much about the catering business, he had friends who did. It was the sort of business that he would have to pay minimum attention to if he got a good guy in to run it. Dining out was a popular pastime in Lima. Even if people couldn't escape the city, they could get out of their houses and Miraflores was a reasonably secure and popular area. Mexican food was sufficiently different from Peruvian cuisine for the project to stand a good chance of success. I marveled at the way he thought he could extend himself into yet another area of business. By this time he was having great difficulty coping with what he had already achieved.

The problems he was having are not unusual when a man starts a business single-handedly. He is the person who makes the proposals, supervises the training, and is the constant factor in maintaining efficiency. It is, therefore, not unnatural that the word-of-mouth system identifies him as a person and does not isolate him from the product. If that man then looks at a task, then says that he will get someone in to do the job, there is a sporting chance that he will be told that it is he who must do it. It is he who has satisfied the friend who introduced them and the new client wants the same service.

Meadows found part of the answer to his problems in turning to a small security company set up by a former naval officer, Wilson Gomez-Barrios, familiarly known as "Cucho." Meadows and Cucho had previously met in the Huallaga Valley. At that time Cucho had only a few vigilantes, poorly trained and equipped, with no real organization. Meadows took the small company under his wing and helped to get it properly structured. Partly armored cars were acquired and drivers properly trained, along with escorts. This improved service allowed Meadows to offer a chauffeur and bodyguard training service as well as providing cars and drivers to meet visiting executives. The company, FORZA, expanded quickly as Meadows got them an increasing number of contracts. All the time he kept checking the contracts to make sure that FORZA was providing a high-quality service. As Cucho grew in stature and experience he was able to further supplement the work brought in by Meadows. There were, however, potential and active contracts that required the Meadows touch. He was still regularly visiting the Romero plantation; new clients were coming in thick and fast and the days were too short to cover all the commitments. Remarkably, within less than five years he had built up the most successful security business in Peru.

For tax and visa purposes, Meadows had to leave Peru every sixty days, and he spent as much quality time as possible with Pam in Crestview. Her career was going from strength to strength, and her status within the community was also rising. A military family accepts separation early on, and it seemed that Meadows, in this respect, was just an extra-long-serving soldier. Both Dick and Pam knew that the situation would not last forever, and meanwhile a solid retirement fund was building up.

14

The Golden Days in Peru

1989–1991

The scope of the business was increasing fast. In early 1988 Meadows was invited to look at the security of a mine. For this he needed assistance, and his mind went back to Tom Smith,[1] who recalled:

> Dick gave me a welcome break to go back to Peru to help with a survey of an Andean mine which had just lost an engineer in an assassination by the SL. It was only a couple of weeks' work, and the strongest memory is my first case of altitude sickness as we flew directly to 15,000 feet and began working.
>
> A year later he had another project for me designing security systems for a couple of Lima beer factories. For some reason, the SL had chosen these facilities as targets for bombings in 1988 and '89. It's hard to figure out why beer factories came high on the target candidate list. The project was spread over a month this time, and it came out pretty well and stimulated some additional work for shooting and driving courses, which we did for another month or so.
>
> At that time, both the SL and the MRTA were beginning to feel their oats after a long incubation period, and there was a lot of fear within the private sector. Dick's initial work in the country had such success that one influential family would recommend him to another. There was as much work as Dick could handle and it was backing up. On top of this, Dick was dealing with a major and very touchy kidnap case.
>
> With all this to be done, he made me an offer of a partnership in a surprise move that makes me feel proud to this day. I jumped in with more enthusiasm and energy than smarts. It was practically nonstop for four years. Selling our services was never a problem. With Dick's reputation and

the momentum of the terrorist insurgency, we would just receive the calls for help, tell the clients what we were going to do, do it, and send the bill.

During this same time frame, Dick was approached by the election campaign manager of Mario Vargas Llosa, the famed novelist who was the front-runner to replace Alan Garcia in the upcoming presidential election. This was 1990 and the country was going to hell in a handbasket after five years under the hand of Garcia. Mario was seen as the "great white hope."

The SL and the MRTA were doing just about anything they wanted with one success after another in 1990. So, naturally, everyone was greatly concerned with the security of the candidate, a champion of everything the leftist opposition despised.

The Vargas camp had contracted a local security company to provide bodyguards and general security. The leaders in the campaign had some reservations about the level of professionalism, but, not being experts, they thought they should contact someone with experience and, most important in Peru, someone who could be trusted. Most in-country security was then done through a system of kickbacks and political favors at the cost of efficiency and effectiveness.

The campaign was already in full swing and Mario was about to embark on a whirlwind tour of most of the major cities and a lot of minor ones in between. Dick saw we weren't going to be able to change things mid-stream, but he accepted the offer in the hopes that we could at least make some improvements. So he jumped in to make the best of a bad situation.

We hit two to three cities a day, getting most of our sleep on air hops between locations. Dick organized it so at least the basics would get done. Advance teams were sent out; protection details were reorganized to make some tactical sense, instead of the near mob formations we inherited; emergency medical and evacuation systems were put online; and team training was conducted.

Everywhere we went there were cheering mobs to greet us. The TV ads were constantly singing the praises of the new era coming, and you could feel the enthusiasm of the campaign organizers; but once you looked past the first rows of supporters and "cheerleaders," there was less animation. People, especially in the Andes, were stony-faced and listened to speeches with typical politeness, and then they just turned and went about their business.

During the campaign we stopped at a jungle town in the Huallaga, called Tarapoto. Mario had the typical fanfare. Seemed everyone turned out. At the airport, sitting in the restaurant with a few tables pushed together, was a small, quiet group of about eight or nine people. When we inquired as to whom they were, we were given a completely unknown and foreign name—Fujimori. This was the Japanese immigrant who upset all of the predictions and beat Mario, by a very substantial margin, in a grassroots campaign that would make textbook history in any other part of the world.

Meadows made a few observations on that particular operation:

Mario would have done better to cut out all the expensive TV support and plow some of the campaign money into tearing down the slums and improving the lot of the homeless. His security was too tight for a politician on the campaign trail. The Indios wanted to reach out and touch the man they were going to vote for and not be contained behind barriers. I guess Mario really lost touch with the people because he'd been in exile in London for too long. In a funny way, I think Fujimori got Alan Garcia's support purely because Garcia hated Mario. I did get on well with Mario, and he had a real plan to work for peace in Peru; it would've been a kind of interesting situation if he'd made president because I got very close to him on that trip.

When the campaign ended and Fujimori took power, Meadows and Smith went back to providing security for the private sector. The energy of Meadows was truly remarkable. Smith mentioned that he was running a kidnap negotiation almost as an aside to all the other work. Meadows left Peru every sixty days or so for periods of up to one month to conform to tax and visa regulations, and one of his first ports of call would be retired general Sam Wilson, in

Hampden Sydney, Virginia, to whom he would make in-depth reports about his activities in Peru and his feelings on the progression of the insurgency. Sam Wilson was one of the founders of the U.S. Special Operations Command, and Meadows knew that anything of interest in his reports would land on the right desk.

During one such break in 1989, Meadows had been visited by Ian Crooke, a much respected ex-SAS lieutenant colonel. Crooke at this time was working for Sir David Stirling, the legendary wartime founder of the British SAS. Stirling's private security company, KAS Enterprises, was looking to the United States for support for an idea they had, and Meadows was the man they chose to represent their very sensitive notions. Ever since then there had been quick trips to London and periods spent in conference in the States. The theme of the KAS idea was to set up an alliance between the United States' and the United Kingdom's retired Special Forces fraternities on a very selective basis and between them produce a pool of experienced former soldiers who were still fit and active. This pool could be offered to both countries for use in deniable operations in areas of limited-intensity conflict. The force would be able to take on classic Special Forces training missions or even be used as a small selective strike force. Stirling already had influential friends in the United States, but Meadows happily introduced him to Generals Bob Kingston, Sam Wilson, and others. He was, to the delight of David Stirling, and through his old Secret Service friend Tom Quinn, able to effect an introduction to President Ronald Reagan.

The idea never really got off the ground, for a variety of reasons. The Oliver North incident created a mistrust of mercenary organizations, and the failing health of Stirling effectively took him out of the picture. Then there was the unwillingness of governments to fund such organizations and the growing idea that the almost romantic ideals behind the project would be treated with skepticism in the modern world.[2]

While stateside, outside of his reporting duties, Meadows liked nothing better than to relax by fishing and setting his lobster pots at the mouth of the Alaqua. His favorite dress while at home consisted of "friendly" old shirts, cutoff jeans, his "crabbing" boots, and army socks. To take Pamela out for a meal in the relaxed and casual atmosphere of Crestview's many restaurants he would make a concession and change his fishing cutoffs for more presentable denims and change his boots. The denims would still be cutoffs and with one leg a little longer than the other and he would retain the army socks. Any efforts by Pamela to throw away these old clothes would be met by determined resistance. Her attempts to get her husband into smarter casual gear for their trips out were only successful after she introduced the idea of "Saturday clothes." Meadows came to accept this dress format, and if they had to discuss what to wear to a particular venue then his first compromise would be, "Okay then, Saturday clothes."

He was now the proud owner of a plot of land alongside the Alaqua on which a stilted house with a workshop at ground level had been built. The house was simply referred to as "The Lot." After selecting the land and sorting out the design of the house, Meadows, of course, left the remainder of the arrangements to Pamela. He let her choose all the internal furniture and fittings with one exception. He wanted a potbellied wood-burning stove, and he eventually found what he was looking for even though he had to transport it in his car across many state boundaries. At that time Meadows's mother- and father-in-law (Sadie and "Spud") were living in Crestview in a mobile home adjacent to the main house. Spud helped Meadows to construct a mooring jetty for his boat and life was then complete for the part-time fisherman. Pamela's parents eventually moved back to the UK because her mother could not tolerate Florida's climate.

Back on the home front, Mark Meadows had gained his ROTC commission at Georgia Military College in 1984. During his academic period he had still found the time to take the Ranger course and attend Jump School back to back. When Meadows and his wife went to visit their son at the end of his Ranger training, the students had just returned from the jungle training phase. Pamela, though warned by the commandant that the students would be in a sorry state, was still not prepared for the fact that her son had lost so much weight and looked on the point of exhaustion as he made his way toward them. She recollected the moment vividly:

Mark didn't know that we would be there for Ranger graduation. He was told at the last minute. As Dick and I stood around waiting, this person started to make his way to us. It was Mark, but I didn't recognize him until he was right up with us. He looked as though he'd just come out of Belsen! I just burst into tears and turned on Dick, thumping his chest and saying things like, "What have they done to him?" "What's the point of all this?" I couldn't see that there was anything worth that sort of effort and physical punishment.

Later, and no doubt with poignant memories of his experience with Neguera so long ago, Meadows took great pride in pinning Airborne wings to his son's chest before returning to Lima.

If Meadows's work in Peru sounds mundane compared to his earlier employment, consisting of security surveys, training bodyguards, and conducting driving courses, then recognition must be given to some of the outstanding missions he undertook. Usually Smith was involved, but sometimes Meadows acted alone. When Mobil Oil began to explore the Upper Huallaga Valley it was a huge operation, and it was natural that Meadows and Smith were called in for advice after one of their camps had been occupied by the SL. Mobil Oil, however, decided to ignore the Meadows assessment and plan. It was not long before their main exploration camp was occupied by an SL force. They commandeered the two Mobil helicopters to shuttle them into the exploration base camp and were in a much larger force than ever before, estimated to be ninety to a hundred men. At that point Meadows could only monitor the situation. Sending in the army would put Mobil's people in the middle of a major shoot-out by forces that had no concept of fire control. The SL occupied the area for a tense week, prohibiting any contact with the outside.

This time they didn't leave peacefully. On the last day, they herded the engineers into a storage enclosure and proceeded to go on the rampage. They destroyed millions of dollars worth of equipment and stole whatever they could use. At midday, they went looking for the two senior engineers to conduct a public execution. By an incredible chain of luck, the engineers escaped by hopping fences, hiding in a pigsty, and slipping into the jungle. A few days earlier the SL had tied up, hooded, and executed a schoolteacher and two others who were accused of being MRTA sympathizers. They also executed a camp prostitute who, it was claimed, had taunted the SL. Having completed their destruction, the SL used the helicopters and captive pilots to shuttle out of the area.

Mobil finally got the message. Their camp was destroyed, a helicopter was missing, and their chief engineers had barely escaped with their lives. But Mobil was in a bigger dilemma than Meadows first thought. They had just acquired seismic data that indicated a major oil discovery. According to the geological patterns and formations, the experts speculated that it could be as big as the Alaska North Slope oil fields. An ideal test-drilling site was identified. As luck would have it, it was right in the area where the camp had been destroyed. Meadows and Smith told the chief executives of Mobil Oil that they could sort out the situation but that they would not become involved in a disaster. They would design the security force, equip and train it, and then deploy and monitor it. They would do it right there in the zone. Mobil agreed and it became a straight-out-of-the-manual Special Forces A Team mission. The project lasted almost a year and Meadows needed to recruit a security chief. Smith had known a Peruvian lieutenant colonel when he had worked in Ucayali and went to see him. Jorge Contreras, who also helped to recruit some top NCOs from the commando school, agreed to take the post if the army would release him.[3]

From that point on the project took on huge proportions. Meadows and Smith decided to recruit and train their own dedicated force and control the payroll themselves. Tom Smith went to Iquitos, a jungle city near the upper reaches of the Amazon River. There he coordinated with an army general to use his base for recruiting the men needed to get the force established. They also did the same thing at the army base at Tarapoto. They wanted twenty-five men to guard the logistics base there and fifty men for the actual drilling site in the jungle. They got their recruits and ran two separate thirty-day training courses on a rice plantation only a dozen kilometers from the scene of the earlier destruction and executions.

The drilling project entailed bringing 120 eighteen-wheeler truckloads of equipment up the Amazon by ship. From there the cargo went by barge on the Marañón and Huallaga rivers to the town of Yurimaguas. Think of Dodge City before Wyatt Earp cleaned it up and you can get an idea of the town. Here the stores were transferred to trucks to be run in convoy along the seventy-kilometer jungle road (which had been specially carved out for the Mobil project) to the drilling site. All of this was in terrorist- or narco-controlled areas. The army supervised only the ground it stood on. There is little doubt that Meadows and Smith had a good time training the force. It was as though they were back in an A Team again, and it was rewarding as well as nostalgic. After their thirty-day course, the troops could patrol, communicate, and hit what they aimed at. They understood fire discipline, knew security procedures, and could deploy tactically.

It was also a nostalgic time for a number of former Green Berets as the training progressed. Assisting Meadows and Smith was Frank Median, who took on the responsibility of the second training cycle and supervised shooting courses. He did wonders in developing the commando NCOs into fine small-unit leaders—a concept practically unknown in Peru and one that made the job much easier down the road. Al Trevino was enlisted to set up the evacuation system and medical training (which he did in faultless style) as well as to develop the air support plan and SOPs to cover the convoys. Walt Shumate was happily employed across a wide spectrum of the mission. All this was done in the heart of "bandit country," so those experienced and well-armed warriors felt quite at home.

Meadows was able to make the Mobil force the most cost-effective, best paid, and most well-equipped unit in Peru. Moreover, the final figure was within a few percentage points of the projected budget. A large allowance was given to the army in order to pay for troops on the ground, the concept being that Mobil would pay for each soldier actually deployed. This clever and perfectly acceptable idea meant that the army would put out as many troops as possible. So, Meadows was doing an efficient job at half the cost of the traditional methods. The reason he could do it was because there was no need for kickback money and, because of the administrative structuring, none of the profits could be hidden. Most importantly, however, they were able to take care of their troops better and thus demand a higher performance. The morale produced by this factor paid dividends to Mobil. There was practically no attrition rate, so the cost of further recruiting and basic training did not exist. As Tom Smith was to say later, they had found a formula that really worked: "I don't think anyone would dispute it was the most successful private security undertaking in Latin America. After all, this was the Upper Huallaga Valley in 1991. The only problem was that there was no oil. I think this bothered us more than it bothered Mobil. It seems such dry holes are a normal part of their life. Anyway, the force was disbanded. The officers and NCOs all found other security work and we went on to other projects. But it was certainly an interesting adventure while it lasted."

This successful project just added to the Meadows reputation—but how long could the golden days last?

15

The Bubble Bursts in Peru

1991–1995

The successes continued and the stream of business seemed to be never-ending. FORZA's operations were expanding and they now had an efficient control center based in Lima.

Under similar threat conditions to Mobil, Newmont Gold had been persevering with their mining explorations right through the bad years of insurgency and terrorism in Peru. About 45 percent of Peru's earnings came from mining, the predominant minerals being lead, zinc, silver, copper, bauxite, and gold. Around 30 percent of the mining companies had applied to the government for permission to cease their efforts due to the SL attacks. Len Harris, a senior executive with Newmont Gold, had first come to Peru in 1983 from Chile:

> The terrorism problem had been building up since 1980. For example, the years 1989–90 and '91 had seen three thousand incidents per year with the loss of fourteen to fifteen hundred lives. This is apart from serious injuries and severe damage to property. In fact, by 1984 nobody wanted to invest in the country anymore. We persevered and by 1992 it was obvious that we had a very viable mine at Minera Yanacocha [Black Lake].
>
> I attended a conference in Denver to discuss the future of the mine, which was showing great potential. I asked the questions: "What about security? How safe is Peru? What do we actually know ourselves about security?" The board pooh-poohed the question, but Tsumeb, who was a colleague very familiar with similar situations in Angola, supported me. He stressed the need for early consideration and a proper plan. The net result was that I was told to look at the situation and report. I was put in contact with the Ackerman Group in the U.S.A.

Ackerman recommended Dick Meadows for any work in South America, but particularly in Peru. I also met a senior ex–Special Forces officer who gave Dick an excellent reference. When I asked him what I should do with Meadows, he said, "Meet him. Brief him. Do exactly what he says." That was good enough for me. I was the general manager and Dick was officially taken on as my security consultant. From the beginning he had said that he would not be "a participant to murder" and wanted full control over the guard force and all procedures.

FORZA brought in a guard force to operate under plans devised by Dick. We had two initial philosophy decisions to make. Did we want to be high or low profile? What did we do about the Peruvian superintendents? They had the habit of vanishing to the villages and having a drink and other things whenever they were off duty. Sometimes they didn't return. On the question of high or low profile you have to remember that Minera Yanacocha was the first foreign mine in Peru for over twenty years and the executives were prime targets for the SL. There was also no board consensus on the security needs, and they ended up pointing a finger literally at Cucho and saying, "You are responsible," and by this they also included Dick. Up to that point over three hundred mining professionals had been killed. Dick's reply to the question of profile was: "We go high profile. Look around you, it's the low-profile guys who are being killed and kidnapped."

Harris continued:

His answer to the question of the Peruvian superintendents was simple: "Lock 'em up."

This we virtually did. They did three weeks on duty at the mine with no alcohol, no women, and no passes to leave the camp. Then they'd get a week off in Lima. There were some gripes at first, but it soon died away when they realized that they were actually pretty secure for the first time.

My wife, who is an ex-police officer, thought I was crazy to take on the job at the mine in Peru. Her attitude changed after she visited and inspected the security herself. She did it right. She checked all the drivers, the bodyguards, and even checked the camp procedures. Let me make two important points: One, Minera Yanacocha is now one of the biggest mines in the world, and two, it is probably the safest. Fujimori said, at a conference in the U.S.: "Two hundred major foreign companies are now investing in Peru. Newmont Gold was the spark of light which showed the way." But it was Dick Meadows who showed us the safe way. There is no doubt whatsoever in my mind that he saved the lives of me and many others!

These then were the halcyon years for Meadows in Peru, but how long could they last? The winds of change, when they arrived, were subtle. Tom Smith and Meadows had decided, amicably, to go their separate ways. This did nothing, of course, to lighten Meadows's workload. He managed to keep most of his business intact, but in late 1993 he noticed that the level of inquiries had fallen dramatically. However, he did get a call from a U.S. company.

Wilkate, supporting a specialist insurance brokerage, retained Meadows to provide response cover for kidnap cases. An excellent and proven consultant, he was also of great assistance on the policy sales front. His calm, commanding presence and his easy and authoritative explanations of security and the duties of response consultants did much to increase the potency of the presentation at the point of sale. Eventually Meadows was contracted to manage the whole of the Anglo-American response team for the company. This made even greater demands on his time.

In a 1995 letter, Tom Smith made many observations about Meadows, and one of them goes some way toward explaining his success in the kidnap and ransom consultancy field:

I do know that Dick continues to do good work in the kidnapping arena, building one success after another. And I should comment on this, as I had the good fortune to see him operate on these from time to time. Dick has a quality to instill confidence in the tightest of situations and with practically all that come in touch with him. I can't define this quality. But it is the magic that makes Dick who he is, in my eyes. Nowhere could you see this more vividly than in his kidnapping cases. To appreciate this, you have to understand the seeming futility in these situations. The bad guys hold all of the cards. You are starting from the worst possible position. What possible resources do you have? In this despair Dick could perform his magic. Not miracles, because rescues are practically out of the question in such situations, but magic.

You see, kidnappings are usually a case of making the best of bad choices. I've seen crisis management committees argue away and come very close to making some disastrous decisions (whereas it's hard to make things better, it's all too easy make them worse). Dick has a sense about when to enter and what to say to get the best possible results for the moment. His air of confidence is contagious, and he uses it to stir others to rise to the occasion. It's called leadership.

I also admire him for his self-discipline in not getting ahead of the case, something that usually spells disaster. His way of putting it is, "They play a card, and then we'll play a card." Quite often Dick's job involved keeping anxious family members and other emotionally charged persons from playing too many cards in advance. For example, there is often the tendency for the spokesperson, the one in direct contact with the kidnappers, to want to make too elaborate a story, usually to draw the kidnappers out. Dick is good at reining them in and keeping them in pace with the unfolding events. Then, when a break would come, usually as a result of this patience, he would take bolder steps to exploit it.

Despite Meadows's enthusiasm, fitness, and huge capacity for work, something had to break. Look at his commitments in 1992: major security operations which still required the personal touch; day-to-day driving and shooting courses; countersurveillance training; property surveys; the unpredictable demands of kidnap and ransom response; his foreshortened rest periods at home (he still reported to his intelligence masters whenever he returned to the United States). Notwithstanding all this pressure, Meadows never lost the human touch. He was very proud of being able to help two young, highly intelligent Peruvian boys obtain places at a U.S. college. His only request in return for this favor was that the boys should not let him down. They certainly did not, and at the last report they were doing brilliantly in their chosen careers.

Meadows would have derived great satisfaction and deep pleasure from that.

A series of incidents in 1994 culminated in a situation that made Meadows question the future of his business in Peru. A surprise setback came when the Romero family appointed their own security manager to oversee ORUS. With the appointment of the new manager, the Meadows contract came to an abrupt end. He was hurt by the news. What needs to be remembered here is the effect that the establishment of ORUS had on a major part of the Lima and general Peruvian community. The security measures designed by Meadows and his team instilled confidence in the owners, and this resulted in a desire to fight back against the MRTA and SL. They, and international companies, began to reinvest their money in Peru. The Romero group as a whole was admired by the wider community, which took its lead from them. Meadows often used the stability of the Romero group as an example to others, and the loss of the contract hit his marketing methods hard.

The general security situation was improving dramatically. The activities of the MRTA and SL were diminishing and business owners and investors felt safer. Inevitably, the "bean-counters" arrived and began to scrutinize the security budgets. Newmont Gold also decided to appoint an in-house security chief. The new incumbent did the rounds of all the commercial companies that had security organizations and did a cost comparison. He also reappraised the threat and risk analysis. In the latter he was at odds with Meadows, who was not yet totally convinced that the dramatic lowering of the threat level was anything other than a temporary situation. This brought him into direct conflict with the Newmont Gold security manager. The company hierarchy in the United States decided to keep their in-house man and dispense with the services of outside consultants, and Meadows lost his contract. FORZA was asked to cut costs by reducing manpower and come into line with the company's reduced threat analysis. It is ironic that the situation that had arisen, whereby the risk to Meadows's clients had lowered and caused them to look at security costs, was a direct result of his efforts on their behalf. Without his work and input the security situation would never have stabilized so quickly.

It is also apparent, with the wisdom of hindsight, that the leukemia of which Meadows was ignorant at that time was beginning to affect him. It did not curtail his ability to think on his feet, but it was making him very tired. Jim McInnis, of Occidental Petroleum and a friend and supporter of Meadows, recalled:

> Dick and I used to meet quite a lot for lunch and some "feet-up" time. He would tell me a lot of what was going on, but only as much as he wanted. I'd pass on any information we had to him on the same terms. We both understood the situation in business and were at ease with that. I have recommended FORZA to a lot of people and still would, as they're the best company around at the moment, and I know Dick helped them become that. You know, about 25 percent of the members of the Lima Chapter of ASIS[1] owe their membership to Dick.
>
> I remember on his last visit to Lima we were scheduled to have lunch and he called to cancel, saying that he was very sorry but that he was just too tired and kept falling asleep. I naturally thought he'd gone to see someone else and what a strange excuse it was that he'd given me. To be "too tired" at eleven o'clock in the morning? Now, of course, I know that it was true. You know, a lot of people in Peru owe that guy a big debt of gratitude.

Depressing though the loss of two good contracts was, Meadows was able to find a logical reason for it in his own analysis:

> I do believe that there was something sinister going on in the background, but even so the writing was on the wall for people like me. The days of the big retainers and high daily fees were fading. This was a natural progression as the situation began to stabilize. Those who criticize the kind of money that was paid for our services in those days conveniently forget the personal risks we, as Americans, were taking. The new security managers of the big companies had never been around in Peru when the MRTA and SL had a free rein to do whatever they wanted. We went to the high-risk areas ourselves to sort out the problems and train the guards; we didn't do anything by remote control.

Meadows was very busy with Wilkate at the time and he was not in a good position to take on the opposition in Lima. He knew that something odd was going on when he had a tip-off that he was going to be arrested for treason by the Peruvian Naval Intelligence Service. He could not fully believe the news, but he had to take it seriously because it came from a highly trusted source. Had information been deliberately leaked to him in order to get him out of Lima?

There were certainly people he knew who had good enough contacts in naval intelligence to pull a few strings had they wanted. He could not imagine what he had done at anytime that could raise a charge of treason against him. His reporting duties in the United States could not have been known. Nothing was ever in writing in his apartment. He decided to go into hiding for a few days to think it through. Before he left he faked a telephone call he knew Maria would overhear. He pretended to book a ticket to Panama on a flight leaving that night. Then he went to ground to let things unfold. He reasoned that if there was a conspiracy against him in Peru it was a battle that he could not win.

He chose to go to ground with a family he knew well. The family trusted him and he them. The place in which he stayed was not in an area that anyone would consider searching for a gringo. He stayed with them for only forty-eight hours. In the meantime, he had taken the precaution of asking one or two of his close American associates to try to check the veracity of the situation.

When he came out of cover he knew that if the people he had spoken to had done their stuff and talked to U.S. embassy officials he would probably be safe. He had no intention of running. Nothing happened to him. He could not think that he had any major enemies but accepted that he might have little ones. Little enemies are like a cancer, they band together and destroy you cell by cell. He began to think of quitting Lima and moving across to Quito, Ecuador, which had its own set of security problems. The question was whether he had the energy to start over again, and Wilkate was keeping him busy. Also, he now had a little granddaughter at home and he wanted to spend some time with her.

Though Meadows shrugged off the treason accusation, it is obvious that it hurt him deeply. The report of an impending arrest was accurate, but he could only conjecture at the combination of circumstances which brought it about. Peruvian intelligence organizations could be forgiven for seeing Meadows as a threat, but if their analysis of their information and suspicions had included a real appreciation of the character of the man, they would not have been so foolish as to try to tarnish his reputation. If those parties had looked at what Meadows had achieved and how he had achieved it, there is little doubt that his operations could come under intelligence scrutiny. It is far more likely, however, that competitive elements within the rapidly expanding Peruvian security industry had decided to try to scare Meadows into closing down his operation. Look at him and his work from a stand-off point of view:

He was a self-imposed man of mystery. He played his cards close to his chest and never let anyone know where he was going when he made any of his frequent and prolonged absences. This apparently covert side to his life made him a hot subject for gossip within that fertile breeding ground of rumors in Lima. His visits to the U.S. embassy heightened the awareness within Peruvian intelligence circles just as his associations with serving and former members of the Peruvian naval intelligence fraternity caused comment among U.S. intelligence operatives. The "man of mystery" facet was also reinforced by Meadows's refusal, except for one or two examples of a short-lived nature, to take on Peruvian partners in a formalized company structure. In a strange way, the fact that all his deals were impeccably legal also drew attention to him in a country where it is almost a national pastime to try to evade the revenue department. While Meadows was away in other countries operating for Wilkate, he was reliant on local associates to follow up on business leads. Often these opportunities were lost or sold to competitors.

Meadows had an innate ability to talk to the indigenous people of Peru, and he created a loyal following. It has been estimated that he was responsible for creating directly and indirectly employment for about twelve thousand Peruvians, many of whom, because of their work in the security industry, were under arms. This could be looked upon (again if one did not take the trouble to understand Meadows) as a solid basis for a "People's Army"—well-armed, well-trained, and owing their allegiance to a foreigner. When setting up a security contract he would argue long and loud with his clients that they owed it to the men and their country to make sure that the guard force they employed was properly paid, treated with respect, and had good working conditions. It was one of their duties in the fight to stabilize Peru.

He had a willingness to stand up to figures of authority (both American and Peruvian) and speak his mind without bias or favor. Certainly the onetime U.S. ambassador to Peru, Anthony Quainton, did not find this an endearing trait. Meadows reported to Quainton before and after his ambassadorship when he was incumbent in one of the terrorism study groups at Washington, D.C. He made no secret of the fact that he would have liked to have seen a FORZA-type organization that covered the whole of Latin America. Ambition and an obvious closeness to indigenous peoples are often mistrusted and the relationship with Quainton was uneasy, but it should be remembered that Meadows was actually employed by the U.S. embassy as an advisor across a broad field of subjects. He helped to provide information relevant to decision making in the drug war. He helped to organize the evacuation procedures for U.S. personnel and assisted in the general security planning for the embassy buildings and employees.

He took a firm and highly vocal stand against the drug business. He staunchly supported the efforts of investigative journalist Sharon Stevenson in her self-appointed task of spreading an awareness of the problem on an international basis. During his many visits to neighboring Colombia he was known to have been involved with a group of earnest Colombians in Medellín who were planning to take aggressive action against the late Pablo Escobar, then leader of the Medellín drug cartel. This aspect of Meadows's life caused suspicion largely because it involved unpaid effort. Unpaid effort from a man who normally charged premium prices for his services? This was an unusual fact for businessmen to accept.

There were petty jealousies in abundance in Lima. In the security industry Meadows was seen to be earning more than a doctor or top lawyer, but apparently this was of little concern to him. There were no outward trappings of wealth; as a host he was generous to a fault, but he never discussed money in a social environment. He made no public outcry when the Romero and Newmont Gold contracts ceased, but in the case of the latter it is certainly at least probable that tongues began to wag when a U.S. company got rid of a U.S. consultant. Why, the gossipers asked, did Meadows take all this so quietly?

The fact that a good security consultant learns a lot about the private and commercial affairs of his clients also caused some disquiet, especially when this was balanced against Meadows's superb social intelligence network. As one person put it: "When you looked at Dick, there was nothing in his expression to even give you a hint of what he knew or didn't know. There was nothing in what he said to suggest that he knew more than he had already told you. But knowing him, you just accepted that he would be holding some cards close to his chest." He would travel to any part of Peru no matter what the security situation may be and he never expressed any reservations about doing that. Did he have some form of official protection? Of course he did not, but there were many who thought that a possibility. He was never armed, at least not in Lima—a city where anyone who can get a permit carries a pistol.

Certainly there were enough aspects of Meadows's field of operations and his manner of conducting them to raise suspicions about him or his motives. But equally, his morality and love of the country were obvious to anyone who spent even a short time with him. To accuse him of treason was ludicrous. There may even have been a political backlash, given his reputation in the United States. Look at what happened and what was said when Ross Perot invited Meadows back to the States for a ceremony at which Perot was being honored with the Patrick Henry Award. He asked Meadows to perform the function, on May 23, 1990, of introducing the president of the United States to the assembled audience. In his response to the introduction, President George Bush said: "I have been introduced by Heads of State and Members of Congress, leaders of every kind from around the world, but I don't believe I have ever been more honored than I am tonight to be introduced by Major Meadows. A fine hero and I just echo everything Ross Perot said about him. Thank you very, very much, sir." Ross Perot had said:

> Ladies and gentlemen, it is my privilege to introduce Major Richard Meadows, whose service to our country spans the entire cold war. Every person here in uniform tonight either knows him personally or knows of his legendary record. He has lived Patrick Henry's words since 1947 when he joined the army. He fought in Korea; he fought for over three years in Laos and Vietnam. He led the first team in to Son Tay prison 20 miles outside Hanoi. They flew in a helicopter 350 miles behind enemy lines over the most heavily defended city in the history of warfare.
>
> The helicopter had to crash land into the compound. Dick was on that helicopter, he and his team took the objective. Unfortunately they had emptied the prison camp; the raid was a textbook success. He is a founder of the Delta Team.

Although retired at the time, Dick Meadows was one of four Americans waiting in Teheran to support the Delta Team the night we attempted to rescue the embassy hostages. Think for a minute what would be involved in sneaking into the country, living there on your own and then having to get out completely on your own. He was in Panama just before the invasion. I can only say that he served in an advisory position but in the great Meadows tradition his son, Mark, was a Ranger platoon leader who parachuted in to the international airport. His platoon was instrumental in securing the airport. Major Meadows continues to serve our country. He has come a great distance tonight from another continent where he has been on still another mission for all of us. He epitomizes the courage that all our special military guests and their families represent.

There was a standing ovation from the audience. All of them knew at least some of the feats that had helped to create this living legend.

Was there a concerted effort to force him out of Peru? Meadows thought that there could have been. We will probably never know, but I think that theory is possible. It is highly probable that some individuals sought to reduce his hold on the security industry, and collectively they could have started such a campaign. I prefer to reflect on the good that Meadows did in Peru, and it is not too grandiose a statement to say that he changed the face of the security situation within a very influential section of Peruvian society. This in itself helped in a big way to bring much-needed business stability to the country.

I believe that he could have won the battle. His standing in Peru and the United States far outweighed the problems he was having. Given time and energy, he could have climbed the greasy pole again. Had he wished, he was well positioned to create an alternative to FORZA, for example. He had important clients other than the Romero family, and he had a host of trusting friends who would have willingly helped him to reemerge. They would, after all, simply be returning the assistance he had given to them. Fate decreed, however, that he was not to be given either the time or the energy. Unknown to Meadows, he was about to be confronted with another battle, this time one which he could not win. Back in Crestview he began to make a loose plan to examine the prospects in Ecuador, but the tiredness which had been afflicting him for the past few months continued. His condition eventually forced him to seek a medical opinion. On being given the news that he was in the advanced stages of leukemia and had but a few months to live, he accepted it in typical Meadows style. The percentage chances of a cure by conventional treatments were, to him, unacceptably low and he opted to die with dignity. He immediately began to put his affairs in order.

During this period a letter was hand-delivered to the Meadows home that demonstrates the high regard in which he was held by the U.S. embassy in Peru:

Embassy of the United States of America
Lima, Peru

Dear Dick,

I was shocked and saddened when I received Sharon Stevenson's call yesterday informing me of your illness.

As both the United States Ambassador to Peru and as an American citizen I would like to express my sincere appreciation for your extraordinary contribution both in service of our country's national security interests over the years and more recently as an active and effective proponent of improved U.S. Peruvian relations. Your efforts on behalf of the United States of America are legendary; your friends and admirers are legion. I am proud to count myself one of that legion.

I particularly want to express my personal and official appreciation for your unselfish commitment to the Peruvian people. The manner in which you represented in both word and deed all that is good, honorable, honest, and caring about our culture and our society has had a significant, and I believe lasting, impact on the lives you have touched here in Peru.

The thoughts and prayers of all your friends in Peru are with you; a grateful American community in Peru and your many Peruvian friends salute you.

Your friend,
Alvin P. Adams, Jr.
Ambassador

There is no better way to close this chapter of Meadows's life than to print an excerpt from a letter he wrote on July 17, 1995. The letter was to Ross Perot, and it clearly shows his affection for Perot and the calmness with which he was accepting his fate:

Dear Ross,

To update you on my situation, first, my health remains stable with blood transfusions (three to date) and should remain so until the immature white blood cells, called "blast" win the war with the red cells. As of July 9, 1995 the blast count had doubled in a period of three weeks. If this continues my mathematics tell me I will arrive at the crisis point in about seven weeks. At that time, some vital organs will break down and shortly thereafter I will begin my last patrol.

My affairs are in order and I will pass on without regret of my time spent in Vietnam, from where it is suspected I contracted leukemia (Agent Orange). I spent a lot of time in zones where the chemical was being used by our forces to defoliate the Ho Chi Minh Trail.

My decision is not to receive treatment due to such a low percentage rate for recovery and the misery involved during the reception of the treatment. If my misery was to benefit someone else I would not hesitate, but this is for me and I have made up my mind. Again my thanks to you for your concern for me and my family, however, we are truly content with my decision.

16

A Special Forces Marriage

This is a good point at which to examine some of the pressures exerted on the Meadows family over the years of continual separation. Some of these strains they shared with many Special Forces comrades. How does a unit, even one as loving and close as the Meadows family, stay together as a cohesive, caring entity throughout the long periods of separation? Being a good husband and a father as a serving Special Forces soldier is not easy. Family plans can be made which then have to be cancelled as military duties, undertaken often at a moment's notice, disrupt the domestic scene. This can create a basic problem to all such families; some find a way to deal with it, while others just struggle ineffectively as their family units collapse.

Absences are many and often lengthy. The results of these can cause severe stresses on the closest of relationships that rarely occur in civilian life. In times of war these stresses are exacerbated by other factors. Take, for example, an assignment to Vietnam. The husband goes off to do his sworn duty for a period of a year, sometimes more. The care of the family and the running of the home then devolves totally upon the wife. She becomes mother and father; teacher and nurse; controller of the budget; mechanic, plumber, and gardener. She takes on all these roles while having also a full understanding of the dangers faced by her spouse, an understanding that has to remain private. She cannot transmit her fears to the young children in case she adds to their anxieties. To cope with this multiple responsibility, routines are devised to make life run as smoothly as possible. Letters to the husband are carefully phrased in order not to add to his concerns.

While the husband is at war he is not immune from familial pressures. He is unable to take a direct hand in home affairs. He must be able to forget his family to a degree for lengthy periods. His trust in his partner must be absolute if he is to avoid niggling worries that may affect his own judgment in action. His letters will be equally carefully phrased to avoid any hint of deep concern or criticism. It is a false situation built on carefully constructed half-truths and hackneyed phrases. During the Vietnam War, of course, things were doubly difficult for a family living on a military post. There were almost daily reminders of the high casualty rate, and no matter how placatory and benign a husband's letters may have been, the family at home knew the reality of the situation. Decorations for valor, while enjoyed and respected by a family, are also a stark reminder of the dangers being faced by loved ones.

When the time comes for the husband to return home, eager for love, companionship, and instant absorption into the family and lifestyle that he left, he may find himself being resented. This is not because of a lessening of love. The fact is that he is an intrusion into a well-established, defensive mechanism of routine that has been set up to cope with his absence. His wife will have become used to decision making and may not take kindly to what she may perceive as interference in the running of an efficient operation. He finds that his young children have grown at an alarming rate while he was away and now they have different attitudes, knowledge, and perceptions. The new interests of the children may not include a father figure, and this may hurt him. He has to go through the process of getting to know them all over again, and this will seem to take a long time. His wife will sometimes jealously protect the special relationship that has grown between her and the children and will resent "third-party" intrusions. How do a husband and wife cope with this knowing all the time that the situation could be repeated for years to come?

Dick Meadows's character made the continual periods of reintegration easier than for many other families. First, he didn't bring the war home with him. He did not feel the need to talk about his exploits unless it was to answer direct questions, and then he would play down the situation. Second, he respected the necessity for the routines that Pamela had designed for herself and the children and he didn't try to take over as a formal head of the family when he returned from his trips. It is obvious that the child initially will develop a closer relationship with the constant mother rather than the periodically present father, and this was no exception with the Meadows children. Dick accepted the routines and house rules that Pamela had established and also the children's closeness to her. Pamela remained in charge of the domestic budget and Dick, with infinite patience and gentleness, quietly gave his children all that he could. Reading to them at night gave him as much pleasure as it gave to them. He retreated completely from any form of physical discipline and never raised his hand to either child.

A highly moral man, as has already been seen, Dick Meadows's methods of putting across to his children the importance of honor and loyalty were by example and patient explanation. A child's question had to be answered. The answer could not be fabricated and it could not be put off until another day. Curiosity showed a desire to learn and it deserved an instant and honest response.

He would never make arbitrary decisions on behalf of the family. Anything serious needed discussion. On minor matters such as the family being invited to partake in something with friends, Dick was quite likely to say that it had better be discussed with the first sergeant (Pamela). If this paints a picture of a man who was totally prepared to stand down and acquiesce in all domestic and family matters, then that is not so. Dick was a totally honest man who could not stand subterfuge of any kind, and if he felt strongly about anything then he would have his say in a very positive fashion. But like many fathers (especially military fathers), Dick found his relationship with his son much easier than with his daughter. There are some things that are more easily discussed between persons of the same gender. It is easy for a father to offer advice to a son who has girlfriends, but how does he cope with a rapidly maturing daughter?

A man will imagine that any boy who escorts his daughter is bent on seduction only. This one fact makes it difficult for a father to actually like any of his daughter's male friends. Apart from that suspicion, there is also a jealousy factor involved—how dare anyone try to take away his daughter. As Michele reached and passed puberty, Dick found it increasingly difficult to discuss some of his concerns. There were other testing times also as Michele, conscious of her father's successful career and her brother's decision to join the military, decided to prove that she was equally capable. Her parents were far from happy when she announced her decision not to go to college but to join the army. Not only would she join the army, but she would enlist into a transport unit. No amount of parental persuasion was going to change her mind. Her first call home to mother was tearful as the realities of service life hit her, but she still opted to forego the statutory opportunity to reverse her decision and off she went to Fort Dix, New Jersey, for basic training.

Her parents' predictions that she would almost certainly be assigned to a transport pool in Germany were of course accurate, and it was an unhappy Michele who flew to Europe. Her discomfort grew, due in many ways to an unhappy clash of personalities with the first sergeant of the motor pool. Scrubbing steps with a nailbrush and pulling what seemed to be eternal gate guard duties were not Michele's idea of serving her country. One unhappy call home led to a highly indignant and thoroughly protective Pamela making the five-thousand-mile journey to check what was going on. (How many mothers would make such a journey to share a guard duty with their daughter?)

Michele left the army at the first opportunity, married, and had a daughter, Pamela Hayley. Coping with her parental duties and financing herself with a bus driving job, she enrolled in college in 1988 and went on from there to earn her master's degree in counseling and psychology.

Although never at ease with small babies (what man is?), the arrival of a granddaughter was a great joy to Dick Meadows, and at a very early age she could be found in his company as he collected his crab pots and fished in the Alaqua. Pamela Hayley, in return, adored her "Poppy" and greatly looked forward to his vacations from business in Peru. The utter trust and unfettered love of a small child stirred great emotions in Dick and he found the relationship totally rewarding.

After years of separation due to military duties, it would not have been surprising if Pamela had objected to Dick's prolonged second career in Peru. She understood his need for action and independence and recognized that he could never have been happy as a company employee in Florida. Herself an independent woman, she was able to concentrate on her own career and take some solace in that. The situation, though not perfect, was quite workable. Unless Dick was out of Lima they were in constant contact by telephone. His visits home were predictable, and they were able to make plans for their time together.

So the Meadows family survived all the separations and stresses that life placed on them. Outside of the obvious love that existed, probably it was those characteristics of morality, strength, and straightforwardness present in both partners that were important ingredients for their good marriage. In short, a marriage has to be worked at extra hard under the circumstances produced by Special Forces soldiering, and Dick and Pamela tackled it as a team. As Dick put it: "I've always been very proud of my family, and life isn't always easy for those we leave behind. When a nation pays tribute to her soldiers, she should also include the families who stand by them and support them on their missions."

17

The Last Patrol

On the morning of June 23, 1995, Meadows received a telephone call to say that three old friends were going to pay him a visit. Generals Wayne Downing and Pete Schoomaker and Paul Zeisman wanted to pay their respects. He had been relaxing and wearing a pair of cutoff blue jeans, his "crabbing gear," but as soon as he heard the news he went off to dress himself in a fresh shirt and slacks. I was able to watch a remarkable transformation. The rather tired man became alert and almost bouncy. He was determined not to show any signs of his rapid physical deterioration in front of these three Special Forces stalwarts and treasured friends. Had an outsider come into the room and witnessed Dick and Pamela chatting to their guests, it would have appeared a perfectly normal situation. I was privy to many reminiscences about SFOD-D and other situations that cannot be related in this book. The generals had a mission, apart from wanting to make their farewells to Meadows.

Meadows was told that he was going to be inducted into the Ranger Hall of Fame, that he was going to be the recipient of one of the nation's highest decorations (the Presidential Citizens Medal), and that a life-size statue was going to be erected at a suitable place. He was also informed about the creation of the Richard J. Meadows Award for Heroism. A personal letter from the president of the United States was also handed over. Meadows had secretly hoped that he might one day qualify for inclusion in the Ranger Hall of Fame and was delighted by the news. Of course, the other awards and the statue pleased him, but he was quietly embarrassed by that sort of attention. The pièce de résistance for him was being presented with the long-awaited HALO Instructors Badge, serial number 001. The farewells when the generals left showed the true warmth and depth of feeling between those distinguished warriors. Afterward Meadows sat for quite a long time in a private reflection on the events and the letter from his president that read:

The White House
Washington
July 24, 1995

Dear Major Meadows,

I was saddened to learn from General Downing that
your leukemia continues to progress, but I know you
are dealing with this challenge with the same unfailing
tenacity and courage that you displayed so valiantly
throughout your distinguished career of service to this
Nation.

In Korea, Vietnam, Iran and many other dangerous
locales, you established a legendary reputation that will
forever be hallowed within the Special Forces and by all
Americans who know of your extraordinary exploits.

Hillary joins me in wishing you every comfort and an
abiding sense of peace during this difficult time. Please
know that a grateful Nation recognizes and appreciates
your exceptional contributions to preserving our
freedom.

Sincerely,
Bill Clinton

The Presidential Citizens Medal was established in November
1969 for the purpose of recognizing citizens of the United States
who have performed exemplary deeds of service for their country
or their fellow citizens. The medal may be bestowed by the president upon any citizen of the United States at his sole discretion.

Induction into the Ranger Hall of Fame was, to Dick Meadows,
the most pleasing of all his awards. To be eligible for selection to the
Hall of Fame, a person must be deceased or have been separated or
retired from active military service for at least three years at the time
of nomination. He must have served in a Ranger unit in combat or
be a successful graduate of the U.S. Army Ranger School. A Ranger
unit is defined as an army unit with a recognized Ranger lineage or
history. Achievement or service may be considered for individuals
in a position in state or national government after the Ranger has departed the armed services. Honorary induction may be conferred on
individuals who have made extraordinary contributions to Ranger

units, the Ranger foundation, or the Ranger community in general, but who do not meet the normal criteria of combat service with a Ranger unit or graduation from the U.S. Army Ranger School.

The criteria for the Richard (Dick) J. Meadows Award for Heroism reads: "The Dick Meadows Award for Heroism is bestowed on members of special operations who distinguish themselves by heroic or meritorious achievement or service. This award honors extraordinary service and accomplishments involving great personal risk. It is presented to special operators who have displayed singular acts of courage while executing special high risk missions of great importance; or who have demonstrated exceptional skill and gallantry on the field of battle; or who have provided exceptional acts of service during peacetime operations."

The award is a replica of the Dick Meadows statue, and it was introduced using the following words:

The heritage of Special Operations has always rested, and still rests, on the quality of our soldiers, sailors, and airmen. Our Special Operations personnel are often called upon to perform extraordinarily dangerous, high-risk missions that have great strategic value.

The success of these missions hinges on audacity, courage, ingenuity, leadership, and integrity. Many in our community have these values to one degree or another, but none more so than Richard J. "Dick" Meadows. Dick Meadows exemplifies all that is the best in the Special Operations Warrior.

During more than thirty years with the Army, from the Korean War through Vietnam to the Iranian Hostage Rescue attempt, Dick Meadows epitomized the meaning of the "Quiet Professional."

His battlefield actions are stories from which legends are made. His beginnings were of the most humble order. He was born and reared in a one-room shack without plumbing or electricity. He enlisted in the Army in 1947. Five years later, he became the youngest master sergeant of the Korean War.

During the Vietnam War, Dick Meadows served with the Military Assistance Command Vietnam—Studies and Observations Group, better known as MACV-SOG. He led teams on clandestine, cross-the-border missions into North Vietnam and Laos.

Because of his extraordinary combat record, General William Westmoreland awarded him a battlefield commission, the first of the war.

Dick Meadows was also a planner for and a leader of the Son Tay Raid, and was the leader of the first assault team to land inside the prison compound.

Probably his most daring exploit came after he had retired from the military and was working as a consultant to the Army. Dick Meadows, posing as a foreign businessman, went to Iran during the hostage crisis in 1980. He scouted the American Embassy in Teheran where the hostages were being held and reconnoitered the Desert II site where he would link up with the rescue force and then escort them into the city.

After the tragic events at the Desert I site, Dick Meadows was able to make his escape from Teheran.

Dick Meadows is the epitome of the Special Operations Warrior. It is his leadership, skill, bravery, daring and intelligence that we commemorate with this award. Those who receive this award have demonstrated the same qualities of military professionalism, and embody that true spirit, daring, leadership, élan, and self-sacrifice that are Dick Meadows's legacy to his comrades in arms.

During the meeting with the generals it had been stated that the award of the Presidential Citizens Medal and the induction into the Ranger Hall of Fame would take place at a ceremony preceding the annual Son Tay Raiders Association reunion dinner to be held on July 29, 1995. Meadows, aware of his worsening condition, had set himself a personal target to attend the reunion. This would require a further blood transfusion the day before the event, and he was confident that this would see him through this one last public commitment.

The next day, Dick Meadows decided that his fishing boat moored at his "lot" on the Alaqua River should be taken out of the water and returned to his yard in Crestview. It was typical of him that he wanted to complete this task himself despite his failing strength. Dick himself drove and his son, Mark, and I went along to assist. That night we stayed in the cabin by the river and Dick and I had our last "porching" session. Sitting on the veranda sipping Old Milwaukee led to one of the most poignant talks I had with Dick. It was dusk, the evening noises had begun, and it was warm and almost balmy. The gnats were also drinking their fill from us, and Dick remarked with a wry smile that they would regret drinking from him.

I sensed that Dick did not want to talk about any of his former exploits that night, but I was keen to ask him one question. Did he, I inquired, really believe that Agent Orange was responsible for his leukemia so long after the Vietnam War?

> Yes, I truly believe that my condition came from exposure to Agent Orange. You know, the veterans association has put a lot of work into trying to prove it for so many who contracted leukemia. There were a number of defoliants used. They all had different color code names, but Agent Orange was the most widely used and it had a constituent of acids that made it the most dangerous to humans. We walked through the dust of that stuff a lot in the SOG days, especially during my tour in 1965 and 1966. I just know that it didn't do us any good, but you just went where you were sent in those days. I would like you to mention this in the book.[1]

By the morning of July 28, Meadows was very weak but very positive as he went to the hospital to receive his last blood transfusion. He was determined that he was going to make it to the Son Tay Raiders reunion and the award ceremony. Tragically, it was discovered that his condition had deteriorated rapidly and a transfusion was not possible. He passed away with Pamela at his side in the early hours of July 29. That same evening Pamela, Mark, and Michele earned the lasting respect of the Special Forces community as they bravely accepted the posthumous awards. The Son Tay reunion dinner that followed was a muted affair.

Perhaps inevitably during our last "porching" session, the conversation had come around to religion and death. Meadows had no formal association with any of the accepted religions, having failed to find one that gave him satisfaction. He did, however, believe that reincarnation was a possibility because he found himself incapable of believing in a complete cessation of consciousness:

I believe that a man should have a conscience regarding his actions during his life. I'm curious about death. I expect a bright shining light to pluck me up to a star or something. Stars that I can see are said to be 4.5 light years away. What the speed of light is I can't remember, but that's a long, long way away. I've always believed in man's insignificance in the order of the world. You've only got to stand in one of the world's great deserts to appreciate your smallness. I always expected to die as a soldier, and in some ways that would have been a fitting end, but it's nice to have my family around at this time. Soldiers don't often achieve that. A man should be allowed to go wherever he's going on that last patrol with dignity.

And Dick Meadows went with dignity. He was laid to rest in the Barrancas National Cemetery at the Pensacola Naval Air Station after a funeral in the packed Naval Aviation Memorial Chapel on August 1, 1995. Those who gave their reflections and remembrances during the service included Colonel Elliott P. "Bud" Sydnor and Mr. H. Ross Perot.

On June 6, 1997, the U.S. Army Special Operations Command officially gave their recognition to Dick Meadows at Fort Bragg when an eight-foot-high statue of him was unveiled. The skies poured with rain and the large tent was crammed with people, leaving many with no option but to get soaked. Hundreds of his former comrades in arms gathered for this final tribute, which was hosted by Lieutenant General Peter J. Schoomaker. General Henry H. Shelton was the reviewing officer. Lawrence "Larry" M. Ludtke, who sculpted the bronze statue, has said: "It's a wonderful opportunity to be able to create a figure of a great American hero. Just by his nature, he was somewhat reclusive and retiring. And his job was of such a nature that he didn't get much notoriety. And so to have the opportunity to pick someone who might have been overlooked and his accomplishments unnoticed is a great honor."

A list of the major military awards and decorations held by Dick Meadows at the time of his death is impressive: the Distinguished Service Cross, two Silver Stars, two Bronze Stars (one with "V" Device), the Air Medal, the Legion of Merit, the Meritorious Service Medal, the Joint Service Commendation Medal, three Army Commendation Medals, the Combat Infantry Badge, the Glider Badge, the Ranger Tab, the Scuba Badge, the HALO Instructor Badge, and many foreign awards.

As a civilian he also earned the Defense Superior Service Medal, the CIA Seal (posthumous presentation), the Presidential Citizens Medal (posthumous presentation), the USSOCOM Medal (posthumous presentation), and the USSOCOM Outstanding Civilian Service Medal (posthumous presentation).

Since Dick Meadows's death, a fund has been established which would have given him enormous satisfaction. The Richard J. Meadows Memorial Scholarship, administered by Command Chapter LX (Richard J. Meadows Memorial Chapter) of the Special Forces Association, is now a thriving entity.

In February 2006 Meadows received yet another prestigious posthumous award when he was nominated to be the recipient of the USSOCOM Bull Simons Award. It would have been particularly pleasing to Dick to have known about this award, as Bull Simons was one his special friends.

Perhaps we should think carefully about this fine, unique, and honorable collection of accolades for the man who said, "I regret that I've not done anything significant."

Epilogue

Dick Meadows went on his last patrol with dignity, the same dignity with which he had lived his full and adventurous life. But there was more than dignity in the makeup of this remarkable and complex man. He had immense pride and a rigid sense of honor insofar as his country, the military, and his family were concerned, but he also carried these characteristics into civilian life. He was unremitting in his search for perfection, and this rubbed off onto all those who worked with him. Perfection in the profession of arms is impossible to achieve—there are too many variables in combat—but it is possible to attain near perfection in planning, training, and preparation, and this is where Meadows shone. Soldiers and civilians alike felt safe with him.

At the beginning of his military life he was a driven man. The army had been an escape for him from a background that offered little love and no privilege. Indeed, he confessed that it was many, many years before he even began to understand the meaning of love. Because it was the army that gave him succor in his early years, it was the army that became his first mistress and attracted his first loyalties. But loyalty to the army also meant not only loyalty to those who served as his superiors but also to those who were placed under his command.

In some ways it is probable that his lack of formal education helped him to become that man who is now a legend. He felt that if he failed in anything that the military threw at him the institution would start to look for reasons, and he was ashamed at his lack of recorded qualifications. This endowed him with a measure of stubbornness that could appear to be as impenetrable as a steel barrier. He took everything as a personal challenge and no matter how simple or complex the task was he would apply the same thoroughness in his approach. This situation did not last. He was a highly intelligent man and he soon realized that the lack of formal education was unimportant if a soldier was capable of understanding complex situations and rendering them to simplicity. Meadows's written reports set standards. Never use a paragraph if a sentence will do, and stick to the proven facts. He spoke out confidently enough as an enlisted man, but from the point at which he was commissioned he took advantage of his heightened status to reach as many ears as possible with his ideas and innovations. He recognized his own leadership abilities but didn't abuse them. He never gave a soldier a task that he was not willing and able to do himself.

Proud as he was, he was happy and eager to learn from others (and to give them recognition for their input), and this instilled in him the ability to pass on his own wisdom in a manner that left the recipient feeling good. Whatever task he was given, he would approach it with the same aim: to do his best for the army and his country. Those tasks were many and varied, but his methods of achieving his aim were a constant throughout his life:

- No matter how verbose the orders, render them down to simple aims.
- Know your enemy.
- Plan every move from the point of departure to the point of return. Keep the element of surprise in mind at all times. Plan boldly and act boldly (but not foolishly).
- Ask the question "What if . . . " at every stage of the plan. Ask that question no matter how outlandish it may seem to be.
- Give honest orders and honest answers to the troops' questions.
- Do not delegate a task unless prepared to do it yourself.
- Select the right equipment, but always remember that it is the man who counts.
- Rehearse, rehearse, and then rehearse again.
- Hope for—but do not expect—good luck. If good luck does appear to be with you, exploit it—fast.

No one will deny that the Meadows-detailed preparation and planning phases for any operation paid off. It is a technique still practiced throughout Special Forces.

All the planning in the world can come to naught in fast-moving combat situations, and it is here that another of the Meadows principles is pertinent. Act with speed and act boldly; do the unexpected. Of course he knew fear; what Special Forces soldier has never felt that demon? The secret lies in controlling it, and Meadows had this down to a fine art and never showed his emotions in a tight spot. His control was rigid and his actions immediate. He led by example and imbued in his soldiers a sense of indestructibility, and in all his years of combat he never lost a man.

In Peru he appeared to be a shrewd businessman, but under that facade was a man who hated the drug trade and corruption and who was a constant supporter of the underdog. The employment slots that he engineered run into many thousands, and most of them still exist. Such was the fidelity of the "troops" he trained in the large security industry of that country that he could possibly have taken control of a civil army, though he would never have been so minded. His intelligence network was impressive, and both the United States and the Peruvian government benefited from his information.

The standards set by Dick Meadows will be there in perpetuity. The statue and the Dick Meadows Award for Heroism record his legacy to Special Forces, reminders to all of what can be achieved in the pursuit of excellence.

Acknowledgments

I owe a huge debt of gratitude to many people for their assistance in putting this work together. Many did not wish to be named and I have respected that. Many people passed on anecdotes during reunions and conventions that I was privileged to attend, and I apologize for not remembering all their names. In keeping with the relaxed nature of the interviews and the informality of this book, I have dispensed with ranks. In particular I thank, alphabetically, Dick Adams, Billy Antony, Geoff Barker, Scott and "CJ" Berwick, Norm Bild, "Bucky" Burruss, Lyle and Mrs. T. Button, Graham and Shirley Cartwright (for a quiet haven at the "Ponderosa"), Chapter LX of the Special Forces Association, Will "Squeak" Charette, Jorge Contreras, Bill and Verda Crenshaw (for true Southern hospitality), Scotty Crerar, Marty Donohue, Wayne Downing, "The Delta Guys," Richard D. Ellmers, "Fred," Chuck Fry, Joe Garner, Bill Garrison, Cucho Gomez-Barrios, "Country" Grimes, Len Harris, Sam Kingston, "The Ladies in Lima," "The Lady in Washington, D.C.," Bob and Pat Lloyd, Earl "Frosty" Lockwood, Joe Lutz, Leroy Manor, Jim McInnis, Ron McKown, Earl D. McMillan, Marty Montgomery, Joan Norris, Charlie Norton, Stan Olchovik, Jim Paxton, Floyd Payne, Ross Perot, George Petrie, Dick Potter, Tom Quinn, Wayne Rich, Peter Schoomaker, Eugene Smith, Tom Smith, "The Son Tay Raiders Association," the Special Forces Association (Fort Bragg), Sharon Stevenson, Elliott "Bud" and Jean Sydnor, Al Trevino, and "The Warden and Jones Team." Many of these redoubtable soldiers served multiple tours in Vietnam, and to those who served alongside Meadows during the notable actions that are described in this book I offer my thanks and gratitude for the memories. Sadly, many of them have already departed on their "last patrol." I must also give a special word of thanks to Shirley Meadows Harvery and Grace Meadows for finding the photographs of Dick as a youngster—thank you, ladies. Thanks must also go to Roger Cirillo, Steve Wrinn, and the whole of the very professional team at the University Press of Kentucky.

My greatest accolades, however, must go to the Meadows family. Not only did they give me tranquil bases at Crestview, "The Lot," and Fayetteville from which to work, but they accepted all my questions (some very personal) without hesitation. I was made a welcome guest even during the period when Dick died and immediately afterward, when the family had every right to grieve in peace and privacy. I was honored to read one of the scriptures at Dick's funeral. To Pamela, Mark, Michele, Lisa, Pamela Hayley, and, of course, the grandchildren that Dick never really had the time to get to know, Carrington, Alexander, and Andrew, my warmest appreciation along with enormous respect.

All of you gave freely of your time and offered me superb hospitality—thank you—and "Keep the Faith."

Appendix

Research Notes on the Use and Effects of Agent Orange

Research into the use of Agent Orange is easy. Tying it in a positive way to causing leukemia is not. Between the years of 1962 and 1971, nearly 19 million gallons of herbicides were sprayed over an estimated area of 3.6 million acres in Vietnam. Agent Orange apparently made up 11.2 million gallons of the total amount. Not only were such herbicides used to clear jungle canopies in remote areas in order to deny the enemy ground cover, but they also were used in areas immediately outside military base camps and fire support bases. Although most spraying was done by fixed- or rotary-wing aircraft, a certain amount was done by boat, wheeled vehicle, and man-packed equipment. Spraying operations began in 1962 and were intensified in 1966 and 1967. The harmful dioxin in Agent Orange (TCDD) was created during the manufacture of the herbicide. I quote now from *Veterans and Agent Orange*, by the Institute of Medicine and published by the National Academy Press:

> As the decade [the 1960s] wore on, concern about possible long-term health consequences of Agent Orange and other herbicides heightened, fueled in particular by reports from growing numbers of Vietnam veterans that they had developed cancer or fathered handicapped children, which they attributed to wartime exposure to the herbicides. Along with the concerns of Vietnam veterans, public awareness increased because of reports of health concerns surrounding occupational and environmental exposure to dioxin—more specifically, 2,3,7,8-tetrachlorodibenzo-p-dioxin (2,3,7,8-TCDD), informally known as TCDD—a contaminant of 2,4,5-T. Thousands of scientific studies have since been conducted, numerous governmental hearings have been held, and veterans organizations have pressed for conclusive answers, but the question of the health effects of herbicide

exposure in Vietnam remains shrouded in controversy and mistrust. Indeed some veterans organizations, researchers, and public interest organizations remain skeptical that the issue has received full and impartial consideration by the Department of Veterans Affairs (DVA; formerly the Veterans Administration) and other federal agencies.

Faced with this lingering uncertainty and demands that the concerns of veterans be adequately addressed, the U.S. Congress passed Public Law 102-4, the "Agent Orange Act of 1991." This legislation directed the Secretary of Veterans Affairs to request that the National Academy of Sciences conduct a comprehensive review and evaluation of available scientific and medical information regarding the health effects of exposure to Agent Orange, other herbicides used in Vietnam, and their components, including dioxin.

In February 1992, the Institute of Medicine (IOM) of the National Academy of Sciences signed an agreement with the DVA to review and summarize the strength of the scientific evidence concerning the association between herbicide exposure in Vietnam service and each disease or condition suspected to be associated with such exposure. The IOM was also asked to make recommendations concerning the need, if any, for additional scientific studies to resolve areas of continuing scientific uncertainty and to comment on four particular programs mandated in Public Law 102-4.

To carry out the study, the IOM established the Committee to Review the Health Effects in Vietnam Veterans of Exposure to Herbicides. In conducting its study, the committee operated independently of the DVA and other government agencies. The committee was not asked to and did not make judgements regarding specific cases in which individual Vietnam veterans have claimed injury from herbicide exposure; this was not part of its congressional charge. Rather, the study provides scientific information for the Secretary of Veterans Affairs to consider as the DVA exercises its responsibilities to Vietnam veterans.

In the conclusions section of the above study, the committee classifies leukemia, along with a number of other "health outcomes," as having "inadequate/insufficient evidence to determine whether an association exists":

> The available studies are of insufficient quality, consistency, or statistical power to permit a conclusion regarding the presence or absence of an association. For example, studies fail to control for confounding, have inadequate exposure assessment, or fail to address latency. There is inadequate or insufficient evidence to determine whether an association exists between exposure to herbicides and the following health outcomes:
>
>> Hepatobiliary cancers
>> Nasal/nasopharyngeal cancer
>> Bone cancer
>> Female reproductive cancers (cervical, uterine, ovarian) and
>>   breast cancer
>> Renal cancer
>> Testicular cancer
>> Leukemia
>> Spontaneous abortion
>> Birth defects
>> Neonatal/infant death and stillbirths
>> Low birthweight
>> Childhood cancer in offspring

Some important notes arise from the research:

1. Agent Orange accounted for 61 percent of the recorded herbicide use.
2. General purpose defoliant (leaf fall within six weeks—control persisting for seven to twelve months).
3. Percentage uses:
   90 percent—forest defoliation
   8 percent—crop destruction
   2 percent—sprayed on ground around base perimeters and
     cache sites, waterways, and communications lines.
4. Of all the herbicides used in Vietnam, only Agent Orange was formulated differently from the materials for commercial application that were readily available in the United States. TCDD concentrations in individual shipments were not recorded, and the levels of TCDD varied in sampled in-

ventories of herbicides containing 2,4,5-T. The level of dioxin contamination in Agent Orange could have been up to 1,000 times higher than the level of dioxin found in phenoxy herbicides domestically available at the time.

5. In October 1969, the DOD restricted the use of Agent Orange to areas remote from populations in response to a report from the National Institute of Health that 2,4,5-T could cause malformations and stillbirths in mice.

6. In December 1969, the American Association for the Advancement of Science (AAAS) declared that recent research showing that 2,4-D and 2,4,5-T could cause birth deformities in experimental animals supported the conclusion that 2,4,5-T posed a probable health threat to humans. The AAAS also maintained that the levels of application of 2,4-D and 2,4,5-T in Vietnam exceeded levels in civilian usage and called on the Department of Defense to cease use of these chemicals (Buckingham, 1982). In April 1970, the Secretaries of Agriculture; Health, Education, and Welfare; and the Interior jointly announced the suspension of certain uses of 2,4,5-T (and therefore Agent Orange) in all military operations pending "further evaluation of its chemical constituents" (US GAO, 1978).

Final comment:

The military use of 2,4,5-T, and thus Agent Orange, was suspended by the Department of Defense in April 1970 (Young and Reggiani, 1988). Following the suspension of 2,4,5-T, the White House announced on December 26, 1970, that it was initiating an orderly yet rapid phaseout of the entire herbicide operation. On February 12, 1971, U.S. Military Assistance Command, Vietnam announced that herbicides would no longer be used for crop destruction in Vietnam and the last Ranch Hand fixed-wing aircraft (C-123) was flown. Subsequent spraying of herbicides was limited to controlled use around U.S. fire bases by helicopter or ground troops (MACV, 1972). On October 31, 1971, nearly 10 years after the herbicide program began in Vietnam, the last U.S. helicopter herbicide operation was flown (NAS, 1974).

It seems unlikely that the suspicions about Agent Orange held by Dick Meadows and many others will ever be proven.

Notes

Prologue

1. General William Westmoreland was then Commander of U.S. Forces, Vietnam. A controversial figure, he eventually became Chief of Staff of the U.S. Army before his retirement in 1972.

2. Dai Uý is the Vietnamese word for captain, but it was often used in the sense of "boss" for sub-unit commanders of noncommissioned rank.

3. The basic content of this mission was provided by Meadows. Confirmation was obtained from Major Billy Antony, USA (Ret.), during an interview at Crestview on the day following Meadows's funeral.

2. The Young Soldier and Korea

1. Floyd Payne was interviewed at Fort Bragg in 1996. His clear recollections of those early days with Meadows was impressive. He also served with Meadows in the Special Forces in later years.

2. The story of the 187th RCT from its inception until the end of the Korean War is shown in a video produced by Butler Military Videos. Interestingly, one of the brigade commanders in Korea was William C. Westmoreland, who was to have a direct influence on Meadows's career some years later.

3. Though Meadows was very young to get the rank of master sergeant, it was policy in the 1950s to give the appropriate rank to the man who was qualified and actively doing the job; as such, he could have been E-6 or E-7. The true test for Meadows would be if he were allowed to keep the rank when he left Korea.

3. Special Forces

1. The 10th Special Forces Group was initially under command of Colonel Aaron Bank, often referred to as the "father" of Special Forces, a veteran of the OSS who had operated in German-occupied France during World War II. The 10th SFG deployed to Bavaria in 1953, and the cadre which remained at Fort Bragg became the 77th SFG. Later (in 1960) it became the 7th SFG.

2. Much later Sydnor and Meadows were to become closely linked at key points in their careers.

4. A Lighthearted Interlude with the Brits

1. A detailed account of this can be found in the book *Looking for Trouble* by General Peter de la Billière, who commanded at all levels within the SAS Group and who was a staunch supporter of the USSFG and SAS liaison.

2. Johnny Cooper was the youngest of the original SAS volunteers in the Western Desert during World War II. After the war he rejoined the 22nd SAS in Malaya before serving with the Sultan of Oman's army.

3. On a visit to Afghanistan in November 2009 I accompanied retired Major Roddy Jones (Royal Welsh Fusiliers), who, while serving with the Trucial Oman Scouts, had visited the Jebel Akhdar at the same time as Meadows. He said, "Meadows was the first American Special Forces soldier that I had met and he was the best possible advertisement for the Green Berets; his skills were obvious; he was knowledgeable and eloquent; he could climb; he knew his military history and weapons; and he was totally at home in the desert/mountain environment."

5. Laos and the Learning Curve

1. This clumsy arrangement was in force right up until the French Army withdrew from Laos at the end of 1960.

2. Master Sergeant Theodore "Ted" Berlett died on January 28, 1962, while detonating faulty 3.5-inch rocket launcher ammunition.

3. The legendary Bull Simons commanded the first group to be inserted into Laos in July 1959. He remained until June 1960 but returned once more in October 1961, coincidental with the name being changed to White Star.

4. Colonel Vang Pao had been selected by the CIA to head the clandestine military operations against the Pathet Lao. He was a controversial figure who eventually became a general in command of some 25,000–30,000 troops who tied down the communists for over ten years.

5. Captain Moon was later reported to have been executed. Sergeant Ballinger was freed by the Pathet Lao on the signing of the Geneva Agreements in August 1962.

6. Spencer Chapman was a highly regarded British member of the SOE and Ferret Force operating in Malaya and Thailand during the Japanese occupation. His book covers, among other things, the long

period he spent alone in the jungles of Malaya evading the Japanese Army.

6. Panama and the Fun Years

1. The School of the Americas provided training for officers of all three services from aligned Latin American countries.

2. In July 1962, Castro announced that the U.S.S.R. was investing heavily to help him to defend his country. Between August 10 and August 31 President Kennedy was presented with evidence that medium-range ballistic missiles were being deployed in Cuba.

3. In 1958 students from Panama University began Operation Sovereignty by placing flags throughout the Canal Zone. This led to the Panamanian National Guard being called out to control the students.

4. Meadows was uncertain of the name and I could not trace it. There is a possibility that he was referring to Captain Ronald Shackleton.

5. The letter, dated July 16, 1995, refers to a conversation between Chuck Fry and a former comrade at an SFA reunion earlier that month. Only the direct references to the HALO Instructors course are used. It is used with the permission of Chuck Fry.

6. Meadows was eventually given his HALO Instructor Badge, inscribed 001, by General Wayne Downing at the Meadows home in Crestview a few days before his death.

7. Much information on life in the Canal Zone was provided by Joe Garner at the Meadows home in Crestview on the day of Meadows's funeral.

7. Vietnam and RT Ohio

1. HQ US Army Vietnam (APO San Francisco) in General Order 6823, dated December 14, 1966.

2. For the definitive explanation of SOG see John Plaster's excellent book, *SOG: The Secret Wars of America's Commandos of Vietnam.*

3. Billy Antony, interviewed shortly after Meadows's death, was later commissioned and retired at the rank of major.

4. APO US Forces 96499, signed by Major Francis J. Sova, dated August 17, 1966, and addressed to Colonel Ho Tieu.

5. Politics dictated that the Vietnamese officer be credited with command, while Meadows officially took the role of senior advisor.

6. This citation was covered under the same order as that for Lieutenant Le Minh.

7. Many years later Meadows met Woods and presented him with the pistol he had taken from the dead officer on the ridge.

8. Vietnam Through an Officer's Eyes

1. Billye Alexander had the reputation of having very much a "soft spot" for SF soldiers and used her significant influence to help them get the assignments they wanted.

2. "Covey Riders" were SF soldiers who flew with air force forward air controllers to assist in directing air strikes. Sometimes they would handle the insertion and extraction of SOG's recon teams.

3. The SCU was a designator used for both Nung and Montagnard mercenaries.

4. It was not uncommon for the NVA to disguise weapons and ammunition caches as graves, knowing that there would be reluctance on the part of U.S. soldiers to interfere with them.

5. Meadows had great difficulty persuading the Marine commander to part with the POW—they had other things in mind for him.

6. This mission reconstruction is based on interviews with Meadows and "After Action Report. TGT Base Area 610 (Dewey Canyon)," dated March 17, 1969.

7. BDA: Bomb Damage Assessment. Most RT One-Zeros (team leaders) considered BDA missions to be a waste of time and an unnecessary risk.

9. They'll Know We Cared

1. The story of the brilliant raid on the Son Tay POW camp in North Vietnam has been well documented in Benjamin F. Schemmer's book, *The Raid*. This chapter provides only an overview of the raid and takes a particularly personal look at Dick Meadows and his contributions to the planning, leadership, and training schedule for the mission.

2. The "Singlepoint" sight was of English manufacture. It was favored by many of the British SAS in those areas where contact with the enemy was likely to be at night. It was also trialed extensively by SOG in Vietnam.

3. FLIR (Forward Looking Infrared) was a revolutionary system that detected heat patterns through foliage and displayed them on a screen.

4. A Raider at a Son Tay Raiders reunion gave me a reproduction of this statement.

5. This account of the Son Tay raid is based on interviews with Meadows, Colonel Elliott Sydnor, and other participants I met at the two Son Tay Raiders reunions I attended. Further detail is taken from after action notes made by General Manor.

6. The official Son Tay after action report states that the support force killed sixteen soldiers and shows the body positions on a sketch map.

10. The Rangers, Mr. Meadows, and Delta Force

1. The story of the raising of SFOD-D is covered in detail in Beckwith's book, *Delta Force.*
2. This paragraph is a condensation of the three-page job description given to Meadows by Beckwith.
3. It is now possible to identify "Pete" as General Peter J. Schoomaker, who went on to become the 35th Chief of Staff of the U.S. Army (2003–2007) and later the 5th Commander in Chief USSOCOM (1997–2000).

11. "Agent" Meadows in Tehran

1. The details of this trip are from an interview with Meadows and notes which he made at the time of the Tehran mission, which he gave to me before his death.
2. Beckwith was to have a great stroke of luck just a few hours before Operation Rice Bowl got under way. A Pakistani cook who had been released from the embassy had been spotted by a CIA agent and taken in for questioning, at which point he was able to provide the precise locations of the hostages.
3. "Fred" kindly agreed to be interviewed by the author at Fort Bragg in November 1995 and his remarks are taken from that meeting.
4. A copy of the letter was given to the author by Mrs. Pat Lloyd at her home in Cheltenham.
5. Meadows was reluctantly interviewed by David C. Martin for the July 12, 1982, issue of *Newsweek,* which featured him as the "Man of the Week" within an article entitled "Inside the Rescue Mission."
6. I found it strange that Meadows does not seem to be accorded any permanent recognition within the confines of the Delta compound, especially in light of his contribution to the formation of the unit, his part in Operation Rice Bowl, and the official commendation awarded in July 1980 and signed by Colonel Charlie Beckwith.

12. Footloose

1. I met with Meadows in London and did not immediately recognize the snappily dressed brash character that he had adopted.
2. Meadows had personally called his old friend Chuck Fry to ask him to assist in getting to the scene. There were five U.S. citizens among the aircrew and Meadows felt that the Honduran authorities should at least be given a briefing on the options open to them.
3. "Just Cause" was the code name for the U.S. invasion of Panama in December 1989. As a result of the action, Manuel Noriega, the nation's corrupt dictator, was deposed. Interestingly, Meadows's son Mark was one of the Ranger platoon leaders who parachuted onto the

international airport as part of the operation. By then Meadows was working at his security business in Peru.

13. Entrepreneur in Peru

1. By agreement with Meadows, I have to be circumspect in giving names within Peruvian high society and some areas of the security industry. Many of the contacts who helped him in the early days still live and work in the country.

14. The Golden Days in Peru

1. Tom Smith, a former SF soldier, had worked with Meadows on the weapons sting outlined in chapter 11. He is a fluent Spanish speaker and he became an integral part of the business for a number of years. In an interview and by letter Tom Smith has contributed a great deal to the story of Meadows's involvement in Peru.

2. This potential activity is mentioned briefly in my biography of Sir David Stirling.

3. I interviewed Jorge Contreras, who had been the commander of a Peruvian SF unit. Contreras had actually met Meadows as part of a Peru/United States exchange program. When he was asked by Smith to participate in the Mobil Oil project in 1991, he was awaiting promotion to full colonel and the army turned down his application to leave. On hearing this, Meadows went to see a member of the Army Chief of Staff's board and fixed the matter. This has to be a measure of the high esteem Meadows was held in at the peak of his business in Peru. Contreras said that he owed a great debt of gratitude to Meadows.

15. The Bubble Bursts in Peru

1. The American Society for Industrial Security.

17. The Last Patrol

1. Some information on Agent Orange is included in the Appendix. These notes were researched by Meadows's daughter, Michele Gilmour.

Suggested Readings

Though not used as source material, the following books give accounts of Meadows's exploits on various missions or mention other facets of his military service and incidents described in this book.

Beckwith, Colonel Charlie. *Delta Force*. San Diego: Harcourt, 1983.

Billière, General Sir Peter de la. *Looking for Trouble*. London: Harper-Collins, 1995.

Chapman, F. Spencer. *The Jungle Is Neutral*. London: Chatto and Windus, 1951.

Clancy, Tom, with John Gresham. *Special Forces*. New York: Berkley Books, 2001.

Garner, Joe. *Code Name: Copperhead*. New York: Simon and Schuster, 1994.

Hoe, Alan. *David Sterling: The Authorised Biography of the Creator of the SAS*. London: Little, Brown, 1992.

Plaster, John L. *SOG: The Secret Wars of America's Commandos of Vietnam*. 1997. Reprint, New York: New American Library, a division of Penguin Group (USA), 2010.

Schemmer, Benjamin F. *The Raid*. 1976. Reprint, New York: Ballantine, 2002.

Index

Names of military units are alphabetized as spelled rather than by numerical order. For example, *77th Special Forces Group* appears before *6th Special Forces Group*.